WOMEN REFORMED,

WOMEN EMPOWERED

IN THE SERIES

WOMEN IN THE POLITICAL ECONOMY

edited by

Ronnie J. Steinberg

Women Reformed,
Women Empowered

POOR MOTHERS AND
THE ENDANGERED PROMISE
OF HEAD START

Lynda J. Ames

with

Jeanne Ellsworth

Temple University Press

PHILADELPHIA

TEMPLE UNIVERSITY PRESS, PHILADELPHIA
19122
Copyright © 1997 by Temple University
All rights reserved
Published 1997
Printed in the United States of America

⊗ The paper used in this publication meets the requirements of the
American National Standard for Information Sciences—Permanence of
Paper for
Printed Library Materials, ANSI Z39.48-1984

Text design by Gary Gore

Library of Congress Cataloging-in-Publication Data

Ames, Lynda J.
    Women reformed, women empowered : poor mothers and the endangered
promise of Head Start / Lynda J. Ames with Jeanne Ellsworth.
        p.   cm. — (Women in the political ecomony)
    Includes bibliographical references and index.
    ISBN 1-56639-492-9 (cloth : alk. paper). — ISBN 1-56639-493-7
(pbk. : alk. paper)
        1. Poor women—Services for—New York (State)   2. Head Start
programs—New York (State)   3. Head Start Program (U.S.)
I. Ellsworth, Jeanne, 1951–   . II. Title. III. Series.
HV1446.N5A54   1997
362.83'8–dc20   96-20537

To Winnie. To Wendy.
To strong women everywhere.

CONTENTS

ACKNOWLEDGMENTS

❖ We must thank, first and foremost, the women and men of North Country Head Start in upstate New York. These are people who let us into their homes, drove out of their way to meet us, took time from hectic schedules, shared their stories and a part of their lives with us. We thank them, one and all.

This research was initiated by Jeanne Ellsworth. For reasons detailed in Chapter One, I (Lynda J. Ames) soon took the public lead, though Jeanne remained active backstage. When it came time to write this book, Jeanne's other responsibilities in life left her too little of that precious commodity, time. I took over the writing (and rewriting). Jeanne continued to read drafts and discuss ideas and analyses. Though the writing is primarily mine, this project has been and is very much jointly authored.

During all of 1994, I was on leave because of a special program jointly administered by our union, United University Professions (UUP), and the State of New York—the Nuala McGann Drescher Affirmative Action Leave Award. When Dr. Drescher was statewide president of UUP, she initiated this leave program to promote the tenure success of women, men of color, persons with disabilities, and Vietnam-era veterans. That leave gave me time away from the rigors and excitement of teaching to drive all over the North Country to talk with people in their communities, to observe Head Start centers, to transcribe notes, and to make sense of it all. I fear that in these conservative fiscal times, this program may be lost to us, and I will deeply regret that loss. Now, of all times, we need a multitude of voices in the academy; we cannot afford to revert, by default or design, to a narrow range of elite experiences and expression.

We also received, very early in the project, a "mini-grant" from the College at Plattsburgh, State University of New York, which allowed us to purchase tape recorders and do a thorough literature search. Obviously, this assistance was crucial.

Michael Ames, editor in chief at Temple University Press (and no relation that we can figure out), provided so much encouragement and useful suggestions at just the right times. I owe a long-standing, profound intellectual debt to the series editor, Ronnie Steinberg, from whom I've learned so much. Her encouragement and friendship have been invaluable and treasured.

We received assistance from Karen Duckett in background research and interviewing. We'd like to thank the staff of the Office of Sponsored Research here for their cheerful and wise administration of the mini-grant and travel funds that came with the Drescher leave, especially Dr. Sue Spissinger for her enthusiastic support—in many things. And to Mary Lou Stahr, who provided near-perfect transcription services.

Jeanne would like to acknowledge the patient assistance of various reference librarians at Feinberg Library. Thanks also to Liz Petrick, Bonnie Walker, and Evelyn Ellsworth for talking and thinking with her as the project progressed (or faltered). Most of all, Jeanne wishes to thank the women she's worked with on Policy Council for their time, openness, and friendship.

I would like to acknowledge the many colleagues, friends, and family who provided moral support during this project, especially: Patty Bentley, Lynn Schlesinger, Penny Dugan, the Women's Untenured Faculty Comentoring and Action Group, the Women's Studies Associates, Marje Brown, Elisa Meredith (and Coyote Central), Jae Burke, Bj Reed, the Ogunquit gals, and my sister, who kept asking, "Is the book finished yet?"

Finally, I thank with all my heart my life partner, best friend, and most constructive (and harshest) critic, Ellen C. Schell. She read drafts and listened to many stories, woes, analyses, gripes, and so forth, providing comfort, encouragement, and some very good ideas (for which I now shamelessly take credit). And, of course, my thanks to the menagerie for constant company and comfort (and an idea here and there).

Part One

◆

INTRODUCTION

❖ 1 ❖

Prelude: The North Country

I love Head Start. Head Start has done a lot for me. Just did so much for my self-esteem. It's teaching me things. And I believe in Head Start. I see what it's done for me.

Before I got involved in Head Start, I wouldn't talk. Not a word. Now I can talk to anybody.

It seems like everybody who is associated with Head Start seems to give you that uplifting feeling.

These are the words of mothers of Head Start kids. Such words are common among Head Start moms across the country and across the thirty years of Head Start's existence. Mothers love the program for what the preschool offers their kids, but love it more for what it offers the women themselves. This widespread and deep devotion makes Head Start unique among federal social service programs.

That is the story of this book, a story of poor women finding resources for living their lives, resources for making changes in themselves and in their communities. It is also, though, a story perhaps more typical of "welfare" programs in general, a story of disempowerment, of policies that drive women deeper into apathy and hopelessness.

In the summer of 1965, Project Head Start came to upstate New York—the North Country—as it came to many communities throughout the United States. The North Country is famous for its rugged beauty—the Adirondack Mountains, the long shores of Lake Champlain, famed Lake Placid, countless forests, rivers, streams. Life here is surely enriched by scenic grandeur—as well as by the tourist trade it attracts. Yet life is also hard. Winters are long and cold. Heating and transportation are costly and a source of routine danger as well. The North Country is sparsely populated, with towns and villages often many miles apart and only a very few small cities. Some of the richest families in the world own vacation property here—vast estates known as great camps. And yet, poverty rates are above the state average, with pockets of extraordinary deprivation often right next door to extraordinary wealth. It is important to note here that the North Country is overwhelmingly white (about 95 percent), rich and poor. In 1965, many, many families were eligible, were poor enough to qualify for Head Start—that has not changed in thirty years.

We began this research intending to write a book chronicling Head Start "success" stories, stories elaborating on quotes such as the ones at the top of this chapter, stories of empowerment. Very soon, though, we became embroiled in the second part of the story. Local administrators sought to override the wishes of mothers, sought to disempower them, all the while professing otherwise. The events leading to the present book, which chronicles both empowerment and disempowerment, serve as a prelude to the multifaceted story we finally tell here. In that story, women seeking empowerment are, instead, often the objects of professional attempts at disempowering reform. As a prelude, this story of beginning and doing our research needs telling.

In the summer of 1992, Jeanne Ellsworth was asked to serve on the Head Start Policy Council (PC) in one of the counties in the North Country, "Lake County." This Policy Council is the local policymaking and oversight body for the Head Start program. PC is numerically dominated by parents of children currently enrolled in the program, but also includes other community members, such as Jeanne. PC is the primary source of parental power over local Head Start operations.

At the first training session for new members, Jeanne heard compelling stories about Head Start women—stories of mothers who had experienced considerable upward mobility, and of innovative community activism. She began talking about this with Lynda Ames, exploring the possibility of a full-scale study of such women. Our initial discussions also included a colleague whose area of expertise was early childhood education. We mapped out a plan to study the whole of this county's Head Start program. There would be three parts to the study: a longitudinal study of several children and their parents; an historical survey of the thirty years of the program and of the organization itself; and extensive interviews with parents, past and present, to examine "success."

Using Jeanne's contacts, the three of us went to the county's Head Start administrators to discuss the possibility. At our initial meeting, the Head Start director and several of the component coordinators were highly encouraging about the project. We especially recall one coordinator's enthusiasm about the third component, the empowerment of women.

In the spring of 1993, Jeanne presented the outlines of our proposal to the 1992–93 Policy Council. The parents on the PC were excited about such a study and were more than pleased to have a book written about their experiences. The PC voted to invite Lynda to attend PC meetings as an observer for the purposes of writing a book, this book. The women love Head Start and wanted to say so in print.

Head Start funds are administered jointly by the PC and by the board of directors of a nonprofit community action program (CAP). The members of the board are local social service professionals and business people. Since we had wished to paint a complete portrait of this county's program, we also made a presentation before the CAP Board, asking for their support of the study. Specifically, we needed access to the organization's archives and we wanted their cooperation in terms of tracking children and parents. We prepared a three-page overview of the proposed study, and Jeanne was invited to be on hand at the meeting when it was to be considered. While three of the board members wholeheartedly endorsed the project, others were skeptical, to say the least.

At the meeting, Jeanne was bombarded with questions. Some of them were very specific and easy to answer: How many children would we interview? Others were vague and confusing: Why didn't we research public nursery schools? At the end of the discussion, the proposal was tabled. Jeanne detected considerable anxiety about the nature and purposes of academic research. In retrospect, we should have been prepared to defuse that anxiety, but we naively, perhaps arrogantly, were not.

Jeanne went to the next monthly meeting and was reintroduced. Questions continued, this time suggesting deeper suspicions about the project: Who are you anyway? Who do represent? Will we get to read and approve of everything? In what would become the death knell for the project as then conceived, someone questioned the timing of the project. The board was just about to begin negotiations with a new staff union, and it was suggested that our research would interfere with those negotiations. After much discussion, the board voted not to approve the project.

We suspect that their reasons included, but were not limited to, concerns about the union negotiations. The board's questions and concerns suggested, also, "town/gown" discord. In this town, for instance, there are the usual problems of interaction between residents and students, particularly on weekend nights. There was also a particular antipathy among a vocal segment of the community to the Women's Studies Program, of which we are both active members. Most importantly, perhaps, there was a palpable uneasiness about publication.

Given this response, our third colleague moved on to another project—she absolutely needed the approval of the board for her research with the children. At the next PC meeting, the research project was on the agenda, and Jeanne reported that the board had voted no. This refusal posed problems. First and foremost, the PC parents genuinely wanted the study to go on, particularly the part about the PC and mothers, and were angry that the board did not want to allow it. Secondly, the procedural question arose of what happens when the PC and the board disagree on an issue—who wins? This became an important issue of control, and a key focus of our larger story.

Jeanne then told the people at the PC meeting—which included the Head Start director and the CAP executive director—that the board could not prevent us from interviewing adults about their experiences. Members of the PC stated that they had already approved Lynda's attendance at their meetings for the purposes of observation for the study and the board had no legitimate say over that. The PC reiterated its desire to have the whole study done and to have Lynda observe meetings.

The CAP executive director was furious that we believed we could "override" the board's decision, and charged Jeanne with misrepresenting the entire issue. He made an angry phone call to Jeanne and sent a letter to the chair of her department, in essence asking him to call us off. Though the chair's response was mild amusement, this brought us the closest we have been to calling off the whole project.

We ultimately felt compelled, though, to continue to work through our difficulties with the board and the executive director. After all, it was in Lake County that we had heard the first moving stories of women's lives and work in Head Start, and we had begun to observe this process at the PC. Most important, these women were so eager to share their stories. At the same time, though, we hardly wanted the research project to become a significant bone of contention between the PC and the board.

We decided to temporarily suspend our plans to interview mothers in this county. Lynda continued to observe, however, and Jeanne continued to participate on the PC. In the meantime, we made contacts with women in a neighboring county, which we shall call "Kent County." As we will show later in this book, the events in that county were eerily similar to those in Lake County. These events revolved around a decided shift of power from the parent-dominated PC to the professional administration. When we interviewed our first mother in the neighbor county in the fall of 1993, we were amazed at the parallels to things we ourselves saw happening in Lake County. This mother also put us in touch with former staff and parents in her county, whom we would later interview.

In the meantime, friends of Lynda's introduced her to their friend, the Head Start director in a second neighboring county, "River County." Lynda met with this friend of friends and told her about the study. She, like most everyone we talked to, was very enthusiastic—at this point, we were still intending only to document success stories. She had her staff call several parents and ask their permission to give out their names. Over the course of the spring and summer of 1994, we interviewed a number of those parents.

Shortly after the difficult Lake County PC meeting, Lynda met with the CAP executive director, without Jeanne. Some troublesome issues were discussed, and the executive director expressed his support for the research project. In the meantime, the PC president, Hannah (a pseudonym), also talked at length with the executive director about the research. She very much wanted this study done. Moreover, the PC began taking formal steps to resolve this dispute between the PC and the board. It was very clear that the issue of the research project was not going to go away or even to be put off for very long.

Hannah brokered a meeting between Lynda, the executive director, the Head Start director, and the president of the board. At this meeting, Lynda made no references to the parents' right to be interviewed without the CAP's permission. She also allowed Jeanne to be cast as the problem, the "bad girl," and uncharacteristically took upon herself the role of conciliator and "good girl"—Jeanne did not mind. Hannah forcefully argued for the research to be "allowed." At the end of the meeting, the board president declared that she would argue for approval at the next board meeting. Indeed, at that meeting, our research was approved. We began doing interviews of Lake County parents in earnest in the summer of 1994.

If that approval had not happened, we would have conducted interviews in Lake County anyway, and we would have continued our observations of the PC. Our decision to give "approval" another chance was not based on any fear of impropriety in research ethics. We talked at great lengths about this issue, consulted with colleagues about propriety, talked with community women about the politics involved. We were concerned, though, that the CAP administration could have made things difficult for individual parents, not to mention staff. We worried. And yet, we believed in the work and the women's wishes to tell their stories.

From the beginning, then, we were decidedly involved in the disputes between parents and administrators. This whole episode had both methodological and substantive effects on the story we tell here. First, the "approval" process was a clear demonstration to the parents that Jeanne and Lynda were *not* pawns or stooges of the administration, but were, in fact, treated by them in an imperious manner, just as the parents were. This gained us quick rapport as equals:

Camille: You're a Ph.D. then?

LJA: Yeah.

Camille: Get out of here! That's nice! You are very down to earth. I would never—.

LJA: I'll take that as a compliment.

Camille: No it is. You know it is. The professors, you know, they carry this, "I am Doctor so and so," but you don't introduce yourself like that.

Our involvement with the moms, though, virtually eliminated rapport with the administration.

Substantively, these events constituted one of many battles between the PC and the administration, and was one of the few that the PC actually won. (A more complete discussion of the "victory" is contained in Chapter Eight.)

So, the study began under a cloud of contention.

DILEMMAS OF PARTICIPANT OBSERVATION

We have never considered ourselves to be disinterested researchers. We clearly saw that there were battle lines forming between the parents and the administration over this research and many other issues. We have always allied ourselves with the parents. Part of this is methodological; we wanted to be taken by mothers to be insiders so that we could have freer access to their views of what was happening. Most of our alliance, though, is political—our hearts and politics are with the parents.

Jeanne was the first of five children born to teenage parents in the rural northeast. Her family's financial survival, like that of most families she knew, was a constant struggle. When Head Start began in 1965, her younger brother was asked to participate as an income-eligible child. Her father found his first self-affirming job with a War on Poverty program. A few years later, Jeanne's mother finished her high school education and completed teachers' college while receiving AFDC (Aid to Families with Dependent Children).

Lynda's family of origin was working class, comfortable, not poor but with very little cushion. Her father was a welder with a large pipe and casing company; he was a foreman at the plant when he died. After his death, her mother finished raising three teenage children working as a receptionist in a doctors' office, finally retiring as the business manager there.

Each of us was able to attend college and graduate school only because of accessible public higher education and generous student loan policies.

Class has always been a salient feature of our lives. We are used to feeling out of place in the academy, used to experiencing the class-based arrogance of our "peers." We saw a similar arrogance emanating from the administrators—some of them, anyway—toward the parents. We sided, quite naturally, even unavoidably, with the parents.

Further, the gender implications of much of the administration's behavior toward mothers were very clear. We were interested in doing this study, as feminists, because we love seeing women win. We hated the times when PC mothers have been beaten down over the last three years. The women we write about here were dismissed and belittled in many ways *because* they were women, as well as because they were poor. Again, our politics put us on their side; it could not have been otherwise.

Actually, the research might not have continued at all after the initial rejection by the CAP Board. At times we believed it was more trouble than it was worth. However, the mothers kept after us. They wanted the study done and the book written. It was the women who rekindled our interest in doing the work and who kept us at it. They are, in many ways, sponsors of this research.

The research has become intensely personal for us. We have made friends among the mothers and staff. We are invested in their success, individual and collective, to a large extent. We have had many conversations about ways to continue the struggle they started, conversations between ourselves and with them. As we withdraw from the field to write and teach, we frankly miss them.

We had promised the mothers from the beginning that we would make our findings available for their use, though none of us was precise about what that might eventually mean. We wanted, though, to find a way to give the research to the women. What we initially told them was that we were hopeful that the research would show Head Start to be a boon to poor women, and the book could serve as evidence to help increase funding. (Overly optimistic, to be sure, but at the time, the early Clinton administration was talking about full funding for Head Start—times have regrettably changed.) However, there is a more immediate purpose now. We believe that the women have been shortchanged, and they want us to tell the world about it. We are doing so.

All of this discussion is to clarify that we are not and never were dispassionate about this research. We like the concept of Head Start. We love the success stories we have heard and retell here. We would like to see poor women—these women—actually empowered. This book is a small contribution, we hope, toward achieving that empowerment.

Passion notwithstanding, we have been very careful in our data collection and analysis. We are not interested in substituting our stories for theirs. This is the crux of our second major dilemma.

We are professional academics, who get paid for spending our time reading, teaching, thinking. We are over-educated and suffer from a learned tendency toward abstractions—an occupational hazard. We "understand" that poverty is a result of the political economy, the particular social structures of rewards and power. We also "understand" that women are caught in a bind in the modern world, expected to be perfect mothers (according to someone else's definition) and adequate providers (in a labor market rife with systemic disadvantages for women and poor people). We "know" that to significantly alter the life-chances of the women in this book, changes must be made to these structures of inequality. Such changes require wide-spread, transformative social movements.

As we will detail, such a movement has not occurred in the North Country. As progressive, feminist academics, we might wish that it would and might be disappointed that it did not. That, however, would be our elitism and arrogance.

This is our dilemma. We know that the changes we report here have had little to no effect on the structures that constrain the lives of these women. Yet, these are changes the women have made, the ones they have chosen to make, the ones of which they are proud. We might argue that they are experiencing some form of false consciousness. In reality, we would like to help them move toward a structural analysis of their lives. Indeed, we hope to share with them, through this book, some of the ways that we in our privileged occupations have come to think about poverty.

But what we must do in writing this book is to present, with respect, our understanding of their analyses, while at the same time placing their analyses in the structural understandings we have. Though we want them to think in structural terms as we do, we want to explicate the reasons they do not, and we also want to validate the ways they do think (Gorelick 1991; Reinharz 1992).

We see the events chronicled in this book as a sort of morality play about many of the critical issues affecting our state and our nation at this time: the politics of poverty, the location of women in the political economy, the respective importance of democracy and efficiency. We will endeavor to tell it as the women see it, as well as how we see it.

These have been singularly difficult tasks, and the tension will be readily apparent.

RESEARCH IN THE NORTH COUNTRY

We have spent three years in the field, talking, watching, listening. Though we sided with the mothers in their endeavors, we did not wish to become major players in events. Especially in the beginning, we just wanted to observe what Head Start did.

As we said, Jeanne was a participant on the Policy Council, and used that position to observe during the 1992–93, 1993–94, and 1994–95 terms of the PC. Lynda, invited by PC mothers, observed meetings for the last quarter of the 1992–93 term, the full 1993–94 term, and the 1994–95 term through the spring of 1995. As participant or as observer, one or both of us attended all formal monthly PC meetings and many PC committee meetings; we attended informal meetings of parents and staff; we participated in training sessions designed for parents and one designed for board members; we attended miscellaneous CAP functions, such as their annual meetings; we visited the centers where children are taught; and we have had scores of conversations with parents, staff, and children. Virtually any occasion at which parents, staff, or administration gathered, we attended.

We kept extensive field notes and, in some cases, tape recordings of meetings and conversations. We have also examined countless documents produced by the program, particularly as they relate to happenings of the PC and decisions made for the program. Much of our data, then, is ethnographic. We will present what we saw and what people told us about what we saw.

We are interested, too, in how women construct their feelings about the program, aside from the events at the PC or in the Head Start classroom. We conducted formal interviews of parents in order to let them tell us their stories. The interviews were loosely structured. We asked parents to explain how they had heard about Head Start; how they participated in it, if they did; what they expected from it; and what they and their children were getting out of the program. Most of the parents had tales they were quite eager to tell and we largely just let them talk, on tape.

We met with parents anywhere they felt comfortable in talking. A mother with a small boy she was baby-sitting for a neighbor met us at a local doughnut shop. (He was much more interested in the doughnut than the conversation.) Another mother met us at the same shop, where we sat with our backs to the wall in order to monitor who came and went—a little paranoid, perhaps, but she wanted to feel free to say many things and this *is* a small town. We drank coffee in truck-stops, and we ate Chinese food on a woman's lunch break from work. A few women came to our offices at the college.

Often, we met mothers at the Head Start centers where the children attend class. Sometimes the center is housed in a public school, sometimes in a church, sometimes in a freestanding building. In a church, we sat with a grandmother and her son in the large congregational kitchen. We sat on a bench outside a school building and watched children play on the swings. In a school, we sat on the floor just after the child-sized furniture had been cleared away for the summer. We met some mothers in the room set aside for parent activities—three of the mothers were silk-screening t-shirts for a special outing for the kids while we talked. In another parent room, the washing machine was going full-tilt while we spoke.

In many cases, we visited women in their homes. It doesn't come as much of a surprise that we found ourselves talking to women in their kitchens or at the dinner table. In one home, we drank iced-tea in the kitchen while the husband watched television in the living room. One woman had a parakeet that kept up a constant commentary, mostly agreeable, on what the mother was telling us. We remember one home that featured a new litter of puppies *and* a new litter of kittens—heaven for Lynda. Children (the resident Head Start child and many others) were a constant. Many little ones squealed with pleasure when they heard their voices played back on our tape recorders.

In the rural North Country, many of the homes we visited were very secluded, many of them too small or too old or in need of repair. Fitchen (1991, 1992) demonstrates that the rural, upstate New York poor often live in substandard housing to minimize costs and to maintain flexibility in household composition and size. In her studies, Fitchen has noted that, in rural areas, trailers are much more available than apartments and are much more easily purchased than conventional houses. Purchased trailers are often parked together on a bit of rented land, sometimes near a settled town, sometimes in very isolated areas. We visited many such homes. Some were single-wides, basically the width of a lane of traffic, where one or more adults and their children lived. Some were double-wides, giving the families much more space. Around the trailers, there were sometimes flower or vegetable gardens planted, sometimes not.

Some homes we visited had few neighbors, the nearest being perhaps a half-mile or several miles away. One mother, active in the events of this book, lived in such an isolated home. She and her husband owned one car, which he took to work each day, leaving her to, as she says, live on the phone. We sat in her kitchen, warmed by the wood-burning furnace, the only heat source in the house. Later in the afternoon, the school bus would bring her two kids home.

Major snow had been predicted, though, and she was not at all sure that all of her family would make it safely home that night.

Interviews with mothers typically lasted forty-five minutes to an hour, though one was fifteen minutes and several were closer to two hours. Lynda did the majority of the interviews; both of us listened to tape recordings and read and reread transcripts.

We also interviewed staff members, both about the parents they had worked with and about their own struggles with the administration. We interviewed the Head Start director in each of three counties, though one was a former director. We had formal interviews with community representatives on the PC, and with the union organizer who serviced the whole North Country. Many of these staff and community representative interviews took place at each individual woman's office, her turf.

In all, we have formal interviews with: (from Lake County) twenty-six parents, fifteen staff members, three community representatives on the PC; (from Kent County) two parents, two staff members, one community rep; (from River County) fourteen parents, one staff member. Our ethnographic data are from Lake County.

Two of the women we interviewed are African American; all others are white. This breakdown is quite different from the stereotypic image of Head Start. As we will discuss in the next chapter, poverty and race are firmly linked in the minds of Americans—poor people are presumed to be people of color. This book, though, is a study of white women who are poor. This does have some consequences for the women's sense of community, as we will later explore.

Throughout the study, we shared analyses with various of our informants. On occasion, if an interviewee touched on an issue we had recently discussed between us, we tested our analysis with her, asking if it made sense. Other times, we talked at length with people active in events about what we were thinking and what they thought of what we were thinking. When we actually began writing this text, we called meetings to talk to groups of parents and staff members about what we would write. We wanted their feedback and their blessing. At these meetings, analyses might be confirmed or modified—or discarded, alas. However, the book and the analyses are, in the end, ours.

At one of these meetings, some of the staff members wanted to know when the book would actually be published, since they expected considerable fireworks and possibly retaliation from the administration. They wanted the book published very much, but wanted to be forewarned about the timing. We promised them advance copies. As we will later explain, though, the majority of staff members who talked to us have since left Head Start, in each case with great reluctance.

"PARENTS" AS "MOTHERS"

Of the forty-two parents formally interviewed, seven are men. Only two men were interviewed alone, the other five with their wives or, in one case, mother. These seven men were included in our interviews because of their involvement on the PC or staff of their respective counties. They were players in the events we report here.

However, we have written here about women, mothers. Empirically, women constitute the vast majority of the parents involved with Head Start at any level. Head Start constitutes one of the very few "involvement" opportunities available and legitimately warranted for women. Women *can* become involved because this involvement and time away from home concerns the children, women's expected responsibility. In this world, there are more opportunities for public and community involvement for men than women. Further, our ethnographic work and our interviews, although limited in number, indicate that the quality and meaning of men's participation in Head Start are different. More research will be needed to fully understand those differences. We report the experiences of women.

We will introduce many women in this book. It is they who make Head Start successful, successful for both children and mothers. However, we are concerned that the kind of administrative behavior that nearly scuttled this research will also dampen the possibilities for those successes. That behavior is not a matter of individual personality only; it is the result of a long history of conflicting goals and premises in Head Start. We turn next to that history.

❖2❖

Two Wars on Poverty

If you're born with a silver spoon in your mouth, you get to keep it, and if you're not, you don't.

It's a stigma to be poor in this country. But, don't treat me like that's my choice. Do you know what I mean, to be poor.

God, don't put me going on welfare because I hate it.

In 1964, a great War on Poverty was launched in the United States. From the beginning of this war, there were multiple, often contradictory assumptions being made by policymakers about the causes and cures of poverty. Project Head Start, a prominent element in the war, still features specific policies derived from various of those competing assumptions, melded uncomfortably together in a single program.

The meld, though, is neither equal nor uniform. In fact, Head Start can be seen primarily as a practical application of deficit theories of poverty. Much of Head Start's content is driven by the assumption that poor children and families have inadequate and inappropriate values and habits, and that this explains their inability to gain a foothold in the economy. Head Start's experts can help them correct those deficiencies through specific training and "enrichment" activities. Such deficits and the "fixing" are assumed to involve both child and parents, to require a two-generation approach.

At the same time, though, some aspects of Head Start are designed from theoretical perspectives charging that the social structure itself is at the root of poverty. Rather than blame the poor for their inadequacies, these structural explanations focus on "the system"—monopoly capitalism, institutional racism, patriarchy. Given these structures, the poor are effectively without power, and will remain poor until the structures themselves change. Head Start thus includes provisions for granting power to those poor served by the program, with the expectation that the poor themselves can and will create programs they find useful, thereby beginning to change "the system."

Because of the melding of these quite different wars on poverty, Head Start seems able to offer something to every policymaker and politician, across the political spectrum. The program has been extraordinarily popular, in fact, leading a "charmed life" (Skerry 1983). The question becomes, though, which of these wars (or which melding) is most useful for poor people?

THE WAR(S) ON POVERTY

As a "welfare" program of the federal government, Head Start owes its continued existence, of course, to its viability as a political entity—political both in terms of narrow partisan politics at all levels of government and the broader cultural struggles for power, resources, and legitimacy in America. The political processes that shaped the War on Poverty, and thus Head Start, constrain its ability to empower women, even today.

As the prosperous 1950s ended and the 1960s began, poverty was a virtual nonissue in national politics and official attention (Katz 1989; Gelfland 1986). During the decade following the end of World War II, poverty in the United States had been declining steadily (Levitan 1969). Indeed, by the early 1960s, the poverty rate had been cut in half due to economic growth and increasing incomes (Danziger and Weinberg 1994). Richard Nixon, when he was vice president, declared the triumph of capitalism in producing a near-classless society in the United States (Public Broadcasting System 1995).

Yet poverty was not erased, and it began to emerge as a public and political issue. Exposés, perhaps especially Michael Harrington's *The Other America,* brought the specter of poverty to the American living room. Americans could no longer quite ignore what Gunnar Myrdal described as the "ugly smell rising from the basement of the stately American mansion" (quoted in Gelfland 1986: 4).

Very significant among the later forces that disclosed American poverty to mainstream, "classless" America was the Civil Rights movement, which turned increasingly to questions and problems of poverty in the early 1960s (Katz 1986; Ross 1979). This disclosure was not dispassionate or quiet. Rather, there was "trouble in the streets and trouble at the polls" (Piven and Cloward 1971: 219), from inner city riots to the 1963 March on Washington. Not only did this trouble bring national attention to poverty, challenging assumptions of unlimited affluence, but poverty and antipoverty programs began to be linked thereby to issues of race, a link that has never been broken (Quadagno 1994; Weir 1992).

Such an atmosphere gave poverty a renewed serviceability in political contests (Katz 1989). While Richard Nixon was arguing that reports of American poverty were overblown, John F. Kennedy would shake hands with displaced West Virginia coal miners. Kennedy was the potential beneficiary of several decades of black migration to strategically important states like New York and Illinois. He needed to win the allegiance of African Americans while avoiding a too-close association. The latter would cost him votes in the south and could destroy the cohesion of the Democratic Party, then threatened by civil rights demands (Quadagno 1994; Katz 1986, 1989). The issue of poverty, rather than the issue of race, per se, became important to Kennedy's campaign.

There was actually little disparity between Nixon's declaration that capitalism was rapidly eliminating poverty and Kennedy's that the government could and should find ways to accelerate the process. It would not have been politically feasible, during the Cold War, to argue that capitalism had failed. With Kennedy's narrow presidential victory in 1960, however, the question for the most prosperous nation in the world was not whether, but how, the government would intervene to affect poverty. Ultimately, virtually all of the answers to this question would rest on a faith in capitalism and presumptions of a male-headed nuclear family. Through education and job training (but *not* new transfer payments), the government would provide assistance in preparing poor men to enter the American system of individual competition and thus move themselves and their families up and out of poverty (Heclo 1994).

After Kennedy's assassination, Lyndon B. Johnson moved boldly and grandly to declare a "War on Poverty," and to develop programs aimed at creating a Great Society. He created a taskforce of academics and politicians to design the Economic Opportunities Act (EOA). Johnson's war—Johnson's *domestic* war—would be waged through tax cuts, Appalachian development programs, community rehabilitation, youth programs, vocational training and basic education, and hospital insurance for the aged. The EOA was signed into law by Johnson in August of 1964, establishing the Office of Economic Opportunity (OEO). OEO served as a command center for the War on Poverty, housing such projects as the Job Corps, VISTA, Migrant Assistance, and Head Start.

MAXIMUM FEASIBLE PARTICIPATION

The most volatile and ultimately the most troublesome part of the EOA was contained in the section authorizing community action programs (CAPs). These CAPs were to coordinate services locally. The "political dynamite" (Donovan 1967) in this was the mandate that all community action programs be carried on with the "maximum feasible participation" of the community. The concept was favored by those policymakers working from structural, rather than cultural or deficit theories of poverty. The radical, structural theory vision of participation was that the poor should "restructure the social institutions by which [they] gain access to jobs and goods and services" (Danziger, Haveman, and Plotnick 1986: 51). The poor were not poor because of individual psychological or cultural traits, but because they were systematically locked out of jobs, power, and influence. The solution to poverty, then, was to provide the means by which power would be transferred to the poor so that they might restructure society in their own behalf. This version of community action was undergirded not by faith in capitalism, but faith in democracy.

The application of structural poverty theories to social service delivery was not new. The dual responsibility of social reformers to provide services but also challenge and change society was recognized at least as early as the Progressive Era (Chambers 1974; Whithorn 1984; Joffe 1977). Neither were community organizing and development wholly devised by radical social theorists now designing the War on Poverty. Ethnic institutions, unions, and the Civil Rights movement, for example, all have demonstrated the power of grassroots endeavors.

What was new, was that the federal government would initiate and fund such activities. This was national policy being promulgated from the top down, not a grassroots uprising (Gilbert 1970). "The War on Poverty was not declared at the behest of the poor; it was declared in their interest by persons confident of their own judgment in such matters" (Moynihan 1970: 25).

Given this top-down approach, it is not surprising that the provision actually written did not even specify that the *poor* should participate, saying rather "residents of the area and members of the groups served" (Donovan 1967: 40). From the beginning, then, the "political dynamite" of maximum feasible participation was a potential only, not at all a sure explosion. Nevertheless, it is curious that such dynamite was provided at all.

It has been argued that the framers of EOA really did not understand what community action or maximum feasible participation meant or could look like in action (Moynihan 1970). A key selling point involved the perception that government social service agencies were sluggish and "creaky" (Gelfland 1986: 10; Gilbert 1970). CAPs were advertised as a way to coordinate antipoverty efforts locally, thus bypassing the federal bureaucracy (Peterson and Greenstone 1977). Policymakers perhaps considered it simply "a nice sentiment" (Levitan 1969: 36). Certainly, most policymakers did not share the convictions of radical reformers like Saul Alinsky, who envisioned true community activism as "a deep, hard-driving force, striking and cutting at the very roots of all the evils which beset the people" (1946: 154).

In practice, CAPs varied considerably in interpreting the concept of "maximum feasible participation." A CAP in Atlanta, considered a model program, had no poor people on its board; a Newark, New Jersey CAP, on the other hand, had no representation from City Hall (Donovan 1967). Where participation by the poor was nominal, the services offered were traditional and "efficient." CAPs with more participation from the community, on the other hand, were generally less efficient than those run through existing structures, but more broadly conceived and noisier (Quadagno 1994; Peterson and Greenstone 1977; Datta 1970; Skerry 1983; Moynihan 1970).

To some poverty warriors, one advantage of sending money through the CAPs was to circumvent existing local political machines (Valentine and Stark 1979; Quadagno 1994; Katz 1989; Skerry 1983). Sometimes these machines were overtly racist; in other cases, politicians merely exploited the poor for political gain. In any case, local politicians did not appreciate the circumvention.

When decision making and funds began bypassing City Hall, some mayors became noticeably "jittery" and others outrightly contentious as they faced the potential "liquidation of their own empires" (Donovan 1967: 45; Cahn and Cahn 1971). The mayors of Los Angeles (Sam Yorty) and San Francisco (John Shelley) sponsored a resolution in the National Council of Mayors accusing Sargent Shriver (director of OEO) of fostering class struggle (Donovan 1967).

In spite of the mayors' jitters, though, there was little cause for their concern about class warfare. There was sometimes militancy and there were some bitter conflicts (Moynihan 1970; Greenberg 1990 [1969]). Overall, though, reviews of CAPs found little revolutionary activity. Review after review of CAPs found that most were essentially social service delivery systems without significant community involvement (Peterson and Greenstone 1977). Kenneth Clark and Jeannette Hopkins found that in those programs where the poor sat on boards, they could be and often were "manipulated . . . outvoted, and then non-represented" (1968: 124).

Professionals and politicians complained that the participation of the poor on boards made no substantial difference because of their lack of skills: "The point was made that many of these poor people, after they fight so valiantly and heatedly to sit on these governing boards, have a kind of deep sense of frustration because of the fact that they don't have all the facilities they need to really wheel and deal on this level" (Clark and Hopkins 1968: 124–25). In addition, these authors found that both politicians and professionals had a certain "threshold of tolerability" for change, which resulted in maintenance of the status quo and in severe limits on the power of the poor.

In a similar study, Ralph Kramer (1969) found that although participation of the poor on policy boards revealed their ability to do policymaking, planning, review, administration, and budgeting, there were no substantial shifts in power in the new organizations. He further suggested that CAPs had been somewhat successful in organizing social service clienteles, but not in fostering a political constituency.

Critically, several of the noisiest and most troublesome CAPs were organized and directed by African American groups with close ties to the Civil Rights or Black Power movements. Some of these—notably the Child Development Group of Mississippi (Greenberg 1990 [1969])—drew wrath more deeply rooted in racism than in concerns about program efficiency or duplication.

Though many CAP programs largely ignored the mandate for participation, or operated in minimum compliance, there were strong pressures on the OEO—from the National Council of Mayors, for example—to relax even these minimum standards. Consequent changes in OEO regulations in 1967 gave state and local government more control over CAP agencies. Local politicians were then more easily able to fit community action into existing patronage politics, reducing its activist potential.

In short, community action and maximum feasible participation produced no revolution. There were some important gains, to be sure. The EOA did provide funds and organizing resources for projects in poor communities, resources that "generated their own power" (Quadagno 1994: 41). There is general agreement, too, that community action did encourage the development of a small but important number of community leaders, particularly in the African American community (Quadagno 1994; Moynihan 1970; Peterson and Greenstone 1977). Nancy Naples (1991) argues, too, that many *women* learned organizing skills and political analysis through work in community action agencies.

In the end, community action drew considerable, if overblown criticism from many quarters. Though it was often clothed in concerns about efficiency, the criticism and legislative reactions certainly reflected concerns about the revolutionary aims and potential of CAPs (Gelfland 1986; Moynihan 1970). By the time Nixon abolished the OEO in 1973, "maximum feasible participation" had lost most of that potential. Though CAPs would continue to exist, the poor had lost the use of these organizations as vehicles for power and institutional change.

GETTING HEAD START STARTED

It was in this environment of conflicting social theories and community power struggles that Head Start was born. From the earliest discussions of the project, Head Start garnered enthusiastic support as an attractive program for "innocent" young children trapped in poverty, engendering considerable sympathy. Lady Bird Johnson was so entranced with the idea that even she became involved in its promotion. Her husband, when presented with the idea, reportedly said, "That's such a magnificent idea, triple it" (Davens 1979: 90). A significant amount of money was therefore earmarked for Head Start—before any analyses of its assumptions, its efficacy, or its impact were done (Cooke 1979; Zigler and Anderson 1979).

Head Start was proposed as a comprehensive program for early childhood development, one that was essentially compensatory in nature and based on deficit theories. According to such analyses, the poor—whether through genetics, culture, or psychological development (depending on the specific version of theory)—lack the personal traits necessary to thrive in a basically meritocratic capitalist society (Riessman 1962; Bloom et al. 1965). The poor, according these views, were not simply economically deprived. They suffered from something larger than a lack of material resources; they suffered from a "poverty of the mind," as Lyndon B. Johnson phrased it (Public Broadcasting System 1995). Deficit perspectives on poverty became popular with social scientists, educators, and the media. Echoing the enduring association of poverty with morality, and grafting on newer psychological theories, "experts" claimed that the poor were "at the bottom of the heap—socially, morally, mentally" (Public Broadcasting System 1995).

Further, from this perspective, poverty is seen to gain intergenerational momentum as families pass on deficient behavior patterns to their children (even if such patterns can be seen as circumstantially adaptive). Working from a presumed set of cognitive, psychological, and social universals, a host of deviant, faulty, or substandard characteristics were cited as maintaining the "cycle of poverty" through their transmission to children. For example, poor children were "scientifically" shown to have sustained language defects arising from the use of various forms of nonstandard English in the home, and from limited or inappropriate conversing with adults (Bloom et al. 1965). Living with an "impoverished mode of speech" could reputedly affect children's ability to think and learn (Ginsburg 1972: 13). Poor children were assumed to observe the wrong kinds behavior being modeled in infancy and childhood, resulting in unproductive attitudes, skills, and habits—the "variety of living patterns available for imitation provided by low-class [sic] adults is both highly limited and wrong for standards of later schooling" (Hunt 1969: 41). Despite immediate and compelling critiques of these perspectives (Ryan 1976; Leacock 1971; Valentine 1968; Patterson 1981; Neisser 1986), this model of poverty was tremendously influential in the framing of Head Start and other antipoverty programs (Bloom et al. 1965).

Stopping the inheritance of this culture of poverty, stopping the cycle of poverty, would require deliberate intrusion into that cycle. Simply increasing material resources available to the poor would be insufficient. Born of what has been termed, in retrospect, a "naive environmentalism" (Zigler and Anderson 1979: 9), the idea of early intervention in the lives of children provided a hopeful solution. A well-planned program for culturally deprived children would provide "a set of encounters with circumstances which [would] provide an antidote for what they may have missed" (Hunt 1969: 39).

Parents—mothers—were a key target of reform. Kuntz (1995) notes that the OEO used the terms "mother" and "parent" interchangeably. Head Start was unlike other War on Poverty programs in that it focused attention on women (Pearce 1990). Mothers could be taught to model "correct," not "wrong," behaviors and attitudes. This formulation was not new. The Settlement House movement of the Progressive Era was based on similar notions, that children of immigrants needed to be taught to be American, so that they could assimilate in ways unavailable to their improperly cultured parents (Mink 1990; Trolander 1987). Indeed, the movement to establish kindergartens was based on the same ideas (Kuntz 1995), as was the PTA (Powell 1982).

Further, Head Start, like the settlement houses, would endeavor to change the mothers of children. These changes were to be in the direction of being more "American," more middle class. Head Start, like earlier efforts, invaded women's lives more than men's in the name of improving the environment for the children—coming into their homes, attempting to change their living habits, modifying their relationships with their children. The "improvements" in mothers were not intended to benefit the women, except as a side effect, but were intended to allow the child to integrate more successfully into mainstream America. The mother was seen as a primary impediment to the child's success. The mother needed to be "fixed" to break the cycle of poverty in the next generation. The War on Poverty thus perpetuated the gendered social welfare institutions that focus on women as carers for children, but not as providers for them (Sapiro 1990; Bryson 1992; Miller 1990).

Such early intervention arguments, supported by a host of "scientific" evidence, were eminently convincing to politicians. Post-Sputnik fears about the superiority of Soviet schooling, new techniques and technologies for teaching infants and very young children to "read," and a popular interest in early intellectual functioning made cognitive intervention more appealing (Zigler and Anderson 1979).

An early area of contention, however, was whether cognitive gains (i.e., raising IQ) were to be the sole or even primary aim of the Head Start program. Such advances would offer a widely acceptable, quantifiable measure of success. Yet, some members of the task force believed that raising motivation levels was far more fundamental (Zigler and Valentine 1979; Zigler and Muenchow 1992).

Others argued that health services were the essential aspect of intervention. In the end, what emerged was a comprehensive social and educational program that would compensate poor children for the various deficiencies of their home lives. A strong and well-delivered program of the "right" sort of experiences, along with good medical and dental care, nutrition, and parent training would, it was felt, render young children better able to function in society.

A primary putative outcome would be that Head Start children would be capable of taking advantage of the public school system. Participation in Head Start would equip them to take their places beside more advantaged classmates and profit similarly from the opportunities a good education would provide. Again, there was the strong, unexamined assumption that American capitalism would provide a good living to anyone equipped to take advantage of the abundant opportunity.

Head Start was, from the beginning, a program aimed at imparting a different, "superior" culture to poor children. Head Start has stressed children's "social competence" through "improvement of the child's health and physical abilities, including appropriate steps to correct present physical and mental problems"; "the encouragement of self-confidence, spontaneity, curiousity [sic], and self-discipline"; and "the establishment of patterns and expectations of success." Regarding children's families, assumptions of deficit are apparent in the program's aims to "increase . . . the ability of the child and the family to relate to each other and to others" (Head Start Performance Standards 1984).

HEAD START AND MAXIMUM FEASIBLE PARTICIPATION

As a CAP program, Head Start had to meet standards for maximum feasible participation. And, as in the larger CAP organizations, there was considerable variation in how that concept worked in practice. In many programs, "participation" meant "education," and the latter assumed deficiencies in the mother (Joffe 1977).

Note the equation of "parents" and "women" in the following; it was presumed that:

> Parents had to learn *with* their children, particularly how to *be* parents. . . . Parents were encouraged to assist in the classroom, accompany children on field trips, and participate in adult education. But it is hard to escape the impression that the women were being prepared to divest themselves of traditional culture. (Valentine and Stark 1979: 297, emphasis in original)

Head Start also provided, though, that parents participate in running the program through the Policy Advisory Committees (PACs). The original Head Start curricular plan devised at the OEO was flexible, allowing a broad range of designs in different communities. Presumably, the PACs could influence—though not necessarily control—the design of local curricula.

At the other extreme from "education" was the Child Development Group of Mississippi, where the primary emphasis was on parent *control* (Greenberg 1990[1969]; Valentine and Stark 1979; Garfunkel 1986). As noted earlier, the MCDG came under particular scrutiny and criticism, in no small part because of its association with the Civil Rights movement.

While mayors objected to the power of CAPs in general, local school administrators and teachers objected to the power of PACs, especially with regard to the staffing of Head Start centers. Such power over hiring, after all, reduced professional control over membership and standards. Despite these objections, the importance of parent involvement was formalized in 1969 with the creation of a staff position to develop such participation (Valentine and Stark 1979). Even so, the guidelines on parent involvement remained ambiguous enough to allow wide variations in parents' power.

In 1969, the Head Start administration moved from the OEO to the new Office on Child Development (OCD) in Health, Education and Welfare (HEW) (Kuntz 1995). (HEW later became

Health and Human Services, HHS.) With this move, parental involvement might have been lost. OEO was the force behind community action, and HEW was hardly known for such participative programs. Yet, new regulations issued in 1970 granted and institutionalized some increased power to parents (Kuntz 1995; Valentine and Stark 1979).

These new regulations contained a clause, 70.2, in which parents' roles in various levels of decision making was exactly specified. The existence, specifications, and intent of "seventy-point-two" are widely known among parents today. The name of parent groups was changed from Policy Advisory Committee to Policy Council—they were no longer to be considered merely advisory but controlling. Parents were to constitute a majority on the local Policy Council, and were to have considerable power over hiring, firing, budget oversight, and a host of other issues. Indeed, when the new regulations were issued, a number of school boards that had been running Head Start programs gave them up rather than share such considerable power with parents (Kuntz 1995).

On the other hand, the new regulations limited the scope of the poor community's power. Though deficit-based theories supposed that low-income people were apathetic, in fact local programs were overwhelmed with parents wanting to participate in the running of Head Start programs and other community action enterprises (Valentine and Stark 1979; Kuntz 1995). The participation structures of Head Start gave people a vehicle to express and pursue a variety of goals and enter into a variety of conflicts. The new regulations were intended to "contain those needs and conflicts in the interests of broad political stability" (Valentine and Stark 1979: 306). Members of the PC were, according to the new regulations, to be "parents," not activist community members; PC's purview was limited to Head Start issues, defusing greater community action. When Edward Zigler became national director of Head Start, he emphasized parent education over parent power, in large part to defuse controversy over the program (Kuntz 1995). Only so much grassroots activity was tolerable to local and national politicians, and that activity had to be limited to within those tolerances.

The basic presumptions of Head Start were deficit-based and incompatible in many ways with activist parents. This, too, contributed to the constraining of parents' power over the program. Even by 1979, Valentine and Stark could write that most programs concentrated exclusively on parent education rather than parent empowerment. As well, the Head Start curriculum, once very flexible to account for local needs, became much more standardized, giving parents less and less control over content (Washington and Oyemade 1987). This occurred partly to counter increasing claims of inefficiency and uneven quality, but also because of Head Start's unquestioning dedication to deficit theories.

HEAD START CONTINUES: PERSEVERANCE AND CONSTANCY

Despite the "small arsenal of ammunition" shooting down deficit theory (Katz 1989: 7), Head Start's central organizational principles have remained largely unchanged. Indeed, it is likely that these principles, however discredited among academics, have allowed Head Start to weather shifts in perceptions of the poor and ongoing talk about welfare "reform." Head Start persisted after the optimism of the 1960s waned, through "indecision" regarding poverty in the early 1970s (Gelfland 1986), into market-based proposals and program-trimming in the early 1980s (Levitan and Johnson 1984), to the "war on welfare" (Katz 1989; Rank 1994) of recent years.

Head Start may owe its continued acceptance to the way it has harmonized in several ways with the increasingly conservative atmosphere in which welfare policies are made. First, deficit perspectives deflect criticisms of larger power institutions and relationships—always valuable for the powers-that-be. The program has not lost its "hand-up, not hand-out" bearing and spirit of self-help, supporting thereby the basic myths of American society.

Second, because of the program's focus on compensatory edu-

cation and child development theory, the overall direction of ame-
liorative efforts can stay in the hands of experts and professionals
(Katz 1986; Funiciello 1993), again, guarding the status quo.
Third, Head Start is cheap. Recently, Head Start funding was increased chiefly because a longitudinal evaluation of another preschool
intervention program showed that every dollar spent on the program
saved taxpayers three to four dollars in future service costs (Zigler
and Muenchow 1992). And, as Peter Skerry (1983) points out,
Head Start centers are modestly appointed, often making use of
church basements and second-hand equipment, thus warding off
"sirloin-and-Cadillac" charges of pampering the poor with lavish
handouts. Finally, Head Start's continued emphasis on the mother
as the "child's first teacher" is supportive of and consistent with
conservative emphases on "family values" and women's proper and
preeminent role as mothers.

This is not to say that Head Start has received no criticisms, chal-
lenges, or funding cuts. On the contrary, beginning with the Westinghouse study of 1970, there have been repeated attacks from
those who sought but did not find clear indications that Head Start
produces long-term benefits for children's school achievement. Despite literally thousands of studies, the "fade-out" effect first noted
by that study has never been thoroughly dismissed.

Throughout the years, in large measure to address this continuing charge, additional service programs were hooked into the Head
Start program options. Parent and Child centers, comprehensive
Child Development, and Home Start are aimed at providing "pre-
ventative" services for low-income parents and their children from
the prenatal period through age five. Similarly, Project Developmental Continuity, Project Follow Through, and various transition
programs continue intervention into the public school years (Washington and Bailey 1995). The basis for these add-on programs is that
a single school year's worth of "inoculation" against the culture of
poverty is insufficient. Billed as "innovations," these programs extend rather than alter the basic deficit premises of Head Start.

The dedication to those premises has indeed constrained the potential for parent empowerment. Nevertheless, the other war on poverty survives, too. While the "dynamite" of community action has long been defused, for Head Start parents, seventy-point-two preserves the potential for poor parents to take charge of the program, to exercise power. And the tension between the two wars on poverty remains. That tension is the crux of our story.

Part Two

◆

WOMEN REFORMED

❖3❖

Taking Control
of Everyday Life

It's just that life is so much more of a struggle when you don't have any money.

Head Start was designed as a comprehensive, two-generation social welfare program, ostensibly to help individuals in that struggle. Its programs are intended to provide a range of child and family services, covering both short- and long-term needs.

As we argued in Chapter Two, these services are aimed largely, at "correcting" certain presumed deficiencies of parents. It is clear in Head Start publications and procedures manuals that the major focus of the program is on children, and that if these parents' deficiencies can be corrected, the kids will have a better chance in school and life. In large measure, this "reform" of parents is expected to happen by way of *involving* the parents in Head Start.

Parents are encouraged in various ways to attend classroom sessions and assist the teachers in activities for the child. They can serve as bus aids, riding on the bus to watch the kids while the driver is driving. They can serve as chaperones for field trips. There are meetings of parents at each center, and Head Start organizes a series of "Looking At Life" seminars and cooking and nutrition classes. As we will discuss in greater detail in Part Three, a few parents are also involved in setting policy for the local program.

The program's stated philosophy and its rhetoric are filled with references to the parent as the child's first teacher. In this respect, program staff seek to bring the parents into the classroom so that parents are able to reinforce in the child what is taught and so that the child sees the parents involved in her or his school, thereby making school itself seem important. Presumably, this is an important deficit in both child and parent that must be overcome.

Parents themselves can be taught subtly while they are helping out in the program. By thus participating, parents are taught by the staff's modeling how, for example, to discipline children appropriately (as defined by professionals) and how to prepare nutritious meals.

Given a deficit view of poverty, the program and its intended results sound like the comprehensive program it purports to be. Yet, what happens through Head Start's parent involvement cannot be captured by considering these policy objectives. The existing academic literature about parents and Head Start is not much help, either. In the first place, that literature is quite skimpy. More critically, though, most authors seem to accept the deficit view, designing studies that demonstrate changes in mothers' attitudes toward child rearing, school, and so forth. Accepting that assumption has kept the studies narrow and limited, and often without significant findings.

In this chapter, we analyze services without making the assumption that parents are deficient. Instead, we expect that women recognize various benefits (and drawbacks) in the services that may not be the same benefits as those intended. Our analysis is of how the women actually make use of the services and of participation. We examine mothers' own views of how these make their lives better or different or neither.

Two things will be clear from this broader inquiry. First, what is taught during the various participation activities are the values and behavior deemed appropriate by professionals. Mothers' own views on discipline, cooking, housekeeping, and so on are explicitly, though usually subtly, rejected (Powell 1982; Joffe 1977). This "cultural imperialism" may tempt one to reject the changes women make as actually disempowering, as taking both culture and voice from the women.

However—and this is the second point—mothers do make their own uses of these "lessons" and their social settings. For many women, Head Start services are the context in which they can take some control of everyday life. In looking from the women's point of view, these services are valued, despite their primarily traditional, even imperial, nature, in large part because of the way in which they are offered.

These two points will bring us, at the end of the chapter, to a more complete discussion of empowerment. We will contend that even the deficit-based services offered by Head Start can be and are used by women in *empowering* ways. In many ways, the joke is on the deficit theorists—women learn to take *control*, learn more than just the narrow lessons offered.

EFFECTS OF HEAD START: RESULTS OF EVALUATION

As early childhood education, Head Start is again and again hailed as a success, despite inconclusive research findings about its long-term effects on children's cognitive development (Nielsen 1989; Schweinhart and Weikart 1986; Zigler and Styfco 1994). There is some indication that Head Start decreases placement in special education classes and decreases the likelihood of being held back a grade (Zigler and Styfco 1994). Further, despite a lack of evidence that the program has had any effect on poverty rates, Head Start has been and remains America's most widely trusted social service program (Katz 1989; Levitan 1969; Skerry 1983).

Some research has been done on the benefits to parents, but too little (Zigler and Styfco 1994; Powell 1982; Robinson and Choper 1979; Health and Human Services 1993). Much of what exists is either very anecdotal (e.g., Sorenson 1990) or experimental and based on a pre/post-test design using various psychological scales. Most studies measure only parent education, not parent empowerment (Valentine and Stark 1979). Only a very few studies seek to examine the actual experiences of parents (e.g., Rosier and Corsaro 1993).

In a 1983 review of the literature, Hubbell cites studies showing participating parents increasing in "life skills," "satisfaction with life," "control over their own lives," "self-confidence," and "community participation." Later literature mirrors these findings.

Parker, Piotrkowski, and Peay (1987) find that, for women in a large city, participation in Head Start led to fewer negative psychological symptoms, greater feelings of mastery, and greater life satisfaction. Leik, Chalkley, and Peterson (1991) find that "enrichment activities" (not regular involvement) increase several measures of psychological health for Head Start parents. Reiner, List, and LaFrenier (1983) report that participation in early childhood programs helps parents to raise self-concept and confidence in their discipline practices. Rosier and Corsaro (1993) conclude that Head Start participation encourages self-reliance.

All of these studies involve *urban* communities. The relevance to rural communities has not been established. Further, most studies include a majority of African American respondents. White, rural women may react quite differently or for different reasons.

In most of this literature, the authors largely accept the proposition that the parents need to be trained and shown by professional social service providers. If there are increases in psychological well-being, for example, that increase is attributed to the intervention. This view and the resulting literature focus on what policymakers say is important for the parents to "become" and how the programs "make" the parents become that.

In any case, the studies do not show (or claim to show) precisely what forms of participation are most likely to result in positive psychological benefits and positive socioeconomic benefits. Each analysis cited uses a different definition of "participation," and purports to measure the effect of very different activities. In order to attribute cause and effect, though, it is necessary to specify how particular kinds of participation will result in specific positive effects. None of the studies have done this.

Each of the studies is clear that not enough is yet known even about what Head Start programs can do *for* parents. What is not at all clear is what parents do with the programs, how they use them in their own ways. We will conclude that a particular "intervention" and its intended effect is largely irrelevant—again, the joke is on the deficit theorists. What happens in Head Start programs everywhere (judging from this literature) is that parents can use the programs as arenas to increase their control over life. We will not dispute the findings, simply the root cause of them.

EASING COMPLICATED LIVES

When we began this research, we seemed to be paying particular, if not exclusive, attention to the ways in which Head Start facilitated women acting and growing publicly and politically. We were reminded—scolded, even—by several staff members and parents that, for the women served by Head Start, everyday life can be so challenging that seemingly small changes make big differences.

Louise has worked with Head Start families and children for many years. She told us:

> Well, we all lead complicated lives. I realize that. But sometimes their basic needs are not being met, and they just are struggling to meet those very basic needs. Can we pay the bills? Will the electricity go off? Will there be someone home when they get home? Will there be a fight? Will there be money? Will there be food? Will the food stamps run out? All these kinds of things.
>
> Sometimes we have to ask questions [of the parents]. I know one of my family workers said she felt awful. She would have to ask someone, what are your goals for the next three years? You know,

> and that's a very logical question, but she knows that this poor
> woman is trying to get through the next three days. She said they
> would look at me and say, three years, my heavens, you know. So,
> that's what I really mean with complicated lives.

Helping women manage these "complications," helping them move past crises large and small, is something that North Country Head Start does regularly and well, according to mothers. These helping episodes happen in many phases of the program and often in a fairly *un*systematic way. That is, when parents express a need or problem, *someone* responds—often a staff-member, but sometimes another parent or the parent group. Joffe (1977) refers to this phenomena in a state-funded preschool program as the program's "underlife."

For example, Genine recounted a time that her daughter needed sneakers. "They [Head Start staff] had extra there, so they gave them to her. We got caught at a bad time, and they were there." Parents discovered that Head Start staff could be called on in emergencies, even fairly critical emergencies. One mother, Lois, did so when she and her family returned from an aborted move out west:

> It was eighty-five [degrees] when we were out there. And then when
> we came back here it was like thirty-two. Yeah, we stayed in back
> of the horse trailer. In fact, when we got back here, we slept in the
> horse trailer. The kids slept at his mother's house. Couldn't find a
> place. Called [a Head Start staffer] up and luckily got the last house
> for rent.

Lois also told us that the staff would find ways to make sure her children received proper health care. "When Head Start started up last year, they [children] had to have a dental exam and we didn't have the money, and [a Head Start family worker] told me that they have a clinic set up. They paid for it with special funds." Lisa, another parent, remembers that "there was a little girl whose parents were in a domestic violence situation. They [Head Start staff] got the mother and the kids into safe housing."

Many poor mothers do not have the knowledge or wherewithal to locate needed resources for their children, especially if the need involves professional treatment or advice. Jody needed help with her son, found it at Head Start, and knows what might have happened without it:

> Well, my son is very active. And as a matter of fact, the people at Well-Baby Clinic recommended I send him [to Head Start] because he was so active. I think if he ever went to kindergarten the way he is now—. I mean, they've [Head Start] been evaluating him and checking him, and they think he has allergies. I thought he had like attention deficit or something, and they think he has allergies, and they're taking me to [a larger city in the next state] next week to have him evaluated by an allergy specialist, and I think if he would have went to school, they would have just said, hey, he's a bad kid.

In fact, resources that are well-known to many people may be unknown to poor, rural parents. Lois tells of yet another basic resource that Head Start helped her to obtain. "I never knew about food stamps until they [Head Start staff] told me. That's helped us a lot. I didn't realize there was so many places out there to get help and stuff."

Getting Head Start families hooked up with existing social services *is* part of the job for the staff, though they seem to go to special lengths to do it. Emma, a former parent (former parent is an odd term—Emma is still a parent, of course; this is the way, though, that Head Start folks refer to parents of children formerly enrolled) and now staffer, explains:

> And I particularly remember this one family. We sat down and we were talking to the wife and looking at the new baby and I was just talking and then the husband came in. And we just talked. And he

> said would I like a coffee and I said, "Sure! Why not." Said, "It
> sounds good." I says, "It's cold outside," you know, it was winter.
> So I had a cup of coffee, and we were talking, and I was just asking
> questions and asked him if he needed help with anything. And he
> said, "Well, I don't have food, except for WIC [services for Women,
> Infants, Children]. My wife gets on WIC for the children." I said,
> "Okay," I said, "well I can help you with that." So we took care of
> that. They didn't have transportation to go down [to the food
> pantry] and get the stuff, so we brought it back to them.

However, it is not only families actually enrolled in Head Start
that may be served. If there is a need that someone knows about,
staff members and families routinely help fill that need, if they can.
Mary, too, is a former parent now on staff:

> We have a family this year [with a] cousin [who] had a baby and
> didn't have a thing, not one single thing, and no money to get it,
> and I was told by the woman that she lives in a dump, that it wasn't
> even fit to live in. We got her a crib, [the teacher] and I. [The
> teacher] had a crib and we got her a crib, and we got her clothes
> and whatever it took for the baby. We brought them down to the
> girl that was in Head Start and she saw that the other girl got them.

Again, these instances of helping behavior are routine, but often un-
systematically delivered—people express a need and attempts are
made to help. The current structure and customs of North Country Head Start allow and encourage that helping behavior. Each instance of helping and assistance means that the women have a little
more space, a little more breathing room, and a little more control.
There were few parents who did not have some story like this to tell.

There are, though, much more systematic, even didactic attempts to "help" parents, attempts to correct deficits. These more
systematic attempts are those that have generated charges of patronization and middle-class cultural imperialism (Cravens 1993;

Polakow 1993; Powell 1982; Mink 1990; Oyemade 1985; Gordon 1990; O'Brien 1991). Some parents also recognize that they are being asked to make changes to a lifestyle that had been "good enough for my folks" and from which "I turned out all right." And yet, parents *still* may value these services.

Two "instructional" areas may be most illustrative: parenting and nutrition/cooking. Both assume a deficit among parents; each area is commonly mentioned by parents talking about how Head Start has helped them.

Parenting

Head Start, in policy and practice, makes serious attempts to train mothers in acceptable parenting skills. Many mothers welcome this training. In almost all of our interviews, this was an especially valued experience, both for single mothers like Amy and partnered women like Genine.

Amy: I mean I'm only twenty-seven, so this all started and I was like, my husband and I separated when I was twenty-two, and I hadn't had my third baby yet when we separated. So it was like all down on me at the same time. So it gives you, you know, I can do this. Like you aren't born knowing all the answers. You know, they say that a mother has an instinct. Well, I didn't have all the answers. And there's other ways to do it. I mean, you put your own touches to it but they give you other ways to do it.

■

Genine: It's been well worth it. I agree, you know, both of [my daughters] were getting out of control. And I didn't know how to get them on the right track. You know, you can't do it the old-fashioned way, you know. So, I let her go [to Head Start] and, you know, I started spending time in the classroom to see how they dealt with it. . . . I've pretty much taken over. I do things at home like they do in school.

The "old-fashioned way" involved corporal punishment. Head Start very clearly steers parents away from physical discipline. Lisa is a current (as opposed to former) parent who agrees with what she has been taught at Head Start:

> You know my parents—if my kids do something, you know, "all he needs is a good spanking." And now, we don't do that, you know. There's alternatives. I think a spanking is appropriate in certain instances, like if they're doing something dangerous or they're endangering somebody else. Not a real spanking, spanking but . . . you know.

Margaret's Head Start daughter is now in middle school. Margaret learned much the same thing those ten or so years ago:

> And there was one time I told them, "I just want to beat that kid until he can't move." They told me it was the wrong thing to do. Well, I knew beating a kid was wrong. And being hit quite a few times when I was a kid, I swore I'd never hurt my kids. And this is what I was trying to prevent. So, anyways, they helped me through that. Which I'm very thankful for.

Corporal discipline is not old-fashioned so much as it is simply typical of working-class parents (Bee et al. 1969; Powell 1982; Oyemade 1985). Noncorporal methods are more middle class, which is not the way most of our respondents were raised. While most parents accept this "modern" form of discipline, not all do. Even some of the ones who find the new skills valuable notice that they are being trained away from what was "good enough" in the past. Mary is a former parent and now works at Head Start:

> *Mary:* These kids have got to learn. Kids today are not brought up like we used to. If you touch the kids today, you're turned in for child abuse. A slap on the ass when we were being brought up didn't hurt us one bit.

LJA: I got quite a few.

Mary: Me too. I come home from school one night. My mother was an outdoor person. She worked on cars. She worked in the woods. She did everything. But she didn't do—she hated—housework. Well, the dishes were still left there, everything was still left there. Dishes were all in the sink, and she told me to do the dishes, and I said I wasn't doing no effing dishes, and that hand came across my mouth, and I never swore back at my mother again. But today, if you touch them like that, it's child abuse.

Camille, a current parent, is also unsure about the "modern" methods: "Yeah, go there and help out in the classroom, see what's going on. I even had [my son's] father go one day. 'That was a joke,' he said. Oh God. Because, you know, you can't hit these kids. There are some kids that you'd like to."

This is not a merely academic debate. Unlike middle-class mothers, poor women are likely to be deemed "unfit" if their child-rearing practices do not conform to accepted standards. A number of parents were quite concerned about being "hotlined," or reported to the state Child Protective Services (CPS). Jamie is a single mother and is critical of the staff's emphasis on preventing abuse:

> If you turn around and if your kid falls and they got a bruise or a scrape, if you don't call them and tell them what happened immediately, they're hotline happy. Do you know what I'm saying? It's, okay, there's not an accident. Everything's done for a reason. It's like, stop. Give me a break. You know, kids do fall.

If mothers learn noncorporal discipline, they are (aside from accidents) less likely to have to deal with CPS. So, while the training may be imposing standards that are unfamiliar to working-class culture, it may well be saving women from disastrous encounters with CPS. This does give the women some control over their lives. As Lisa says, "See, I learned you don't do that [spank]."

Part of the reason the parenting "training" is so valued among

Head Start mothers is the same reason middle-class mothers regularly seek the support and advice of friends, relatives, and more formally organized groups, such as Mothers of Toddlers and Mothers of Twins. Mothers like and need to talk with other similar mothers about mothering (Greenberg 1990; Wickham-Searle 1992; Horowitz 1995; Brophy 1994; Calhoun and Collins 1981). Again, in Lisa's words, "And we've been through about the same thing, so you meet other parents that—I'm not all by myself."

Being a mother is a large, even consuming part of everyday life for mothers everywhere, and may be harder, in many ways, for poor, rural mothers. One of the features of rural North Country life is the degree of social isolation poor women endure. Great distances, poor road maintenance, particularly in winter, bad weather, and lack of adequate transportation (there is almost no such thing as public transportation, even in the larger towns) all contribute to the physical isolation many women experience. Further, many poor, rural women lack strong, supportive family ties, and most lack strong networks with other mothers of small children (Fitchen 1991).

Given such isolation, Head Start offers perhaps the only forum for coming together that these women have had. In interacting with other mothers, Head Start women (like, presumably, members of middle-class mothers' groups) often move toward new ways of thinking about their children and different ways of mothering. They find support for their mothering trials, large and small. This may be especially true for single mothers like Allison and Amy:

Allison: I enjoyed it. I enjoyed the other people. Like I said. I was a single
   parent. I enjoyed, you know, doing things like that. I never got
   involved with many people. . . . I've lived here almost two years and
   I don't know nobody.

■

Amy: Because I was a single parent, kind of, it was being more like, I
   don't know, friends. I hated being the bad guy because dad was

the one with the presents, and he always got to be the good guy.
You can't look at it that way. I'm more like friends with them now.

It's also very important for mothers with partners. Carol and
Eileen are friends and found that involvement in Head Start helped
them adjust to changes in their children's lives, though in very different ways:

Carol: To be honest with you, I was with Kimmy till she was three. I didn't
go back to work after her [birth]. I got pulled out the first time until
she was three years old, and she was with me, clung to me, stuck to
me. I mean, she first started coming [to Head Start], she cried all the
time and stuff. She didn't want to ride the bus, and I'd be here at
school. She'd come in on the bus and she'd be crying and stuff. She
was clinging to her mommy and stuff.

Eileen: See, like little Frank, he's never been away from me. It's like Carol
said about Kimmy. Little Frank's never been away from me. I was
married ten years. I was five and a half months pregnant after five
and a half years. It took me five and a half years to have little
Frank. I never thought I was going to have him. So he was awful,
awful special and precious to me, so it was like after I had him, he
was clung to me and I was—he wasn't clung to me, I was clung, I
am clung to him because when he came here [to Head Start], he let
go. I'm here every day because I miss him and I want to be with
him, but he doesn't—you know, he—it was just funny, as Carol said
Kimmy clung to her, well Frank's not really clung to me, I'm clung to
him.

Lisa has also learned to "let go": "I think as parents, we don't
mean sometimes to suppress them or keep them down, but it's like,
oh, let me do that, you know, or let me pour that. We can come to
Head Start and see how good they do and when—you know, it
makes us think, you know, they can do it."

What women learn by participating in Head Start, even if it is just confidence in themselves, is a considerable boost to their lives. Further, mothers have used the parent-training services and instruction to create a network among themselves, a network of mothers. They have transformed the instructional services into a support group that they can really use.

Nutrition

Head Start furnishes two hot meals a day for children and parents who volunteer in the centers. From assisting in the kitchen and in serving and eating the meals, women report to us that they have learned how to cook with less fat, more vegetables and fruits. Meals are cooked by a paid-staffer (often a current or former parent) but are designed by a professional nutritionist. There is much emphasis on fresh fruits and vegetables, and on low-salt and low-fat foods. Meals are served "family style" in large bowls that are passed around the table. Children are encouraged to taste before they decline a new food.

Centers also organize miniclasses on cooking and nutrition, with emphasis on affordable and healthy meals. Mothers' reactions to the need for or the content of this instruction are mixed. For some, like Margaret, the Head Start way of cooking is foreign—as it might seem to the children, too:

> There was one day that the cook was ill, and they had asked me if I would try to get the lunch ready. And I tried doing exactly as [the cook] would do. And she didn't have something that they had on the menu that day. And I substituted it. And it wasn't what the kids were supposed to have. They said it was loaded in sugar. And I said, well, they're enjoying it. That's all. Boy, did [the Head Start nutritionist] come down on me. . . . And it was for almost a week after, the kids wouldn't eat lunch unless I helped [the cook] put it together.

Other mothers, like Evelyn, felt the cooking and nutrition classes to be unnecessary—at least for themselves: "I think a lot of times it teaches nutrition. I mean, some of the things that it teaches—. Now, I didn't have a problem, although I did learn things about nutrition that I didn't know. I, you know, I knew how to cook. But there are some mothers who really don't."

While the direct educative benefits of cooking instruction were not universally appreciated, cooking classes *were* universally described as enjoyable times to get together with other parents. For instance, when parents attended Head Start meetings, a standard component of their center's reports concerned their cooking classes. Women routinely reported how much they had laughed during the sessions, how much they had enjoyed the process of fixing the meal, what good friends they were making. Often, the actual content of the meal or the nutrition lesson was not mentioned; always, the fun was emphasized. These sessions are very valuable to the women, but not necessarily because of the specific didactic intent. Again, the services allowed them to build community in their rural isolation.

TRANSFORMING SERVICES

It *is* clear to us that women learned much of what they were intended to learn in these targeted instructional programs. The content of these programs, though, was based on a presumption of the women's deficiencies. Inherently, such programs seem to be patronizing and demeaning, and have long been criticized among feminist and radical academics as attempts to coerce working-class women to act like middle-class women—cultural imperialism (Mink 1990; Joffe 1977; Gordon 1990). Our acceptance of these critiques likely accounts for our initial focus on "important" changes visible in the public and political spheres.

Because so many of the women we talked with were so adamantly positive about these programs, though, we began to carefully examine what it was about Head Start that might cause us to temper these critiques. As other researchers have noted, women simply do not use services they deem demeaning or irrelevant (Horowitz

1995; Quadagno and Fobes 1995). What our data show, is that women transform services, when they can, into services they can use as they see the need, regardless of the intentions of policymakers.

Head Start, in its structure and culture, provides for that transformation in ways other social service agencies, including public schools, do not.

Structural Provisions

Head Start centers provide the needed structure for the transformation of programs. In the first place, each center sets aside a space designated as a "parent room." Often, this room doubles as the center's office, and in one case, as the janitor's closet for the entire school building. Yet, the space formally belongs to the parents, to use when they wish. Parents meet each other there informally and for regular center meetings; they met *us* there for interviews; they prepare special events for the children there, such as silk-screening t-shirts; and they wait there to chat with staff.

This room is a significant statement, we believe, about parents' rights and importance. Because of the parent room, parents are not guests in someone else's place; they have a legitimate place to be in Head Start centers. This is decidedly not the case in either public schools or other social welfare agencies (Washington 1985; Calabrese 1990; Gowdy and Pearlmutter 1994; McAtee n.d.; Arroyo and Zigler 1993).

Head Start centers are also relatively close to parents' homes; other social service agencies are located in cities, often a great distance from their homes. Parents may ride the Head Start bus into the center with their children in the morning, making it less vital to have one's own transportation—many women do not, in fact, have a car. Family workers also regularly provide transportation for a variety of purposes, picking up parents and delivering them to meetings and events for example. In addition, younger siblings of Head Start students are welcomed at the center, as well, allowing parents with more than one child to spend time in the classroom.

Finally, Head Start supports, with funds as well as transportation and space, regular meetings of parents at each center. Each center's parent group is given a formal budget and may also request additional start-up funds for projects.

All of this allows, even encourages, parents to transform didactic services into community-building collectivities. Evelyn, for one, clearly recognizes this potential:

> My dream has been to have a parent room [in the larger community] like we had here because you had five or six mothers who got together. I don't know if you're a mother of small children, but when you are, you get to feeling like there's no—, you know, adult conversation is just a wonderful thing. You'll grab the Electrolux salesman and keep him there having coffee for an hour because you want to talk. So, you had this social structure [at Head Start]. It teaches you to lean on each other. . . . I mean, it's not easy to be in that position and not have money, and then if you have a jerk of a husband who drinks and beats you up, and that's not by any means the majority of them, but it's just that life is so much more of a struggle when you don't have any money.

Other mothers also understand how important community building had been in their own lives, especially if they were rebuilding after a family crisis, like Amy:

> Like last year, I had gone through a divorce and a custody battle and all that. And I was not without sleeping pills for anything. And about halfway through Head Start last year, I started coming more often. More parent meetings, more classroom visits, and as a result, I believe, of getting out and doing Head Start, I started school.

Patty's family had only one car, which her husband took to work, leaving her in their isolated home. Nevertheless, she could participate in Head Start, relieving some of her loneliness:

> I love Head Start. Head Start has done a lot for me. I moved here; [originally] I had been from the Elba Lake area [of the North Country]. I been in California for ten years and I moved here and I didn't know a soul. Didn't have a car. Sat home depressed. Gained weight. Just nothin'. Got my kid into Head Start; met people. Just did so much for my self-esteem; it's teachin' me things. And I believe in Head Start. I see what it's done for me. . . . I'd like to [continue being involved]. But I'm so far away right now. And with the financial situation we're in right now and not having a vehicle, it's really hard on me to get to these meetings and stuff. Which I desperately want to. And I have my family worker running me amuck [driving me to meetings].

Parents' sense of community often became very strong as a result of Head Start participation. The centers' parent groups often engaged in fundraising—raffles were very popular. (Both authors had our hearts set on winning a quilt, hand-made by one of the mothers, in a raffle. Alas, neither of us did.) The funds generated are sometimes used for special social outings for the parents. The groups also use the funds for emergencies. On at least two occasions, for example, a local low-income family lost everything they had in a fire. (Many homes here are heated by wood stoves—cheap but sometimes dangerous.) Parents' groups used money they had raised to help these families buy some of the items they needed to start over.

The amount of money given was not large, but the act of raising and giving this money was an act of building community. The parents did not simply assume that government social services would help the family. The parents took for themselves the responsibility of helping. It was the structure of Head Start (the required parents' group) that provided a mechanism for these parents to help their community.

Respect

The day-to-day culture of North Country Head Start builds re-spect. Women almost universally report that they respect and are re-spected by front-line staff. (See McAtee n.d.; Arroyo and Zigler 1993.) The activities in which they engage, they tell us, build their self-respect, allowing them to "step out of the supplicant role" (Solomon 1976: 354). This is a crucial element in explaining why seemingly demeaning and imperial services are useful to the women (Swap 1990; Skerry 1983).

At the very simplest level of participation, mothers are always welcomed into classrooms, any time, unannounced. Teachers rou-tinely incorporate present parents into their lessons and actively make use of them. Many parents report that this is highly reward-ing. These women's remarks are typical:

Lisa: I know that my daughter loves it when I come to school. And a lot of other little kids in there, I hear them asking [the teacher], is my mommy coming today? Is my mommy coming today?

■

Genine: You know, it feels good to sit down and play with Playdoh and people not look at you as if you're—you know. But I love going to the Center.

■

Clara: It's almost like a family. If you're not there, it seems, gee, I should be there today. . . . I already miss it with the kids not going in today.

■

Rita: I volunteer a lot. I go in. You help out, make them lunches. [Help at] playtime. I enjoyed being with my kids, doing things. Because a lot of schools, they won't let you be with your kids in class.

Obviously, some mothers very much enjoy being in the class-rooms and around the centers. The women who choose to spend much time in the centers are most often those for whom mothering is a full-time occupation. Working in a center provides public recognition for the abilities around which their lives presently revolve— the very abilities that poor and "welfare" mothers are so often expected *not* to have—the kinds of abilities for which women, particularly poor women, are almost never recognized. This public recognition allows women to claim some dignity, some sense of self-efficacy, as well as the enjoyment obvious in Genine's description:

> I don't know of any child that wouldn't want their mom or dad or somebody there. I walk in down there and [my daughter] is like, "Mommy!" All the other kids know me on a personal level. "It's Genine!" You know, I'm there if they fall, to kiss their boo-boo. Or give them a hug. I don't care what child it is.

Vital to women dropping in, and vital to the sense of reward they get, is the welcoming atmosphere the centers and staff members provide.

Lois: They didn't make you feel like you just came in for the day. They really make you feel like one of the people, you know. . . . But down at Head Start, you can mix right in and ask them anything you want, talk to them, tell them if you don't like something.
LJA: And they'll listen?
Lois: Oh yeah. They listen. All of them do. . . . It's like a big family. That's what it makes you feel like. Like the teacher she says, and like [the family worker] told me, "If you ever have a problem or something, you don't have to keep it to yourself. Tell somebody."

Other mothers speak the same theme, that Head Start staff treats parents as a member of the *team*.

Hannah: And I guess that's probably the biggest thing about Head Start is that teachers rely on parents, as well as the parents to teachers.

And the family worker, the same way. The family worker relies on parents just as much as they do the family workers. And then going up to the office levels, the same thing. They make you feel like, you know, that you're a part of them. That means you don't have to be afraid to ask questions, and that everybody's a person, and you are a person, so don't feel afraid to ask questions, or whatever.

∎

Allison: Because they make you feel like more of a family probably. They involve the parent, they involve you, you know. That's all I can think of. They offered, "Do you need help?" You know, I was going through a really bad relationship with a boyfriend, and [the teacher] was really supportive. . . . She just made you feel comfortable. I enjoyed going there. I enjoyed being around.

The mothers' comments suggest that there is an interpersonal tone, a manner of caring and respect that encourages them to feel at home. And this tone is all the more evident when women compare Head Start to the public schools and other social service agencies. Public schools are not very inviting; as Lois says, "It's more like you're a parent [in the public schools]. You stand over there and you don't participate. I don't know the word to use. They scare me a little bit or whatever." Mary agrees, "You can't just walk in [to public school classrooms]. I just walked in and I've talked to the counselors, but not just to the teachers you can't."

Margaret, too, prefers Head Start's treatment of parents:

LJA: You've got older kids and Head Start kids. Is there a difference between the public schools, the way they accept parents or want parents to participate?

Margaret: Yes. The only time the school calls you for anything for participation is like for the school concert. The parents have to bring them. Which I don't mind [doing]. But the only time they call you is if the kid gets in trouble. That's the only time they call you.

LJA: Do you ever call them?

Margaret: I call them for annual reports. And they say, well, you just have
    to wait till the report cards or deficiencies come out.

Evelyn's son has developmental disabilities and she tried to stay
involved in his school after Head Start taught her how. However,
she found it difficult. She stayed involved, she said, "to the extent
that public schools would allow it, which was fairly rare. Classroom
teachers are not always very conducive to having you there."

Some parents recognized why this occurs. Janet says, "I think
that the general public schools are just so caught up in bureaucracy
and boards and, I mean, they're just trying to get through everyday." In contrast, Head Start sees their families quite differently.
Lila and Doris are both long-time staffers and strong advocates of
parents.

Lila: Like the Department of Social Services. [Parents] can go down and
    get their food stamps and their Medicaid and their monthly check,
    but nobody cares. Nobody cares. They don't want to listen to [the
    parents], they don't want to hear them, they don't care.

                                    ■

Doris: The Department of Social Services has treated them like children,
    and other people have treated them like children, and I come along
    and I treat them like an adult.

Though the structures of Head Start noted above are important
in creating this difference of treatment, clearly the individuals on the
staff are instrumental as well. One of the things that makes Head
Start workers different from other teachers and social workers is that
many of them (during our time in the field, from about a third to
nearly half) are themselves parents of children formerly enrolled in
the program.

Preferential hiring of former parents is a legacy of the War on
Poverty's drive to provide job opportunities for poor people. The
policy helps maintain a staff that, to some degree, reflects the com-

munity it serves. These former parents, found at all levels of the staff, contribute strongly to maintaining an atmosphere in Head Start that engenders the trust and loyalty of families.

Clara, who volunteers regularly in the center where her grand-daughter was enrolled, notes a "little" thing that has major impli-cations for women without much formal education: "[The Head Start staffer] was down to earth with us. I mean, she said things that we understood. She didn't say these long words that nobody un-derstood what they were. She always talked with us in a common language that everybody knew."

Moreover, the presence of former parents and their very low salaries also blur the social class divisions that so dominate the rela-tionships of poor women with public schools and other social wel-fare agencies. Jody explains:

> As a matter of fact, they're very helpful. I was collecting
> unemployment. I lost my unemployment and one of the teachers had
> called me to set up a parent meeting and I had told her. She like
> talked to me for like an hour about all my options, and what I could
> do and what to try, so they're very helpful. I think because they're
> like us. They're not very highly paid themselves, I don't think.

Where those class distinctions are not so salient, mothers may well find services useful, even if the theoretical assumptions of pol-icymakers are demeaning. In this atmosphere, women often use the language of self-esteem to describe the reward they receive. For ex-ample, Janna has expressed resentment against other social services, but has found Head Start important in her own growth: "It's got me motivated, which is a very hard thing to do. My self-esteem is a lot higher, well, with going on those trips [to Head Start parent conferences]. And then we had that parent recognition day. I al-most started crying."

And some women describe their new self-confidence as directly responsible for enabling them to take some control over their lives, to seek new avenues of growth, or to stand up to a husband or not be intimidated. Jody describes how she has changed:

> People that are on PC, it builds up their self-esteem, I think. I had a really low one, and now I think I can do more than I thought I could before. I don't want to give up things as easy. I'm like a vacuum lately, sucking up information everywhere. I'm actually thinking about going to college.

In fact, we watched as Jody's self-confidence grew over the time we knew her. She began PC very quiet and withdrawn, even timid. She finished the year chairing meetings. Similarly, Hannah found new avenues open to her:

> And everybody was so supportive that [serving on PC] wasn't a hard thing to do. Everybody made it very easy, you know. Oh, you can do it. And there's gonna be people here to help you and back you up. And it seems like everybody who is associated with Head Start seems to give you that uplifting feeling. Do you know what I mean? . . . I wouldn't be in college right now if I hadn't went through the Head Start program. I don't think, anyway. . . . If I hadn't gone through the Head Start program, I think I still would be intimidated by people.

As we will learn in the next few chapters, Hannah is not intimidated by very many people at all anymore. This growth in self-assertion is something Evelyn noticed for herself, too:

> [Head Start] is helping me gain self-esteem and courage and confidence. I was able to go back to school, which certainly helped my family financially. It also helped my family in that I was able to say, number one, I had learned that it was not good to keep shifting these kids around from place to place every six months. And number two, I had gotten the courage and self-confidence to be

able to say [to my husband], I am not changing school systems with these kids again. If you want to move again then go ahead, but we are staying here.

For many women, what they described as self-esteem was a new feeling. We did not solicit stories of abuse, but we heard several, such as Mary's story:

I haven't been with my husband in fourteen years, because [my son] was eight months old when I left him. He held a thirty-ought-six to my head three times, twice loaded. A knife to my throat. Came home and caught him in bed with another woman. One thing I can say, he never hit me.

McAtee (n.d.) reports that of ninety-one families in one local program, 73 percent had experienced or were currently experiencing domestic violence. For these abused women, the activities of Head Start did help them regain—or newly build—a sense of themselves as *worthy* people. This is not a trivial accomplishment. Such changes have been well-noticed by long-time staff members, such as Louise and Lila.

Louise: And we will hear parents say this, that they felt that they were not worthwhile. If there's been abuse, if they've been put down so much, it takes quite a while, quite a lot of interactions to make them feel, "Hey, I am a better—. I'm not worthy of this kind of treatment. I should be treated better."

∎

Lila: You take a person who comes from, say, an abusive home and has been brought up to believe they're worthless, no good. You're a tramp, you're a bitch, you're this, you're that. And they're young, they got pregnant, were in a poor relationship with a man, as well as their parents, and so finally, they get to Head Start and somebody says, but you can do this. You can. You can be a better parent. You can be a better mom. You can go back to school. You can. And letting them know that they can do whatever they choose to do. Well, that's a pretty powerful morale booster for anybody suffering from low self-esteem.

Another woman we met at the Policy Council is Dorothy. In talking with us, she alludes to a difficult life with her first husband. The evidence of her growth in self-esteem is suitable for framing:

> I was never allowed out of my home when I had the boys in Head Start. So when I had my girls in Head Start, I was allowed to get out of the house, do the things that I wanted to do. My family situation, so. Actually, it was more like with our family worker, she knew there was potential with like—I could draw, I could do different things.

Dorothy had told us how she had so much loved to draw in high school, but that she had completely abandoned it in the ten years since she had dropped out. After her youngest children started Head Start, she was "allowed to get out of the house." She had become very active in Head Start, where we had watched her confidence grow. She left her controlling husband and remarried. She completed her GED and returned to her art. We interviewed her in her home, where she proudly exhibited her many recently completed, framed charcoal and pastel drawings. Dorothy was still poor, to be sure, working as a chamber maid. But she had regained her sense of herself as an artist and as an important being.

Transforming Services, Developing Autonomy

Some of the positive effects we observed were largely side-effects of program features designed for other purposes. For instance, the centers' parent groups were designed to bring the parents into their child's learning environment. Yet, as we noted earlier, these groups could serve as mechanisms of community building. The classes on cooking were designed to change the eating habits of the poor, but functioned as networking opportunities for isolated mothers. The connections mothers made gave them a firmer hold on their daily lives, a support network, and different methods of coping. All of this led to a more positive self-image and a somewhat easier day-to-day life.

These positive outcomes could, perhaps, be more directly attained. Head Start staff members could directly facilitate the organization of baby-sitting networks. The "Looking at Life" series could include forthright sessions on self-confidence and assertiveness, as well as cooking.

However, a key feature in the positive view women developed of themselves and of Head Start was due to the fact of the women doing the work of networking and community building on their own, without the direct intervention of the staff. The women literally transformed the services into the kinds of assistance they decided they needed at that moment (Ellsworth 1992). It is important, perhaps, that these positive features were side-effects, rather than engineered effects. Women cannot be told to take control, but they will take it on their own when it is possible for them to do so.

We noted above that the few systematic studies conducted with parents of Head Start children show positive psychological benefits of participation. One implication of this current analysis is that these effects may be due, in large part, to what has long been called the "Hawthorne Effect." In a famous series of experiments designed to increase labor productivity, researchers decided that simply paying attention to any group of workers increased their attention to their work, regardless of the changes made in physical surroundings. Thus, it matters less what is done than that it is done.

The Hawthorne studies, though, also involved giving the workers (women assembling parts for Western Electric) some control over how they did the work—there was no direct supervisor in the test groups (Perrow 1986). It was perhaps not so much that the workers simply felt attended to, it was that they felt themselves to be in charge to a greater degree than at any time in their lives. Analogously, the respect (attention) offered mothers in Head Start is important, but it may be the staff's encouraging the mothers to take charge, indeed expecting the mothers to take charge, that is key here. Mothers were shown alternative paths and resources; the staff engaged them in active problem-solving. Then, when they succeeded, competence—their own competence—was reinforced as a good thing, not something they would be abused for.

In the end, giving women control over their lives, even the small things in their lives, may be the biggest Head Start success. Though parent services in Head Start will not directly end poverty—and may not reduce it much even for the small number of families served—it may be that these services lay the foundation for poor women to make those changes themselves.

EMPOWERMENT FOR EVERYDAY LIFE

We began this chapter's inquiry by noting again that Head Start social services are based largely on a deficit theory—parents' deficiencies could be corrected through their participation in Head Start programs. Programs like this have been deservedly criticized for their inherently demeaning character and their futility in *empowering* recipients. And yet, there is something indeed empowering that the women take from these seemingly patronizing social services.

"Empowerment" is a term loosely thrown around, both by scholars and by politicians, especially regarding their proposals for welfare "reform." It is seldom, though, elucidated. When it is explained, when attempts are made to characterize the phenomena, some writers delimit what counts as "real" empowerment.

One common view is that empowerment requires an understanding of structural and institutional forces and action against those forces. Morgen and Bookman, for example, argue that empowerment is "a *process* aimed at consolidating, maintaining, or changing the nature and distribution of power in a particular cultural context. . . . [E]mpowerment begins when [women] change their ideas about the causes of their powerlessness, when they recognize the systemic forces that oppress them, and when they act to change the conditions of their lives" (1988: 4; emphasis in original). Collins (1991) argues, too, that empowerment requires women to see their powerlessness as a result of systems of domination, or, citing C. Wright Mills, to see their personal troubles as instances of public issues.

From this perspective, our use of the term empowerment for the changes we noted in this chapter could be termed shallow or, in Morgen and Bookman's view, merely "fashionable," referring only to "individual self-assertion, upward mobility, or the psychological experience of 'feeling powerful'" (1988: 4). Indeed, the services valued by the women in this chapter could be seen as fostering an accommodation to, rather than changing, women's circumstances. Services are aimed not at encouraging women to reject or challenge the middle-class standards by which their lives are judged, but rather at training them to imitate those standards.

We marvel in and celebrate stories of women's collective struggles against institutions (Morgen and Bookman 1988; Rowbotham and Mitter 1994; Tiano 1994; West 1981; West and Blumberg 1990; Milkman 1985; Eisenstein 1983; Orleck 1995). Indeed, we will tell such stories in Part Three as these histories contribute greatly to understanding power and empowerment.

And yet, if we were to accept the argument that empowerment requires a reasonably well-developed understanding of structural social forces and action against those institutions, we would have to call the growth documented in this chapter a "false" empowerment. To us, this seems arrogant and quite as imperial as the social services are said to be—we recall the scolding we received about small changes making big differences in poor women's lives. It is important to give *authority* to the experiences and voices of poor women themselves and to understand the constraints in their lives (Fraser 1989; Pearce 1990; Gorelick 1991).

Poor women suffer disproportionately from abuse—personal abuse, to be sure, but also abuse from institutional sources. The public discourse is scathingly critical of their morality, their intellectual ability, their worth to society. They have few resources, whether educational, economic, or institutional. This is the context in which poor women live their lives. Empowerment must be understood in that context. "People's perceptions of themselves and their possibilities are very much affected by their position in the social and economic structure of our society, . . . [which includes] efforts on the part of the authorities to undermine the development of a sense of efficacy" (Ackelsberg 1988: 298).

Though Collins wishes for a Millsean view for women, she also argues that empowered acting need not mean participating in formal organizations of the working class, such as unions, or in electoral politics. Empowered acting does, though, necessarily mean changing that view of oneself that is engendered by the oppressor (1991). Similarly, Naples defines "doing politics" as including "any struggle to gain control over definitions of '*self*' and 'community'; to augment *personal* and communal empowerment; to create alternative institutions and organizational processes; and to increase the power and resources of their community" (1991: 479; emphasis added). In the case of the women we knew, changing an oppressive view of oneself, augmenting personal empowerment, means rejecting stereotypes of poor women as such applied to themselves, via enhanced "self-esteem," a feeling of contributing, and a sense of importance.

Further, the context in which poor women act involves *actual* powerlessness, not just feelings thereof. Poor women have *very* little power to change institutions; other actors have real power to maintain those institutions. This we cannot forget. As Collins puts it, women become "empowered through self-knowledge, even within conditions that severely limit [their] ability to act" (1991: 111).

Women's reports of not being intimidated, about standing up to a husband, being tenacious, going to school, all tell of personal triumphs, but they are also *political* triumphs in personal lives. Triumphs also came from standing *alongside*—rather than standing up to or against—people the women respected. Women worked together to accomplish a range of tasks; they worked with other Head Start moms and they worked with professionals, perhaps for the first time, as equals. These are small but important instances of challenging relations of power and domination in the women's lives. We need to consider these changes as political transformations, even if they *are* in women's everyday lives, and neither collective nor carried out in broader political arenas.

Similarly, Fantasia (1988: 11) recognizes that certain activities by workers, while lacking "the will or capability to make revolution, represent a transformative associational bonding that can shape class relations in significant ways." Even without an abstract theory of class relations, these "cultures of solidarity" can represent *political*, empowering consciousness. These acts can only be understood as such by looking at the context for the actions and "bondings," not at abstractions.

We do not see empowerment as an end state or a linear process. We see "empowerment" as an activity, an action, the act of using or seeking to use power. Empowerment begins, we think, with women laying a claim to dignity (Rowbotham and Mitter 1994). It begins with "doing politics" as Naples describes it above. For poor women, "becoming" empowered may mean recognizing as open particular avenues of action they had believed closed. It may also mean opening up avenues that *were*, in fact, closed. It means, following Delgado-Gaitan (1990), that women come to maximize control over their lives.

There are, then, many empowerments. Particular empowerments may be more or less *emancipating* (Edelsky and Boyd 1993) and more or less *critical* of existing power structures—some empowered acting is aimed at institutions of power and may result in structural changes, some is not. Following Piven and Cloward (1977), we note that people seek change in the institutions they actually experience and on the level at which they experience them. (See also Costello 1987; Susser 1990; Gowdy and Pearlmutter 1994.) Empowered acting, even critical or emancipating empowerment, does not require an abstract understanding of social structure (Naples 1991; Gorelick 1991; Fantasia 1988). As Tiano (1994) argues, empowered acting requires a belief in one's efficacy, which can be an enormous accomplishment for poor women. When women "act to change the conditions of their lives" (Morgen and Bookman), they likely will not do so according to theoretical predictions. Our understanding of the concept of empowerment must be grounded in the experience of the women, not imposed abstractly.

Thus, the empowerment we presented in this chapter will not likely change "poverty." The instances we presented, though, *are* examples of empowerment—women using power to make changes in their lives. We will return to this argument in Chapters Five and Ten.

❖4❖

Making Good Work

I thought I was born to wash dishes and take care of kids. I thought all I could do was wash dirty diapers.

I want a job that pays good money, or I want to work at Head Start. If I can get the satisfaction of doing something with children, for children, then I don't care about the money.

If Head Start has given many women ways to make their everyday lives somewhat easier, even while remaining poor, it has also given a few women paths to upward economic mobility, or at least economic stability. The number of women who have taken these paths is small, relative to the number of families served and to the number of poor families overall—one study reports that 17 percent of parents get a job or further education through Head Start (Calhoun and Collins 1981). In the North Country, the proportion is also surely quite small—our sample does not allow us to measure exactly. Yet, for those few, Head Start has made a profound change in their individual lives. Those few, too, are important as models for others.

While we will celebrate the strength of those few women, we must also note the structures that prevent more than a few from achieving such relative economic success. Nationally, labor markets, especially rural labor markets, are not favorable to women, contributing instead to their poverty (Bayes 1988; Cautley and Slesinger 1989; Fitchen 1992; Lichter, Johnston, and McLaughlin 1994).

Women are concentrated in low-pay, low-power, low-opportunity jobs. This societal-level phenomenon has worsened, here as elsewhere, by the lack of human capital—at the time of their Head Start involvement, nearly half of the women we talked with had not finished high school.

Human capital or not, opportunities for women to earn a comfortable living are hardly plentiful in the North Country. The North Country labor market is based on several industries: the government sector, including a military base, a number of state and federal prisons, schools, small state colleges, and state parks; service and retail businesses, which are often heavily dependent on buyers from Canada; summer and winter recreation and tourism; and some forestry, farming, and light manufacture. During the late 1980s and early 1990s, all of these except the government sector recorded job declines (New York State Department of Labor n.d.). In the mid 1990s, the military base closed, taking with it not only military but civilian jobs and a portion of the consumer base. A conservative Republican governor was elected in 1994, bringing severe cuts to state jobs and state college funding—not to mention cuts to social services. Finally, the exchange rate with Canada has discouraged many cross-border shoppers, putting local retailing and tourist attractions in jeopardy.

In this depressed labor market, the women described in this book find themselves in and out of work, some of them on and off public assistance. Many will work (usually at minimum wage) for a tourist season and then be laid off. Others will take part-time jobs (usually at minimum wage) around their children's school schedules; these jobs are also subject to sudden lay-offs. A number of the women were looking for full-time work, but could not find it. Sometimes women can depend on their partners' earnings. If something happens to his job or to the relationship, women have to seek work or welfare.

Head Start, the employer, provides one of the few genuine opportunities for low-income women's advancement in the North

Country. As we noted in the last chapter, Head Start offers a preference in hiring to parents and former parents. This legacy of the War on Poverty means that parents, even those with no formal training or experience, might be hired into steady jobs. These parents are then encouraged and assisted to increase their formal training, including college, and to seek promotions within the organization.

Lake County Head Start serves perhaps 180 families a year and there are currently about forty front-line staff members. Obviously, even highly motivated and talented mothers may not find room in this organization. Some of those closed out may instead seek training and education in more general fields. Indeed, the individual, noncritical empowerment described in the last chapter—development of self-esteem, support networks, taking charge of everyday life—do give some women the aspiration to return to school or pursue other training outside of Head Start.

Again, though, such upward mobility (within Head Start or without) may serve primarily to reinforce deficit views of women in poverty—because of Head Start, these individual women's deficiencies were corrected and they achieved success. Yet, to take advantage of the opportunity offered, women had to overcome a view of themselves as incapable and undeserving. Taking the opportunity offered them did constitute a step toward changing the structures of their lives. Again, the distinction between reforming the poor and empowering them is not necessarily so clear cut. And, in case after case, the upwardly mobile women found jobs and careers in occupations that serve poor women and children, helping other women manage their complicated lives.

In this chapter, the women describe the paths they have taken toward economic stability and success. We think these women are extraordinary. Their involvement in Head Start provided the mechanism, perhaps the spark, they needed, but they themselves provided the drive and vigor. We will also seek to understand the women who do not appear, at least for now, to have changed their lives in this way.

LILA

Well, let me see. I got started in 1965. I had eight children, and the school nurse had called me and—. Of course, the school is right here, so I go to school frequently. So she had called me and said there was a summer program for children that were going to kindergarten that fall, and would I want to send Christine, and Christine was my youngest daughter. And I said, "I'd love to send her." It sounded terrific. She said, "Well the teacher will be making a home visit and we'll be contacting you."

So, [the teacher] came that one afternoon, and she had a little paper duck and it had "Christine" on there, and Christine, being my youngest daughter, clung to me, you know. So, she's sitting here and the teacher's sitting there, and I've got my arm around her. So the teacher said, "I have a nice little duck with your name on it, Christine, and you can come to school." And she looked at [the teacher] and she said, "I don't care if you have a duck with my name on it. I'm not going to school. I'm not going to leave my mommy."

So they talked to me about getting involved, and I had to work things out because I had the other children, you know. And so I asked my sister. My sister lived next door. And I said, "Will you keep the kids, and I'll go up to school a couple mornings and see how it goes?"

Well, after I'd been there three, four days helping out in the classroom, and Christine was going to school, she was loving it. I was there, right? They wanted me to work in one of the other classrooms. So I said okay. It meant a few extra dollars. I think I got fifty cents an hour back in 1965.

So, I started working in another classroom. It was difficult leaving Christine because when I—she'd go by the room I was in, had the big glass doors, and she'd be crying and the teacher said, "Just let her be. She will be all right." And she was, and she started school. She did very well all through her school years, and so I was glad. And that was my beginning with Head Start.

So then I worked a couple more summer programs and then,

finally, at that time, Edna James was the Head Start director, and I got to know Edna a little bit, and then she asked me to go to a conference, a national PTA conference in Chicago. And here I am, with eight kids, you know, and they're all bing, bing, bing like that, all in stairs and my husband drove a truck, and I'm thinking, how can I go to this conference? It was the end of August. So I talked to Harold and he said, "Well go."

So I baked for two weeks before I went and put things in the freezer and I went to Chicago to that first national PTA conference and it was absolutely wonderful. I was getting on an airplane. I'd never flown. The Head Start director and her husband both had gone, and myself, and it was absolutely fantastic for someone who had been born and brought up in [a small, rural village], and we'd lived in [a larger town], but, you know, we never really went very far. We didn't have the money to go very far.

Going to parent conferences sponsored by Head Start broadened Lila's life experiences. Louise, another long-time staffer, tells us:

We would take big bus loads of people. Any staff, parents, and staff and parents would share rooms. And we would just have such a good time. We went to Japanese restaurants, and some of the parents who—. Well Lila, too, was one. She thought she should just eat at McDonald's, and we would take her and make her go and eat in the Japanese restaurants and all sorts of places like that. She loved it, you know. She's so different now. She just knows she can go anywhere.

Lila's life was changed in more profound ways, also. She goes on:

And on the way back from the conference, we're circling over Montreal, and I said, "Well, Edna, school starts tomorrow." It had to have been way the end of August. I said, "School starts tomorrow." This was on a Sunday night. I said, "So, did I go to this conference and now I just go home?" And she said, "No, you come to work tomorrow morning."

And so I went to work in a classroom. I worked for a couple of years in the classroom, but it really was not my calling. I loved the kids, but that was not it. I was more content with—when a parent came in and I had to talk with the parents, and going to the parent meetings and doing that type of activity—so I was going to quit during the year and Edna James said, "Don't, don't, hang in there." And she said, "Come fall, we'll give you a different position."

So that fall, I went to work as a family worker, family aide, I guess that's what they called us back then. And I really loved that. That was really my—truly my calling.

■

I'd never held a job. Raising eight kids, I never thought I'd ever be able to find work. I thought I was born to wash dishes and take care of kids, until I got out there and realized that there were a lot of other things that I could do, you know.

■

I've always, up to the past two years, found Head Start extremely rewarding. I always felt I did. I knew I did an excellent job. I knew that parents learned a lot about themselves and their kids, how to be better parents. And for a lot of them, what they wanted out of life. You know, some of them came—like me, when I first started. I didn't even have my high school diploma. I had gotten married at sixteen. And then I went back. Mrs. James, was the director, said, "Lila, you need to get your high school diploma." So I did. My son helped me, and I studied and got my high school diploma and then started taking college courses.

■

And I like to see the parents when they would come to us, and gee, "I'd like to get my high school diploma." "Well, gal, I know how you can do that." You know. And so we always encourage parents to go back to school, get [their] diploma and take [their] college courses, if that's what [they] want to do, or go to work, whatever

their choices were, you know, encouraging them to do what it was
that they wanted to do. And so many. I've seen so many come
through the ranks from the beginning. You get them, they were shy
and didn't know anything about the program, and boy, being in the
program a year or two years, they learned a lot. You know, they
learned a lot about their community and their schools and they're
getting involved in their churches.

■

So, just a lot of things through the years that gave me a lot of
personal self-satisfaction. There really never was much money. . . .
We always felt that the children needed us, the families needed us,
and we all worked together to provide the services that were
required in order to make the program effective, and it is a good
program, and I feel that it's done a whole lot for the families in Lake
County. . . . And I have a lot of faith with what the program stands
for.

Lila has been an inspiration to many, many parents over the last
quarter century. And for some of them Head Start has provided careers: "That's another real big benefit—is because three-quarters of
the Head Start staff here in Lake County were parents in the program, and that's a very important part."

Nationally, about a third of Head Start staff are made up of parents of children formerly enrolled (Zigler and Styfco 1994). For
many, as Lila says, and as for Lila herself, that employment has made
the difference between poverty and security.

I know for ourselves, you know, my husband and I, he drove a truck
and I was a mother. We had eight children, and it took all Harold's
paycheck to make the house payments, pay the lights, pay the rent,
pay the phone, keep food on the table.

And when I went to work, I was able—we were able to do more
things that you would like to do for your family. You know, when
the kids needed special things, or they needed things at school, or

the girls were going to the prom, you could go buy them a gown.
You know, I mean, there were a lot more things that you could do
with that extra income, than if it wasn't there for certain.

Lila's husband later became disabled, and Lila's income kept the
family going. Lila is certain that she would not have entered the
paid-labor force without the influence of her Head Start participation. It was she who was quoted in this chapter's epigraph: "I
thought all I could do was wash dirty diapers."

Though rewarding, Head Start employment is not high-paying,
not in 1965 and not in 1995 (Granger 1989; Granger and Marx
1990). Emma, another mother-become-staffer, tells us, "I'm eligible for all the programs [like food stamps, Medicaid]. I've been
working in this program for ten years now. So. You know, and I'm
still eligible for all the programs."

Yet, for people like Lila, Head Start provided a job working with
their own children. It provided rewarding work, giving assistance to
mothers like themselves, giving back assistance that had been given
to them.

If Lila never became economically rich with Head Start, she nevertheless increased her family's economic stability. And, she broadened her worldview, developed a rewarding career, and helped individuals and her community. Lila considers herself to have been
empowered.

HANNAH

One of the mothers Lila worked with is Hannah. Hannah was
moved to tears when she recounted her early adult life. At the time
she began her Head Start involvement, she was raising two daughters alone.

Hannah: I was interested in a preschool program for my children. I
thought that would be a better alternative than baby-sitting, a baby

sitter for them, you know, because I went to work. Baby-sitting has been a problem for me, to find somebody who I felt comfortable with, and you know, making sure my kids would even be okay and all that. And I started looking in Catholic schools and the expenses and whatnot.

And I'm not exactly sure how I got in contact with the Head Start department. I know. I remember seeing a poster at Social Services, but I don't think that's how I contacted them. God, I wish—. I can't remember.

When I did contact them, I was told that I was being placed on a waiting list and someone had suggested that I keep calling in case there was an opening. And I did keep calling back. And I was speaking with Lila. An opening came up and Heather got accepted.

I was really impressed that they had someone come out to the house with the school bus so that Heather and I could both get on the bus, and, you know, it was—. I don't know how to explain it. Made me feel comfortable, and I'm sure it made her feel comfortable, rather than having to walk out and get on a bus all by herself, or for me, just to take her without her seeing it first, I mean, being able to go on it together. That impressed me.

And then the family worker came to the house. She came out to the house a couple of times before Heather had actually started school. And I was invited to the school with or without Heather, to see what the setup was like. And she did her assessments. The family-needs assessments. And then they had family orientation at this time, which you could bring the kids or not. And it just explained the whole program briefly. And it was everything that was needed to help families. We got a lot of support. You know, not financially, of course, but the Head Start being free, yes, but how do I say it? It really boosted our self-esteem.

LJA: For all of you, not just Heather?

Hannah: Not just Heather at all. Especially me.

LJA: How did it do that, do you think?

Hannah: Because of the activities that I got involved in. We had parent meetings. And I was encouraged to get involved with them to see how the program works and stuff. And so I did. And then, when positions became available, I was curious to try, you know, accepting positions and seeing how I did. And everybody was so supportive that it wasn't a hard thing to do. Everybody made it very easy, you know. Oh, you can do it. And there's gonna be people here to help you and back you up.

LJA: When you say "everybody," you mean other parents or the staff?

Hannah: Parents, staff, everybody involved with Head Start. Even the people in the community. And everybody—it seems like everybody who is associated with Head Start seems to give you that uplifting feeling. Do you know what I mean? Whereas if it wasn't for Head Start, I think I'd be very shy and sitting in a corner and not talking to anybody.

■

The difference between my past and then after being in Head Start was I started looking at things differently. I wasn't down on myself so much, and I started realizing that people are people, you know. I used to be intimidated by, like say, a professor or a doctor, even just going to the doctor's office. And in my experience through Head Start, it has made me feel like they're just people too.

LJA: Do you remember what it was about Head Start that taught you that?

Hannah: The whole cycle that you go through in the program, really. About the introduction of the program, and then once you're in the program, people work with you in different ways, and it's all guided by you, what you want to do. Like I got into Policy Council. Not everybody does. But that doesn't mean that everybody wasn't affected positively.

They choose. Like, you could go in the classroom and just observe in the classroom. You can go to their nutrition meetings. I kind of got involved in everything. I was curious. I wanted to know what everything was all about. And in doing so, I feel that I was helped out a lot.

■

And I guess that's the biggest thing about Head Start is that teachers rely on parents, as well as the parents to teachers. And the family worker, the same way. They—the family worker relies on parents just as much as they do on the family workers. And then going up to the office levels, the same thing. They make you feel like, you know, that you're a part of them. That means that you don't have to be afraid to ask questions, and that everybody's a person, and you are a person, so don't feel afraid to ask questions, or whatever.

LJA: Did the family worker make any referrals for you?

Hannah: Yeah. The literacy volunteers. Because I had expressed that I wasn't good in that, and then my writing skills, English. I didn't think I was very good. And she had asked me if I had a desire to go to school, and I told her yes, but I wasn't confident enough, that I didn't think I could do it.

■

I wouldn't be in college right now if I hadn't went through the Head Start program. I don't think, anyway. I mean, there's a possibility that, you know, my husband could have encouraged me because when I got involved in Head Start was when I got married to my second husband. And he's very positive. If I hadn't gone through the Head Start program, I think I still would've been intimidated by people. . . . I mean, I'd walk into an office and a secretary could intimidate me. Where I've learned not to be intimidated. But, you know, I have a right to ask a question. Head Start really made me understand that, in being involved in Policy Council, encouraging me to ask questions when I don't understand, and that nobody's going to put me down for it.

Hannah attends the college at which both authors teach. When we were first thinking about doing this study, we had mentioned the possibility to a colleague. That colleague taught one of the courses in which Hannah was enrolled. From a class project, the colleague knew Hannah was involved with Head Start. She introduced Hannah to Lynda. Hannah expressed enthusiasm about the project and pledged her participation. As Chapter One makes clear, we did not get this project under way as soon or as easily as we expected to. Some months after being introduced, Hannah and Lynda were both at an unrelated community event. At a break in the presentation, Lynda was in front of the auditorium chatting with some of the evening's presenters. Hannah strode up, reintroduced herself, and asked when the study would begin, and when could she be interviewed. (In fact, had Hannah not made this approach, reminding us of how much the mothers wanted it done, we *might* have let the whole project slide.)

After coming to know Hannah better, it is obvious how much this nearly cold call at the community event was unusual for her, at least at the time it happened. All of her comments above about being intimidated and shy were reflected in her behavior, for a time. When we first met her, Hannah was less than perfectly self-confident. At this community event, she was obviously uncomfortable in speaking with Lynda, though nonetheless determined. She was generally quiet and reserved, and very rarely spoke in strong terms. She did not make waves. Yet, she says that even this hesitant demeanor was a marked improvement over her previous self. This assessment was seconded by Seraphina, one of the staff:

> Look at Hannah. Hannah's a prime example. Because she was my parent [Hannah's child attended Seraphina's center], and she was nothing like she is now. She was nothing like she is, and I have to say that the majority of that was probably done by Lila, because that's who she worked with mainly, through PC and everything else, and among herself. I mean, she did quite a lot of it herself.

Lynda did interview her shortly after that community event. She again clearly displayed discomfort and timidity.

LJA: You'll forget about [the tape recorder] after a while.

Hannah: The only thing I worry about is that I don't express myself too well sometimes.

LJA: If you're uncomfortable, I can turn it off.

Hannah: No. That's okay. It just makes me nervous. But it's not that I don't want it taped. It's—. I'm just nervous anyway.

LJA: You mean about this interview?

Hannah: Yeah.

LJA: How come?

Hannah: I'm not sure. I know that sounds funny, because I'm the one that tried to get you to talk to me and everything, because I wanted to tell you about it. Sometimes I need coaxing to just get things out.

During the next year and a half, Hannah became a different person, in many ways. As we will discuss in much greater detail, she became the Policy Council chairperson and actively led a fight against an administration grown unresponsive to parents and their rights and needs. She spoke at public rallies. She contacted federal regulators. She led a letter-writing campaign to state legislators. When the state budget was cut drastically for the state university system, she joined a group from the college to personally lobby senators and assemblypersons, and was very articulate in presenting the needs of low-income students. She made waves.

The time period we observed and got to know Hannah was her second go-around with Head Start. Given the growth we witnessed during this time, we fully believe her description of the growth that occurred during her first experience.

Hannah had seized the opportunity offered her:

LJA: What are your goals now for your family?

Hannah: I would definitely like to get a college education, finish my college, and hopefully do the same for my children. Encourage them that, you know, to get an education, that it is extremely important no matter what you do. Even if you, you know, even if

you get married and don't work, I think that college education is
very important, whether you work or not.

In addition to her other activities, Hannah works during the summer at the Board of Cooperative Educational Services (BOCES),
which offers vocational and special education. She finds it hard to
decide on a career path:

Hannah: On a day-to-day basis, I get very confused. When I'm working
  at BOCES. I think that's what I'd like to do. When I was working
  with Head Start, I thought that's what I would like to do. Then, when
  I get into different studies, it just confuses me more.
LJA: Because there's so many opportunities?
Hannah: Right. I'm sure it'll all come together in the end, and I'm just
  starting out. So.

In a recent conversation, Hannah said that she now wanted to
become a school counselor, which would require a master's degree. Her main obstacle to that is finances; the state is cutting aid
to low-income students, and cutting the state university system in
general. This makes it quite difficult for her to finish her formal education. There is yet another possibility looming for Hannah's
mobility. As we will describe in Chapter Nine, the Head Start staff
has unionized. Hannah has been working with the union rep here
and there, and is now considering working for the union as an organizer.

For Hannah, these are options she would not have had without
having been active with Head Start. She, too, credits Head Start
with empowering her.

OTHER STORIES

However exemplary, there are many stories like Hannah's and
Lila's. This is just a smattering from our data.

Celeste, a Teacher

Nancy: But then Celeste, who was the most shiest, most withdrawn—. I mean the first time I went to Celeste's house as . . . her family worker, the only thing Celeste did was nod her head, yes and no, for anything. No matter what I said. She just nodded her head, yes or no. And now, she's running the classroom. I mean, you know!

Celeste was also active in forming the new union of Head Start staff, showing courage and self-confidence.

Evelyn, an RN

Evelyn: I had come from a family that had very little self-esteem. I had very little self-esteem. I would not have sat here and talked to you. I would not have talked in front of a group of people, ever. I was a meek little mouse, and I was raising a child with a speech problem. And I had a new baby when we came to Lake City.

And I went to the first parents' meeting. . . . And they made me feel good. I had a child that had problems. And I had lots of family problems, and I felt that I was really stupid and didn't know anything.

And through the course of time, coming into the classroom, working. . . . But I think the most important thing was the fact that people would say, come and do this, come to the parent room. And I was the kind of person who thought, you know, if they sent a letter home from school saying we'd like you to come, I'd say, yeah, but they don't mean me. But that never happened in Head Start.

I don't remember what it used to be called. But anyway, they used to pay them. CETA [Comprehensive Employment and Training Act]. That was it. They got me under CETA funds. And I worked for Lila, and then they would have pushed me into a big thing. When there was an opening, I would have had a job [at Head Start], but we had moved by then.

But that was always something that stayed with me. That, wow, you know, this was something that really I was able to do. Not by myself, by any means, but you know, it gave me some worth.

And I really think that it gave me the confidence to go on and apply for the job. There was another interim kind of DOT grant job that I had a few years later that got me back in school. They paid for some school, some college courses. And I thought, boy, I'd been talking about going back to college for a long time and I'm going.

And then, you know, I went from there and I got my LPN, then I got my RN. I've developed ease of talking, too. I mean, I'm not afraid to talk to a group anymore. I can go on, and it's just been such a growth in my own personal life.

■

I was able to go back to school, which certainly helped my family financially. I mean, we struggled until I began making a living when the kids were in school and I started working. That made a tremendous amount of difference.

Emma, a Head Start Family Worker

Nancy: Emma. Who was so strong in the union, she was another parent. Her husband was in the Air Force in Guam. Some place like that. And I mean, she did not move without his okay. I mean, a thousand miles away, but still she did not move without his okay. And now, she's like, you know, fighting. She was one of the negotiators [for the union]. She was fighting for one penny.

■

Emma: When I did it as a parent, my thing was, I told my husband, I said, [my son] is going to school in September. I'm going to work for Head Start. And he said, "How do you know that?" I said, "Because *that's* what I want to do." And that's what I did.

Holly, a Head Start Bus Driver

Holly: Well, I'm a former parent of Head Start also. My son went. Well he's seventeen now.

LJA: When your son was in Head Start, were you part of Policy Council?

Holly: No, I was not. Nope. I used to go and help out in the classroom a little bit and help out with field trips and that, but I never really got into Policy Council.

LJA: Any particular reason?

Holly: No, well, probably just a lack of confidence in myself back then. . . . I started out as a bus aide, substitute bus driver. . . . For myself, I want to get within transportation in Head Start. I'd really like to be—. I'm kind of trying to work my way into the [transportation coordinator job]. . . . That's my goal. You know, that's how I would like to move up.

Helen, a Head Start Teacher

Louise: Helen. Helen was a former Head Start parent, and she came to work with me, and she's just such a sweet young woman.

LJA: She's a teacher now.

Louise: Yes, she is. And she wouldn't mind me talking about her because she knows I love her dearly, and she came to be—. She was working elsewhere, and we needed a cook. And I said, "Oh, let's ask Helen if she would do it," so Helen came to be the cook. Then when we needed a teacher assistant, she was my teacher assistant.

And she hadn't got her GED, and she needed to have it to have the job, so I said, "She's a bright girl." And I said, "Call and find out about it." And it was like Tuesday, and she said, "Oh, it's going to be on Friday." I said, "Just do it." In fact, Helen and I, we laugh, because "Just do it" became the big saying we had. I said, "Helen,. . . Just do it. Just do it. Go for it." And she did, and she got through it because she had been over at [a Catholic school] and she was a good student. She just passed it [the GED] very, very well. Very easily.

Mary, Head Start Family Worker

Mary: I was a parent when both of my children were in Head Start. . . . I volunteered. I was on Policy Council. I was—. It was a rough time for me at that time because I had left my husband, and I was raising two kids on my own. So, Head Start was a big help to me then. And . . . they didn't have a family worker, and [a family worker] came to my house and she said, "Mary, apply for the job. You can get it."

I was working at the time. I was working at Howard Johnson's cleaning rooms, and she took and—. And I said, "No. I got a job. I'm not going to apply for it." A week went by and she comes back, "Mary, go apply for it." So I went and applied for it. . . . I've been here for six years. . . . I like working with the parents. I like working with the kids. I enjoy my work. I enjoy helping people.

It doesn't matter what age group or anything, because I also drive for the Office of the Aging. I work for—. I also drive for Medicaid. I work with the elderly and everything, on top of working with the people in Head Start.

Penny, a College Student

Penny: [Being on Policy Council] made me stand up for my rights and, you know, what I believe in. I guess it's just made me feel more important, you know, in my child's life, than just being a mother. You know, that I do—. That I had a say in the programs she got and the places she went and the things she did in school. . . . I got my two-year degree then I enrolled here [at a four-year college]. I was a late admission but I got a four-point-oh.

But I want Judge ———'s job; that's my goal in life is to be a family court judge. Because, after working with domestic violence and seeing how he handled family cases, I just think I could do a much better job. The only way I'm gonna be able to do that is to get an education. So I'm going here full-time and I work part-time. I'm like thirty-seven years old and I'm still in school.

HEAD START AND UPWARD MOBILITY

Our ethnographic data do not allow us to make explicit assessments about the number or proportion of women in the North

Country who have utilized Head Start experience to expand their career options or become economically stable. At this point in time, the nation-wide data, too, are only anecdotal, like the stories of Hannah and Lila. However, there seem to be *lots* of anecdotes.

Sorenson (1990) compiled over thirty brief stories of poor parents. An Apache woman, for example, unemployed when her child was in Head Start, went on to earn a bachelor's degree and is earning a master's. She has worked in progressively responsible positions in child development programs. An Oregon woman, a single mother, is now working on a Master of Social Work degree while serving on a number of boards of community service agencies. And so on. Other success stories appear regularly in the National Head Start Association Journal. In 1989, the National Head Start Parent Association published *Twenty-Five Voices Celebrating Twenty-Five Years*, containing twenty-five more, very similar anecdotes of upward mobility through Head Start.

Parental upward mobility is regularly cited as a critical feature of the program (Washington and Bailey 1995; Zigler and Muenchow 1992). Though the absolute numbers are surely relatively small, there is, nonetheless, something good going on here. Increasingly, the national debate on poverty and welfare focuses on work and workfare schemes. While we will have a number of criticisms to make of that agenda in Chapter Ten, Head Start seems to provide one positive model for achieving individual upward mobility.

There are likely two key elements here that make Head Start a *safe* space for women to explore their strengths. First is that the front-line staff respects the women. Second is that the substance of Head Start provides a socially respectable outlet for the *mothers'* activism.

The first element is clear from our discussion in Chapter Three. Women make a sharp distinction between Head Start and other government social services. That distinction comes, as staff members and parents say, because Head Start cares about and respects them:

Lila: You know, you try not to leave people hanging out there, and oftentimes I think that's what happened [to parents]. . . . You [as a service-provider] can't believe that you're better than these people. You've got to meet them wherever they are at.

■

Emma: These people need to know that you're not up here somewhere. Above their heads. They need to know where you're coming from, and you know where they're coming from. And just relax with them. You know. You don't have to be all business-like, you know. Because they're not gonna tell you anything. And he [a parent] said something about Social Services. And I said, "I know how that is. I was on Social Services." I mean, I know how they treated me when I went down.

■

Doris: Because the Department of Social Services has treated them like children, and other people have treated them like children, and I come along and I treat them like an adult.

One aspect of this safety and respect is, perhaps, that the mothers can see themselves in the staff. Many of the staff also benefited from Head Start services, and some of the ones who did not are nevertheless from similar class backgrounds. Camille notes how parents see themselves following in the staffers' footsteps:

I think if parents, or new parents coming in, could see—. "Oh, wow, she used to be a Head Start mom. Look at what she is doing now." It would boost their esteem a lot, and they'd be like, "Wow, maybe while my child is in there, I might want to come in and help out, and then I might want to be a teacher's aid," or "I might want to help out and cook sometimes when the cook is not there," or, you know, "I might want to participate a little more and be the bus aid," and this, that, and the other thing.

When it is *safe*, when women feel they are among people like themselves, people who care, women can take advantage of learning opportunities and opportunities to develop networks. As shown in the last chapter, women then can use the programs for their own purposes, including achieving upward mobility. Women will not necessarily make much use of mandated, disrespectful job training (Quadagno and Fobes 1995; Horowitz 1995), but they will make their own use of respectfully offered opportunity (Gowdy and Pearlmutter 1994).

Of course, working for Head Start, whether for pay or as a volunteer, can be seen as "proper" women's work, and this seems to be an important aspect of women seizing opportunities for participation. Working with one's child's educational institution is acceptable, even laudatory for women, perhaps especially poor women. Naples (1992) shows this to be true for poor African American and Hispanic women, whose first activism in the community involved their children's schools. Smith argues that working in the paid-labor force requires a shift in women's expectations away from motherhood (their "proper" role). Even so, "women wage earners must consider their domestic roles the most salient ones" (1984: 138).

Among women in the North Country, we overheard a conversation that illustrates this phenomenon: Before the first PC meeting of the new school year, an outgoing mother complained that she would like to stay and work with Head Start, but her husband had declared otherwise. He had said that if she was going to be involved in that much work, it had to be with the school her son currently attended. In other words, if she was going to be away from the home, it had better be directly related to her kid.

This is one major reason we have focused on *women*, rather than parents in this book. We believe that men, even poor men, have more, or at least different, respectable outlets for participation. For example, men can join the volunteer fire departments that dot the North Country; women can only participate in auxiliaries if their husbands are members. Men do not seem to need "permission" to participate, in Head Start or elsewhere, in the ways that women seem to need it.

Women have permission—explicit or otherwise—to be deeply involved with their children's education. Active involvement with Head Start is seen as legitimate for mothers. This aspect of participation may have helped ease the transition from work in the home to work in the paid-labor market. Lila, for example, went to work caring for her child in Head Start, never thinking she *could* do any other work.

For women who had already been working in the paid-labor market, the content of the Head Start work was important in giving meaning to working. Working with children and parents can make working a more rewarding activity. As Jody explains:

> But the teachers that are in Head Start, they care. They're not there because they're making thirty thousand a year. [The pay is *much* less.] They're there because that's where they want to be. And I want a job that pays good money, or I want to work at Head Start. If I can get the satisfaction of doing something with children, for children, then I don't care about the money.

Mary had been working cleaning hotel rooms. She now finds that she loves working with people, helping them. Emma wants to work with children and families. Penny wants to help women in family court. For these women, then, not only is increased financial stability important, it is also important that their work is intrinsically satisfying and meaningful (see also Naples 1992). Even if the jobs they eventually take are not in Head Start, the jobs share the same character, that of helping people.

Our argument here is *not* what Head Start does *for* women, reforming them, encouraging them to want to take jobs. In the atmosphere Head Start structures make possible, women can do that for themselves—some women, at any rate.

THE WOMEN WHO GOT AWAY

Notwithstanding the many anecdotes available, Head Start reaches only a few women this dramatically. From the stories in the literature and from our respondents, we know that these women credit Head Start for their own success. And yet, the majority of women served by Head Start do not have such compelling stories of conventional accomplishment.

This is not surprising, given the structures we have already discussed. Recall Louise's description of "complicated lives"—not knowing if there would be food, or a fight, or money to pay the electricity. The all-encompassing nature of these complications prevents many women from seizing the avenues made visible or possible by Head Start. It *is* an achievement to reformulate self-image—an achievement not every one makes. Further, women's lack of job opportunities are not due to a personal lack of drive or ambition. The jobs simply do not exist in the quality and number necessary. Only a few women *can* actually make it. Others adjust to this reality and live the lives they understand are dealt them.

All the women we spoke with during our research believe they personally got something out of Head Start. These are women we knew from our field work or women someone recommended to us. We did not do a random sample of mothers—recall that we did not have the full cooperation of the North Country Head Start administration. Thus, our sample did not include people who were indifferent about the program, and very few who had not made some movement toward empowerment. We asked all of our respondents, though, mothers and staff members, why some mothers participated and reaped the benefits described in Chapter Three and this chapter, while others did not; why some seemed to be empowered and others not. We wanted to know something of the mothers who were lost to us.

In describing these women, the staff tended to be more forgiving than other mothers. Louise captures the general view of the staff when questioned about how Head Start helps families:

> Okay. Well, that's a very big question because it helps some and where you can see it, and others, we don't see it so clearly, but that happens in all education, doesn't it? You see it affects some students

and not so much in others. There are many that I feel have been helped. We know that for sure. . . . And some parents are ready for it and receptive and some are just not.

Similarly, as teachers ourselves, we understand that students are in different places with regard to the material we present in our classrooms, some more ready to hear it than others. We always hope that others will come back to it in later years. The following interview is illustrative of our point:

LJA: The parents that don't participate and that don't volunteer, why not? Why don't they?

Lila: Why don't they? Well, I think society will always have the people who—[for them] it's not as important. They haven't learned yet why it's important, and sometimes, and, you know, I've seen through the years. A family might have had five children. Say they had five children. The first two or three that were in Head Start, you never saw them, and then all of a sudden, there they were, and they said, I should have done this when my first child came, but I had the other children. So, they're not having the time, not being able; they can't afford baby sitters; they can't leave the house; moms are pregnant; they're having babies; and when you got a newborn, it's hard to get away. . . .

LJA: Do you think some of them are afraid?

Lila: Oh, yes. I'm sure they're afraid. Yes. Because different ones through the years would say, I didn't realize this would be this much fun, and, you know, getting involved.

Unlike the staff, active mothers tended to blame nonparticipation on laziness or other character flaws—supposed inherent qualities of poor women.

LJA: Why don't [other mothers participate]?

Jody: Do I have to answer that?

LJA: You won't be identified.

Jody: Some of them are working. I know some of them are working. Some
of them just really don't care. They're where they are, and they
have no burning desire to get out of it. Head Start is a place where
their kids can go for free and they don't have to put up with them.
And a lot of them, I mean, it's an awful observation, but a lot of
them, I really think, are like that.

There is a great deal of agreement on this topic among the mothers. Genine tells us, "There are a few families that do abuse, like I
said earlier, not going in to volunteer. That's abusing the program.
That's using Head Start as a baby sitter, which isn't right." Another
mother agrees:

Camille: I think parents got to get in there and got to know what is going
on this program.

LJA: And if they don't?

Camille: Then they're just going to leave their kids there to go on and be
pushed through school and everything else and say, so, "Oh, just let
them go, let them go. It's seven hours out of my day, that I don't
have to worry about them, almost like a baby-sitting service." That's
how some of them look at it.

Clara, who has been a volunteer for several years, even after her
granddaughter graduated from Head Start, tells us much the same
thing:

LJA: Do you think the kids whose parents come get more out of Head
Start?

Clara: No, I think the kids all get useful things. I think that a lot of parents
think that this is a free baby-sitting. This is my impression.

LJA: Do they work?

Clara: Some do, some don't. It's no good to send a kid with a runny nose
or anything. That's why I say, it's a free baby sitter.

This opinion is not new, either. Margaret's Head Start involvement was more than ten years ago, yet she shares the current mothers' opinion: "The way I looked at it, the bus used to pick the kids up about eight thirty and drop 'em back off about two. To me, it was like, after that kid was on the bus, 'I'm free, I can do what I want.' That's what it looked like to me [that some mothers were doing]." It may well be true that participating mothers are stronger than those who stay away, at least for this moment in time. We know that the women we've met in this chapter are exceptional, in many ways. And yet, there is an eagerness to paint nonparticipating moms as different. This view of active mothers toward those who do not participate comes out of, we think, the former's hopes for their children's and their own futures—"There must be some reason those women don't succeed, but I will." This view is perfectly in keeping with deficit theories of poverty and with faith in the American Dream. In many ways Head Start promotes that theory and that limiting dream, even as it provides some women with avenues of empowerment. The view is worth exploring in more detail.

❖5❖

The American Dream

That's why I'm saying, I hope the Head Start program gives Frank the extra boost so he doesn't have to struggle, so he'll have, you know.

I'd very much like [my children] to go to college and get a degree. Go make something of their lives.

The only way I'm gonna be able to [achieve my goal in life] is to get an education. So I'm going [to college] full-time and I work part-time.

As we've noted, Head Start programs for mothers are largely premised on a deficit theory of poverty. And, "success," especially of the type described in the last chapter, may well reinforce that idea. This feature, we have argued, partly accounts for the continued popularity of the program among politicians—Head Start does not threaten the powers that be. This also, we think, helps account for Head Start's popularity among mothers, by seeming to provide them with a way out of poverty and despair that depends only (or at least primarily) on their own ambition.

We have also argued that we should consider the changes in both Chapter Three and Chapter Four as empowerments. Women have developed new conceptions of themselves as able and competent, identifying or creating new avenues of action for themselves. These are important achievements in a world that demeans and insults, not to mention abuses, these women mundanely. For some women, these new conceptions have made life a bit easier, and for some they have made possible a new economic stability.

However, these empowerments have not (yet) led either to an explicated understanding of the institutional forces arrayed against poor women or to collective resistance against those forces. On the contrary, the mothers of North Country Head Start believe in the power of hard work, believe that their own (and their children's) chances in life depend primarily on what they as individuals make of those chances. They believe, in short, the American Dream—"work hard and you can be anything." This might be quite distressing to the original radical poverty warriors, who had wished that community action *would* lead to class-conscious collective struggles to change fundamental power structures in America.

Yet, many women *also* have clear understandings of class-based differential access to chances in life. They know well that it matters whether one is born rich or poor or in-between. Vanneman and Cannon argue that, indeed, Americans have an "instinctual if not fully articulated" sense of class (1987: 14). They go on to note, though, that even if people understand class power, they may not understand what to do about it. To make the point, they quote one of Studs Terkel's respondents, Ed Sadlowski: "[The worker] understands who's screwing him, but he doesn't understand how to get unscrewed" (1987: 14).

The women here do have some concept of "who's screwing" them, but believe that getting "unscrewed" depends on their own, individual hard work, rather than collective, class-based action. This belief is hardly unusual for Americans, but it has decided consequences for the emancipating and critical empowerment that radical poverty warriors wish for the poor. However, those radicals—perhaps the present authors, as well—may wish for the women differently than they wish for themselves.

Again, in thinking about what the women have told us about poverty and getting ahead, we must keep in mind the reality of their lives.

POVERTY

When we talked with women about poverty, the first thing that struck us was that most of the women did not consider themselves poor. They used words like "low-income" and "tough times," to be sure, but "poor" people were generally someone else. Further, when people were "poor" (as opposed to "low-income"), it was generally because they did not work hard enough. Their solution to poverty is for people to get jobs:

LJA: One of the reasons they originally started Head Start, they said it was part of a set of programs to end poverty. Do you think it will do that?

Lois: No.

LJA: Why?

Lois: I don't think anything will ever end poverty until people themselves want to stop. If it's easier to sit back and draw the welfare and sit home and have children, then do it. Then, of course, they're not going to want to get out and get it themselves. There are some people, you know, that just can't get out of it. But they can try. As long as people just sit back, they are trying not to do it.

Lois had told us (in Chapter Three) that she and her husband had once had to sleep in the horse trailer, lacking the resources to find housing on short notice. When we talked with her, she was receiving food stamps and had had to rely on Head Start to pay for her child's dental care. Lois had also just been laid off from work as a cook in a retirement home and had little prospect for another job any time soon. And yet, she insisted that people must try to "get out of it."

Carol and Eileen, too, are critical of people who do not work.

LJA: Do your friends and neighbors think that Head Start is a good program, as well?

Carol: Yeah.

Eileen: Yeah, yeah. But then you take some of the welfare people. If they send their kids. I've heard some of the welfare people say they don't want to send their kids [to Head Start]. It's not because they wouldn't want to send them. They send them. They wouldn't want to go to work. But if—I didn't know this—if they send them, they have to get out and get a job.

IJA: Oh. I didn't know that.

Eileen: Yeah. If they send them, I heard they're supposed to get a job. So a lot of them are saying, "No, I'm not going to send my kid just for the satisfaction of—"

Carol: That's probably why the girl—

Eileen: They don't have to get out and get a job.

Carol: That's probably why the girl down the road that I know. Sorry, but I think she's had three kids. I think every time it comes due for her to go back to work, because I know after the kid's like three years old, three or four years old, welfare tries to push them to get a job. Well, she keeps popping up with another one in the belly. Well, she's fixed now. And it come due for her to go back to work and she has a job for like a week or two. She doesn't want the job.

Eileen: Poverty breeds poverty. They don't want to.

Janna's remarks provide a particularly clear example of the contradiction between women's actual life experiences and their unexamined beliefs about poor people:

IJA: Okay. So here's another question. What causes poverty in the first place?

Janna: Oh, gosh. You got me on this one. I would say that it's people that want something for nothing.

IJA: Yeah?

Janna: So, these people are out there on social services, three-quarters of them can get off their ass and get a job, but they won't because they're getting free money. They ain't got to pay it back and the only way they got to pay it back is if they get caught frauding them and most of them are.

LJA: Oh yeah?

Janna: Oh yeah!

LJA: Anything we can do about that?

Janna: As far as making it harder for the people who really need it, I don't know about that.

LJA: Because there are people who really need it, right?

Janna: Yeah, but then you got these idiots who won't get off their ass and—. Lazy bums! Do you know what I'm saying?

LJA: Yeah.

Janna: It's very frustrating, you know?

LJA: Especially to people who are trying to make good in their lives.

Janna: Exactly. Exactly. Because as it stands right now, I get Medicaid and food stamps. I don't want total public assistance because they're always breathing down my neck, you know. You got to get a job; you got to get a job; you got to get a job. Leave me alone! You know, it's like—. I should be getting unemployment soon, so I don't have to worry about that too much.

And women who themselves escape poverty may be critical of those who do not. Janet's two sons are Head Start graduates and she now works in a professional community service job.

LJA: So you didn't do that [give up on yourself].

Janet: No. No, because I had a different orientation than some of the families, too. Some of the families that were involved, you know, I knew them from town. Generational welfare. You know, lots of kids.

"Poor" versus "Low-Income"

Many of the Head Start women, then, did not use the words "poor" and "poverty" for themselves. Further, they often believed that the "poor" were deficient in terms of a work ethic, including being deficient in a work ethic of mothering. And yet, we (Jeanne and Lynda) continue to use the word "poor" to describe these women. This is part of our dilemma, first described in Chapter One. We have learned to see poverty and class in structural rather than individual terms.

In structural terms, poverty *is* a lack of resources, and these absent resources include income *and* power. Poor people in this society have no political power, no economic power, no social power— as well as having little money. "Low-income" does not fully describe this lack of power nor the structural reasons for it. When we use the terms poor and poverty, we intend to situate the women discussed in this book in a class structure where different classes have very different degrees of control and command over their lives and the lives of others. "Poor" people have the least of that command and control. We recognize that the word poor has extraordinarily negative connotations in this culture. Ours is not a pejorative use of the word.

We are mindful, too, of Susser's (1990) admonition to use the term working class rather than underclass or lower class. As Susser notes (for people in general), the women of this book "find themselves in unstable jobs, in and out of work, on and off public assistance" (1990: 297), and hence deserve to be included in the working class. Yet, there is an important distinction between members of the working class who have stable jobs and comfortable incomes—people such as Lynda's parents and Lila after her Head Start employment—and those whose work does not offer that comfort. Again, we use "poor" to make that distinction. This is an imperfect term, clearly, but we lack a credible alternative.

Getting Out of Poverty

When it came down to what was likely to make life easier for the children, the American Dream came into play—the answer was education and self-esteem. Rosier and Corsaro (1993) make the same point about urban Head Start parents. As we know from Chapter

Four, Lila is a former mother herself who has spent nearly three decades watching other parents go through the program.

JE: Head Start was created to end poverty.

Lila: Yes.

JE: Do you think it has had an influence? I mean, it certainly hasn't ended it. We all know that.

Lila: No. No. I don't really know what all the studies show. I do know that it helped a lot of families certainly get out from under Social Services because it put a lot of people to work. It provided jobs for people. And I don't even know how many people there are working for Head Start now, but, you know, through the years, people have started working with Head Start, went back and went to college, moved out of the field and into other jobs, and went to work in their communities. Some got jobs, you know. Some of them went on and got their master's degrees and taught school, so I know that it certainly helped a lot of families get out of poverty. But I think for every—. Probably for every person you get out of poverty, there's probably one at the door. You know, I don't know if there will ever be an end to it. I really don't know.

JE: Why is that?

Lila: I don't know. I think that's a million dollar question. Why is that Jeanne? Do you know?

JE: Do you?

Lila: Do you have some ideas?

JE: Yeah. Do you think maybe it is that way because people at the top want it that way?

Lila: That could very well be, yeah. Well everything is political, and there's a reason for everything. But I never really studied, you know, any of the—. Well, I was too busy doing to be studying about why, so I don't know, to tell you the truth. I guess, I really—. I don't know. I'd have to think about that. I suppose if I got some books out and read about it, I would know, huh?

JE: I don't know though. I think you might be more of an expert than you think. I'm not sure book-reading would help you. You have in-depth knowledge of what it's like to be low-income, to live that way, to change things.

Lila: I know for ourselves, you know. . . . When I went to work, we were able to do more things that you would like to do for your family. . . . And I've seen a lot of, you know, males and females going to work in Head Start, and it helps them just to be able to do for themselves. You feel better about yourself and are able to say, "I did that," you know. So it helps them have feelings of accomplishment with their own families.

Lois, with more limited Head Start experience, agrees.

LJA: Do you think kids that go through Head Start have a better chance with getting good jobs?

Lois: I don't know about that, but I think they have a better chance at feeling better about themselves. They're getting a better start toward doing something better for themselves. I do. It makes them feel good. "Oh, look I can do this," and "I can do that." And if it continues on, then I think they will do a lot. It will help them.

Eileen, recall, believes strongly that people can work their way off welfare and out of poverty.

LJA: Did you like school?

Eileen: I found it awful hard, awful hard. Common sense wise, I think I had a lot of common sense, but it was just the book work I couldn't get past. It was hard. It was hard, you know. It was like a struggle all the time, all the time. So I says, "Oh, it's not worth struggling any more."

LJA: And your sister [who is a Head Start graduate] likes it?

Eileen: Yeah and she's going to [an out-of-state college] for architectural drafting.

LJA: There's good jobs in that field.

Eileen: Yeah. . . . That's why I'm saying, I hope the Head Start Program gives Frank the extra boost so he doesn't have to struggle, so he'll have, you know. Because I found it always came hard for me.

Genine, as she tells us here, is not employed and hopes that her children will "make something of their lives."

Genine: When [my younger daughter] gets involved in Head Start, it's going to be rough. I can't work because I have a bad back, plus with my asthma. In fact, I've applied for SSI disability because of it. I'm not going to have anything really to do, so why not get involved with my children, get their education on the right track.
LJA: Do you have any particular hopes for them? Expectations?
Genine: I guess what every mom wants out of their child. I'd like them to get a good education. I'm going to push the issue of high school graduation. College is a personal decision. That I'll let them make. I'd very much like them to go to college and get a degree. Go and make something of their lives. But if for some reason that doesn't happen, I'm not going to love them any less.

Genine's wish may be especially poignant. Both she and her husband are themselves Head Start graduates. Both finished high school, but did not attend college. Their work lives are quite unstable and they need to rely periodically on assistance programs. They continue to hope for a different life for their daughters, believing that Head Start might make the difference, though it clearly did not in their cases.

Lynne is taking care of her grandchildren for the time being. Her daughter, their mother, is not able to do so. Lynne's daughter, like Genine, is a Head Start graduate. Lynne recognized that Head Start made little difference in her daughter's life; it did not stop her from making critical mistakes. Lynne, like Genine, still believes that Head Start and other formal education will make a difference in the lives of her grandkids:

And that's one thing I've always preached hard and long to
everybody, is education. It's everything. You can't be anything
without it. You can always be a housewife, you can always be a
truck driver, not that those are down jobs, you know. [Lynne was a
housewife and her husband a truck driver.] But there are other
things that you can achieve with an education.

Lynne herself gained a master's degree late in her life, in between
her two stints at child rearing. Other mothers agree about the importance of education, at least for their children. Jamie, for instance,
did not finish high school. Her dreams for her child, though, are,
"to finish school, go to college, get a degree. Do more than I did."

Lisa and Amy, friends who met at Head Start, seem somewhat
less sure about its magic, but are nevertheless enthusiastic about education.

LJA: When they started Head Start, what they started Head Start for, it
was designed as part of a package to end poverty. Do you think it
does that? Do you think your kids have a better chance at a good
job?

Amy: Well, they have the basics to build on. I mean, the only way out is
school, so they have their basics. I mean, they're getting taught it's
the way it could be. I mean, I don't know. They're still young.

Lisa: I think it's a big boost in that direction.

Dorothy, as we noted in Chapter Three, works as a chamber
maid and returned to her artwork after her Head Start experience.
She knows that there are differential chances for education, but also
that education is important. (Karen Duckett, our research assistant,
conducted this interview.)

KD: It's obvious that there are people a lot richer than you or me. How do
you think they get that way, and how do you think that we may
have missed out?

Dorothy: School.

KD: Education?

Dorothy: Education. I really think that. And for myself, my parents didn't really have a lot. So I wasn't really allowed to go to school myself. I mean, I was up until the 12th grade. My brother enrolled [in college] in the Army. But I've seen other families where they have a little bit more money, where their kids go to college; they make out. I don't know. It's hard to describe. I think education [is the difference], though.

For the women we talked with, making it, getting out of poverty, depended on individual effort, not collective action. Head Start was just that, a head start for their children, a way to make it easier for the kids than it had been for them. For the women described in Chapter Four, Head Start was also a path for their own upward mobility, primarily through education and hard work. However, whether their own lives demonstrated the effectiveness of hard work or its futility, women believed it was important for their children.

RICH AND POOR

While expectations, or at least hopes, for individual upward mobility through education are strong and nearly universal, there is also recognition that opportunities are not completely open. Further, many women know that there are strong prejudices against poor people:

LJA: Do you think that by your kids being Head Start they'll have a better chance at not being poor?

Jody: I don't know. My opinion is that if you're born with a silver spoon in your mouth, you get to keep it, and if you're not, you don't. So, my father busted his butt from day one to give us kids what he wanted. He's been married forty-five years, he finally got the car he wanted.

And I'm looking at forty-five before I actually get a car that doesn't have rust. So by the time we can afford one with air bags, they'll be [old-fashioned].

So, I don't know. I think Head Start maybe helps the kids, the parents, to feel like they might have a choice, rather than the kids. It gives the kids—. But I think they lose it. They get in school and they lose it. They get stereotyped. Everybody in Head Start has no money so they're not stereotyped. People aren't looking at the kind of pants you're wearing, and then you get in school, about third or fourth grade, and you start with the Calvin Klein and the Adidas and Nikes, and the—. And you become a stereotype. . . . Being low-income is like the worst brand you can have, I think.

Like Jody, Abbey knows that people look down on those without money.

It's a stigma to be poor in this country, and it's too bad that as many people do. We don't consider ourselves poor. My boyfriend works hard and we raise two kids on what he makes. I came from a family where my father always worked two jobs, and my mother always worked. We had five kids, so I mean, I know what it's like not to be able to have everything you want. But, don't treat me like that's my choice. Do you know what I mean, to be poor, and they do.

Betsy knows how the rich stay rich. She knows, too, that she'll have little to pass on to her eight children, and has little chance of changing that.

KD: Slightly different topic. It is obvious that there are people a lot richer than you or me. How did they get that way, and how do you think that we missed out?

Betsy: I have no idea, but I wish I knew. I used to play the Lotto every week.

KD: You think they got lucky, maybe?

Betsy: Probably, in areas. But I think most people inherit it anyway.

KD: Inherit their—

Betsy: From the family. It's passed down and passed down.

We've also heard Eileen and Carol talk about the necessity of work. Carol now tempers that opinion somewhat, taking into consideration the ability to get a good job. She has a disabling illness and is on Supplemental Security Income (SSI). Interestingly, Eileen is not working. Her husband recently deserted her and their young son. Shortly thereafter, she discovered she was pregnant.

LJA: They keep saying that Head Start is this wonderful program for kids, and it does help end poverty. How do you think poverty happens?

Eileen: I think poverty breeds poverty.

Carol: I was going to say that there are some people that plain do not want to learn to get themselves ahead and then there are people that try and work and they still can't get themselves ahead.

LJA: For people who work, why can't they get ahead?

Carol: They just can't get good jobs.

Eileen: Their own personal—. I don't know. Pitfalls.

Carol: I was going to say, my husband and I went on—. Well he wasn't working, was working, and then he found a job, and then I was still working and our income was good, and then I got taken back out of work. I admit I still get my Social Security, but our income is not like it was when I was working for myself and he was working for somebody else. The income is still not the same. There's the ups and downs. It just depends on whether or not you can do it [get a good job] or not.

There is a belief among the women that poverty can be overcome by hard work and that poor people *should* try to do so. Often, this belief contradicts what the women's lives have actually been like. This belief is held by women who have overcome poverty to lead a

more economically secure life, *and* held by women who can be clas-
sified as poor on any objective standard, and yet have worked hard
all their lives.

There is also, though, an understanding that hard work will not
necessarily pay off. There is acknowledgment that a "silver spoon"
is important in assessing life's chances. When we asked what could
be done about that, the answers focused on giving poorer people
more chances to succeed by their own hard work. No one suggested
appropriating or even sharing the silver.

Jody: You know, you can't just go gradually because we tried that. And
    we were gradually going up, and the further we got ahead, the
    more in the hole we were. They raised the baby sitters. They took
    our HEAP away, they took WIC away, and we lost our house. We
    lost everything and moved up here because he found a better job
    up here. Now we're starting all over. We worked for ten years to
    be right back where we were when we started.
LJA: Well, what would change that? I mean, if you were president, what
    would you do to change that?
Jody: The biggest thing is that I wouldn't make everything so cut and dry.
    I'd kind of say, okay, if you make five dollars extra more a month,
    so there's four months out of the year, so instead of three hundred
    sixty-five dollars HEAP, we'll give you three hundred and forty or
    something like that. But to cut people off because they're trying to
    better themselves?

                                    ■

    Give them a little boost, help them out so they can get past that fine
    line. Help them make that leap a little better. Because what we're
    doing is, we're starting to leap and then we're falling in the gutters.
    It's like, we don't need that. God, don't put me going on welfare
    because I hate it. I hate people looking at you like you're disgusting
    when you pay for things with food stamps. I hate people treating
    you like crap when you have Medicaid. It's not right. I always cash
    my husband's paycheck when I get my food stamps so that they
    know he is working. It's like why, why should I have to feel that

way? It's my right. We pay taxes. We have the right to get help if
we need it.

Blaming assistance eligibility rules is common as Jamie and
Mickey illustrate. Both are single mothers.

LJA: What do you think would end poverty?
Jamie: Economy. It's the economy. The economy has to come down. The
economy keeps going higher and the pay rate stays the same.
Mickey: I think another thing that would help out, too, is Social Services. If
you're willing to go get a job, they cut you off, I mean, and then
you can't make it for your medical or anything like that. And then
you're still in the gutter. So, if they can help you out a little bit while
you're working, just to make ends meet, so you can better yourself.
Then you can get off it. Instead of cutting you off, and being lower
than you were.
LJA: Because they take away the medical and everything?
Mickey: Right. You know, because when I worked, they took me off of
everything. I had to come up with my rent. I had to come up for the
medical, and the food, and everything else. And around here, I
mean, a hundred fifty bucks around here, a buck just ain't going
too far.
Jamie: When me and Phil were first working, Phil made close to 200
dollars a week, and I made 130 dollars, and what we made in a
month was 300 dollars over their budget with three children to get
food stamps or Medicaid.
LJA: So you were worse off?
Jamie: Right. He had to draw unemployment, and I had to draw welfare
in order to get anything.

What needs to happen, according to these women, is for the government to supply a little bit of help, so that individuals can continue
to try to get ahead. Notice that this prescription for individual achievement is given despite the recognition of deeper, systemic forces ("silver spoons" and the economy). Yet, the systems that the women can

see and recognize on a daily basis are the strict, unwavering eligibility requirements that make any increase in salary a net negative.

THE AMERICAN DREAM AND EMPOWERMENT

In Ed Sadlowski's terms, Head Start moms did have insight on who and what was screwing them: the economy, lack of good jobs, and social prejudice against poor people. This is social structure, of course. Yet, in looking for ways out of poverty for themselves and their children, they did not target class structures or the labor market or inequality itself. Instead, they praised hard work and wished social service agencies would not penalize their hard work with reductions in benefits.

It is clear that many of the women do not have a sense of community and identity with "poor" people. Even if individual women recognize larger social structures as "screwing" them, they have not made common cause with the whole class of screwed people. In fact, many women take great care to carve distinctions between themselves and the less "deserving" poor.

This is not surprising, of course, given the relentless attack on the poor coming from many quarters in our society, perhaps especially from politicians and pundits (Rank 1994; Katz 1989). It is also absolutely in keeping with the larger structural forces of monopoly capitalism, institutional racism, and patriarchy.

Locally, the North Country is very politically conservative—the majority of its elected officials are and have been Republican; thus, there is a strong distrust of government.[1] These forces have prevented a coalescing of the "screwed."

---

1. This distrust centers around the Adirondack Park Agency (APA), created to (as the state's constitution requires) keep the Adirondack Mountains "forever wild." Large portions of the three counties of our study lie within the park. The APA maintains the park's wildness through a set of regulations about building and development. This "government interference" in private property matters has resulted in militia-like attitudes and behavior among many North Country residents.

Nationally and locally, collective action in recent decades has not focused on class per se, but instead on local community and identity issues (Posner 1990; Croteau 1995)—ethnicity, environmentalism, various feminisms, and often, in the North Country, anti-environmentalism.

People necessarily first organize around and combat those structures they actually experience day-to-day rather than abstractions such as "monopoly capital" (Piven and Cloward 1977; Plotkin and Scheuerman 1990; Susser 1990). However, for poor, white, rural women, there may be little sense of community at all. There may be no culturally available axis on which to organize as a community—except around their motherhood and their children.

An anonymous reviewer of some of our work stated that it would be "especially valuable to have a study of welfare mothers that cannot be read with the lenses of race." In other words, readers cannot attribute these mothers' poverty to presumably inherent characteristics or cultures of people of color. Such explanations are common among politicians, some academics, and the public. But this also means North Country women do not have race and racism as a partial explanation of their economic condition. Naples (1992) showed that African Americans and Latinos in New York City and Philadelphia *do* organize around promoting the rights of their racial and ethnic communities. Indeed, that concern was an integral part of those women's mothering. Poor women in the North Country do not experience racism, do not see it as the reason for their place in society. Thus, racism is not a concern around which to organize; they do not have racism as a visible social structure against which they can clearly battle, as Naples' respondents do. It cannot serve as an axis for forming a "culture of solidarity" (Fantasia 1988).

Neither can the women easily organize around class—there has been no widespread class-based collective action in the United States for a very long time. The American Dream as myth has been credited with reducing, even preventing class consciousness in the United States. "American exceptionalism" is the notion that the

United States is virtually alone among Western societies in lacking a strong tradition of labor militancy and class-based politics. The argument runs that class is not an issue with Americans because we, as a culture, firmly believe in the reality of equal opportunity, and believe that we have a classless society. Further, where there is equal opportunity, poverty exists only where it is deserved, where there is a deficit in the poor person. We should expect, according to this argument, that the dream could not coexist with a structural understanding of poverty.

However, Vanneman and Cannon (1987) argue that there is a difference between people's understanding or *consciousness* of class differences and the *results* of class struggle. That is, theorists cannot infer lack of consciousness from the fact that working-class institutions are weak or nonexistent. The latter fact is a particular result of historical struggle—the dominant class has won big in this country. Similarly, Gorelick (1991: 467) cites Giacaman, who notes that Palestinian women "did not necessarily need their consciousness raised. . . . What they needed was the power and authority to change their lives." Piven and Cloward (1977) also argue that a major reason poor people's antistructure movements do not succeed is the forces brought against them by the powerful dominant class (see also Fantasia 1988; Plotkin and Scheuerman 1990).

The ongoing victory by the dominant class and the genuine powerlessness of others means that there are few, if any, class-based models of resistance for women to see. Certainly, there is no successful model of resistance for poor, white, women to emulate. The community action programs of the 1960s might have provided such models, but we discussed that disappointing history in Chapter Two. Croteau (1995) argues that many working-class people have become disillusioned with electoral politics and with movement politics (such as peace, environmentalism, etc.) because they do not see either avenue as effective in making changes in their lives. There are some movements, such as the old Welfare Rights Organization (West 1981), and some current groups, such as the Welfare Warriors (Gowens 1993). These groups, though, are not well known and are, like "welfare" itself, associated with African Americans. For white, North Country women, these would not be seen as models. It is not surprising, then, that the women in the North Country do not seek to join poor people's movements—such movements do not now exist in any meaningful way and were not particularly successful in the long term when they did exist.

Though there may be structural causes for poverty and structural solutions for the social problem of poverty, the way out of poverty for these women *is*, in fact, through individual effort and perhaps a government policy to aid (rather than hinder) that effort. Overt class struggle may end poverty in the long run *if* the struggle is successful—a very big "if" and a very long run. It is unlikely to end poverty for these individuals in their lifetimes.

Indeed, beginning or joining such a revolutionary movement would mean an immediate and profound decrease in living standards and comfort. Let us not forget that very, very few of those people who *have* a structural understanding of oppression are willing to join or start revolutionary movements. We have too much to lose and are quite unwilling to sacrifice whatever comfort we have. Why would we expect others with fewer resources of formally acquired knowledge and power to do this when we would not?

EMPOWERMENT FOR WHAT?

In examining the effect of the American Dream on empowerment and these women's analysis of inequality, we need to ask the question, empowerment for what? As we've shown, what women want for their children is a good life, perhaps a better life than the mothers themselves had. No one reported that they wanted their child to be rich or powerful, only happy. Women's dreams for themselves are similar.

When we say that the women did not use any class-based, systemic analysis to envision changes they would like to see, there is an implicit criticism. We, after all, do use such an analysis and believe that no significant change can come without deep changes to the social system. So, in returning to our dilemma introduced in Chapter One, is it that we wish more from their empowerment than the women wish for themselves? What is it that they should be empowered for?

In the next section of this book, we analyze instances of mothers' and staff's collective resistance to the immediate structures of the local Head Start administration. We know, therefore, they are capable of such collective resistance. We also believe (like Bookman and Morgen, like Collins, and like Mills) that it is desirable, even necessary, to develop forms of collective resistance.

And yet, we come back again to the issue of imposing abstract categories and conditions on actual lives. What these women tell us they have gotten from Head Start is *empowerment*. It may be tempting to dismiss their "empowerment" as instances of cultural imperialism from middle-class professionals or as "feel-good" measures aimed primarily at making them happier to be poor. Indeed, much of the process we have documented so far does just that, making women more comfortable in their poverty.

As the moms we talked to recognize to some degree, there is a class system in the United States. The dominant class has power and resources; subdominant classes have less power and fewer resources. Having power generally allows people to do things that benefit themselves and their kin. Power and resources, though, have been withheld from poor people (which class we take to include our respondents). Therefore, they are unable to live the way they want to and as is best for themselves and their kin.

Croteau (1995) notes that the tools of the dominant class are more effective in establishing and maintaining control over the world-as-it-is: "You can pound a nail with a wrench, but success is more likely if you are equipped with a hammer" (1995: xii). The social structure is currently set up around pounding a nail, and hammers are among the tools of the dominant class, not of the subdominant.

If women active in Head Start learn to use hammers in some small ways instead of wrenches, they become empowered in dealing with the real world. They can make changes that benefit themselves and their kin, even if they make no immediate, fundamental changes to that world.

For example, one issue we've already talked about that is of great concern to many of the mothers is parenting and learning to parent. We argued that the specific content of what the mothers learned was middle-class child rearing. Though this may well be cultural imperialism, it is undoubtedly effective in helping mothers simply keep their children. In New York state (as most likely everywhere else), Child Protective Services (CPS) can be a very powerful adversary—being "hotlined" is a concern often mentioned by mothers. If CPS argues before a court that a poor mother is unfit to raise her children, she will very likely lose custody (Schell 1995). The kind of child rearing approved by CPS is the kind of child rearing mothers learn in Head Start.

Many of the families served by North Country Head Start programs are those with "dysfunctions," as defined by social service professionals. Hence, for many of them, learning to use noncorporal forms of discipline, for example, may well mean the difference between keeping a child and losing custody to CPS. Mothers learn, in other words, to use a hammer rather than a wrench, and the difference is critical in the world in which they actually live. If the women lack a thorough analysis of collective resistance to systemic forces, they know what they need to make their lives better here and now.

The next part of this book will document collective resistance to demeaning administration. We will return to the question "empowerment for what?" in the final chapter.

Part Three

◆

WOMEN EMPOWERED

❖6❖

Power and Ceremony

Well, they [the PC] have a lot of say in what goes on in the Head Start and everything, which I didn't realize. I thought it was just something, meeting of people. I didn't know that you could have so much say as you can.

You can't tell me that those parents, who are maybe illiterate, have the skills to hire somebody.

I don't think we make any real difference. They don't really listen to us. They don't have to.

The last vestige of the War on Poverty's community action program lies in Head Start's Policy Council. Through the Policy Council (PC), parents are to exercise *genuine* power over the running of local Head Start programs, over the way their children begin their education. Here, one might expect to find empowerment more of the sort practiced by the Child Development Group of Mississippi (Greenberg 1990 [1969]), which we discussed in Chapter Two.

Here, though, the contradictions between a deficit-based education program for children (and tangentially for parents) and the more radical conception of participation, aimed at changing social structure, become very clear, as do the difficulties of actual, practical involvement by the poor. In the first place, traditionally disenfranchised people are plunged into policymaking and implementation—arenas jealously guarded by professionals and elites

(Moynihan 1970; Clark and Hopkins 1968; Powell 1982; Joffe 1977). Even more problematical, parents, presumed to be unable to provide appropriate experiences for their own children's development, are expected to plan and control a program designed to compensate for the parents' own failings (O'Brien 1991; Kuntz 1995). By the time parents are elected to the PC, "experts" have long since decided the "needs" of low-income children *and* presupposed the foibles of the parents. Significant parent input would seem impossible, as well as unwanted.

The situation is further complicated by the fact that Head Start is only rarely a freestanding organization. The local grantee agency for Head Start typically also controls other programs for the poor that do not have provisions for participation in decision making. Head Start is alone in such a requirement. Thus, program administrators may be quite comfortable with merely doing *for* poor people, and be unwilling to share any power with Head Start parents.

The promise of exercising real control even over this one small institution governing their lives would seem largely a cruel hoax for parents.

THE STRUCTURE OF NORTH COUNTRY HEAD START

The three counties we have studied share an organizational structure. This structure is quite common to Head Start programs throughout the country. Within that structure lie both the promise and the hoax, power and ceremony.

Recall from Chapter Two that community action programs (CAPs) were instituted by the Office of Economic Opportunity to receive and administer funds for the War on Poverty. These organizations were extra-governmental, often bypassing city governments entirely. Head Start program funds were channeled through CAPs that, theoretically, were able to customize the program for their own community's needs. The benign reasoning behind CAPs was the coordination of funding and elimination of duplication.

The more radical reasoning was to provide a forum for community organizing and political change. CAPs very soon, though, were stripped of their radical potential.

In Lake, Kent, and River counties, CAPs have become private, nonprofit organizations controlled by volunteer boards of directors. Each county's CAP receives funds from the federal government to administer a Head Start program.

In Lake County, the CAP Board is made up of local business people and social service professionals—it is no longer specifically composed of people who themselves receive social services. It does not see its mission as changing the social structure or organizing local poor people. It administers several federal and state programs for assisting low-income residents of the county: Head Start, a home-heating program, a food pantry, and so forth.

The CAP Board employs an executive director, who oversees all the programs and their staff. The Lake County Head Start program is run by the Head Start director, who reports to the CAP executive director. The county's program includes ten centers, scattered around the county. Direct service staff at each center (teachers, cooks, family workers, bus drivers) report to coordinators located at the central office (education coordinator, transportation coordinator, social services coordinator, etc.). These coordinators report to the Head Start director. Administration of the ten centers is thus centralized under the ultimate control of the CAP, through the executive director.

On the outskirts of this very ordinary organizational hierarchy is the county's Policy Council, which, by federal edict, is to oversee policy and operations of the county's Head Start program.

The Policy Council

The Policy Council is statutorily supposed to be made up of at least 50 percent parents. In Lake County Head Start, the PC is composed of at least twenty parents of children currently enrolled, two elected from each of the ten centers. There are six to eight community representatives drawn from various other social service agencies in the area, from schools and colleges, from local businesses, and sometimes from parents of formerly enrolled children. The PC elects officers (chair, vice chair, secretary, treasurer) and sorts its members into committees (Personnel, Budget, By-Laws, etc.). Policy work is typically done in a committee, and the committees bring issues and recommendations back to the whole PC for action.

Monthly PC meetings are often long, regularly lasting three hours, sometimes longer. New PCs are constituted in October, after elections at the centers in September. Meetings in the early fall are often chaotic, since many parents attend and since they have not yet fallen into a meeting routine. Meetings often do not start on time. Refreshments are furnished, and people move back and forth from seats at tables to the coffee pot and plates of fruit and bagels. Most of the PC meetings we attended were held in a room located in a federal housing project and either overheated even in winter, or not heated at all. It was rarely comfortable.

Further, there are often staff members coming in and out of the meeting, to give reports, drop off and pick up parents, or deliver needed documents. Baby-sitting is furnished by Head Start, so there are few children in attendance, though occasionally a very small child is brought along. Especially at the beginning of the term, when people are excited about their new roles, when they have not yet mastered Robert's Rules of Order, people often talk out of turn—including professional staff members.

The issues that routinely come before the PC are varied. The PC is required to approve all personnel actions, including hiring, firing, giving raises, and so forth. At almost every meeting, resignation letters are read, and the resignation is approved by those present. Similarly, new hires and their qualifications are discussed and approved. This business often takes quite a bit of time. Note that, almost always, the staff members resigning have already left by the time their resignations are read and approved, and that new hires have begun work before the PC approves them.

Other standard monthly business includes reports from each center, delivered by the PC center representatives, about what the children and parents are doing. These reports are often quite detailed and are regularly marked with laughter and expressions of having had a good time at whatever event is recounted. There are regularly reports from administrative staff about the various components of the program and about the state of the budget.

The budget is one of the very crucial matters the PC is asked to deal with. The PC is supposed to maintain routine oversight on expenditures and supposed to help formulate budget and program priorities. Occasionally, matters of crisis come before the PC, including sudden staffing shortages or acute personnel difficulties.

In this chaos, in the mix between tedious routine and crucial issues, is the potential for parents' power, real power. However, here also is the likelihood of only-ceremonial power. As is true for many, many organizations and boards (including the CAP Board, too), full-time professional staff members are likely to dominate meetings simply because of their full-time status and their consequent knowledge (Gruber and Trickett 1987; Iannello 1992; and personal experience). There are other, less "innocent" reasons the PC's power might become only ceremony.

Policy Council and the CAP Board

In theory, the PC and the board jointly oversee the program. The board is given "general responsibility" for the program, while the PC must explicitly approve (or not) virtually all decisions affecting the program. There are formal liaisons between the two groups—one member of the board is assigned to attend PC meetings and the PC chair is invited to board meetings. In the ordinary course of affairs, there is no conflict between the board's oversight and the PC's. Any potential disagreements are routinely smoothed over and mediated by the paid administrators—that's their job. The smoothing over by the staff is ordinarily so effective that neither body typically pays much attention to the other.

An organizational chart in the *Parent Manual,* assembled by the Lake County Head Start administrators, shows the PC as *under* and reporting to the board. However, as we will see, that picture may not capture the intent of the federal policies *or* how parents saw their role. Those federal policies *do* require the CAP to obtain the PC's approval, and, if the PC does not approve, the CAP's decision must be changed.

The chart is, however, how the board sees its relationship with the PC. The board clearly presumes that its oversight functions are more definitive, that the PC is at best an advisory body, and that PC parents have no authority to challenge the board. This view leaves the PC with only the mirage of power, ceremonial power.

PARENT POLICYMAKING AS COMPENSATORY EDUCATION

From the deficit-based model of social services, "participation" by parents on the PC can be seen as compensatory education. Actually, such participation serves as educational from either the radical view or the deficit view. We have surely observed women learning confidence in themselves and learning to function well in a bureaucratic arena by way of their work on the PC, learning to use a hammer instead of a wrench (Croteau 1995). Most of the women we observed started their PC term with little or no experience in running formal meetings, no confidence in speaking before a group, even a small one, and no expectation that they had even a bit of information or opinion worth sharing with a group. We observed reticence and extreme nervousness, and our interviews confirm that women felt unworthy and intimidated at first.

For most of these women, this was their first exposure to using bureaucratic modes of decision making. The rules of the game were largely unfamiliar; the sense of power quite alien. As the year progressed, many became much more facile with both the rules and the power. Women came to see themselves as more capable than they had thought—empowered. Further, through participation on the PC, some mothers gained experience and skills that have human capital value—working with budgets, interpreting and complying with federal guidelines, and expressing themselves orally and in writing.

Working on the Policy Council can and does have the important effect of compensatory education for women who have led economically and educationally disadvantaged lives. Naples (1991) noted similar educative benefits for women working in other community action projects. However, as noted earlier, the compensatory education notion is bound up in patronizing and demeaning attitudes toward the women. Patronization often means power that is merely ceremonial, not genuine. The ceremony of pretend power is intended to teach, only—a virtual reality power that can be switched off at any time. When ceremonial power is given for educational purposes, actual power is retained by professionals.

This pretense is often seen for what it is by parents. For every parent who found the Head Start policymaking experience empowering, there was at least another, if not several more, who found it only frustrating. Too often, the women who initially found empowerment later found frustration.

In formal federal mandates (70.2), the Policy Council is clearly intended to hold real, not ceremonial power.

If Head Start children are to reach their fullest potential, there must be an opportunity for Head Start parents to influence the character of programs affecting the development of their children. The organizational structure of every Head Start program must provide this opportunity by increasing the effectiveness of parent participation in the planning and implementation of programs on the local level, in order that parents may also become more effective in bringing about positive change in the lives of their children. . . . Successful parental involvement enters into every part of Head Start, influences other antipoverty programs, and works toward altering the social conditions that have formed the systems that surround the economically disadvantaged child and his family. Project Head Start must continue to discover new ways for parents to become deeply involved in decision making activities that they deem helpful and important in meeting their particular needs and conditions. (Head Start Performance Standards 1970: 1–2)

Though this statement incorporates a deficit view of parents and their social life, it also implies that parents themselves can be empowered to change the social structures limiting their life chances. (Note again, though, that most of the emphasis is on the children's chances, and not on those of parents.) Yet, in most Head Start working documents, it is clearly the training role that predominates, not the empowerment role (Kuntz 1995; O'Brien 1991). To reiterate, in Lake County Head Start, this training function is very gratifying and useful to some parents. However, in this county, the conception was lodged in particularly demeaning and patronizing attitudes and behaviors. The manifestations of patronization begin at the top, with administrators at HHS, with the board of the North Country CAP, and with the program administrators they hired.

Because the CAP mostly administers other programs without requirements for participation by those served, the members of the board seem only vaguely aware, if aware at all, of the specificity and binding nature of 70.2. The board has ultimate authority in its dealings with other CAP programs and assumes that this is true for Head Start as well.

A lack of enlightenment about 70.2, though, is certainly not the only or even the main reason for the board's arrogance with the PC. Rather, it is that low-income parents are seen as distinctly unqualified for policymaking. As one board member stated, "You can't tell me that those parents, who are maybe illiterate, have the skills to hire somebody." The view of most—though decidedly not all—board members and CAP administrators is that the PC's main function is as a tutorial for socially and intellectually deficient, even child-like, parents.

Ironically, this notion was supported in a "workshop" requested by the PC to clarify its role to the board. The PC had noted the disdain of the board and that the board tended to ignore the PC's decisions. The PC wanted the board to be told that the PC had a legitimate, *decision* making role that the board had to honor. In this workshop, though, a trainer from HHS described the PC as a "training ground for how to behave as adults in the world." She went on to say, "For many parents, decision making is a unique opportunity, like a Christmas present. So we ask them what they want. . . . And it's important that we not interfere." She later used the analogy of letting a child use scissors for the first time: "It's natural to want to take the scissors away, but we have to let the child learn."

When explaining how PC meetings were conducted, she said that parents used "Roger's Rules" because they could not quite get to using Robert's Rules. Several of the Head Start and CAP administrators snickered over this, catching our attention.

In her statements, there are two things going on. First, the trainer *is* telling the board that they must not interfere, they must let they PC operate as it chooses. However, the stronger message is that the parents are like children. There is no conception that the parents can teach the board or administrators anything, only that the parents can learn to grow up. This latter, stronger message is the only one the board took home from this "workshop."

However well-meaning this may have been—and there is no evidence that it was well-meant at all—this is hardly an endorsement of the respectful sharing of power. Poor people are clearly assumed ill-equipped to make decisions.

These attitudes are not, apparently, unique to Lake County. Kent County parents active on the PC told us similar tales:

Penny: I know it's been said by certain board members that parents really shouldn't have a say because we don't know what's going on. You

know. Basically the underlying thing is that we're not smart enough
to make decisions about our own children.

■

Patty: We had a board member tell us we were nothing but a bunch of
drug-addicted, alcoholic, uneducated people. What did we know.
"Listen to us. We know what's best for you."

LJA: They said this in public?

Patty: Well it was to another person but it happened to be my sister. She
said, "What?" But, isn't that the point of Head Start to take us, even
if we don't have an education? And build us up so that eventually
we can be productive? Not them. No. "You listen to me, I know
what's good for you." So.

GENDERED ASSUMPTIONS

The paternalism apparent in these reports is based on more than
just class. These are not just poor people, deficient in many ways;
they are poor *women*. In general, the history of U.S. welfare policy
shows that women's needs have been largely discounted in developing policy to combat poverty or ease its effects (Sapiro 1990;
Miller 1990; Abramovitz 1988; Gordon 1994, 1990). Women are
treated as appendages to men (widows, deserted wives) or to children
(mothers of the innocent, deserving poor). We've noted several times
that Head Start programs are aimed at the children, primarily, and at
their mothers, in so far as the latter can help the former.

What Head Start policies *intend* for mothers—which is not necessarily what Head Start front-line staff or the mothers themselves intend—is that they become better parents to their children so that the
children won't suffer another generation of poverty. Chapter Three
shows how didactic Head Start programs aim to change the way
women mother their children more than they aim to assist the women
themselves. In this view, women are not *supposed* to be policymakers
in Head Start or anywhere in the world. Women are supposed to be
good mothers, and *poor* women need training in how that happens.

These presumptions clearly operated at Lake County Head Start,

at least at the administrative level. It was the opinion of several ob-
servers, for instance, that this was a particular issue for the Lake
County CAP executive director. We first heard comments from
mothers. Jody, who was gaining steadily in self-confidence working
on the PC, told us, "He just doesn't want to share [power]. And he
hates women. Thinks they should all be little dollies at home." The
staff—predominantly women—tended to agree.

LJA: What do you think he thinks about the parents on PC?
Seraphina: I don't think he would like to think that they have a mind or
   that they're able to do this kind of thing. You know, that's just my
   opinion. I mean, I have no proof of anything. At this point. But I
   really also don't think that he believes that women—.
Nancy: Have a mind.
Seraphina: He has a problem with women.
Nancy: Definitely. . . . I think he thinks that they need to be taken care of,
   you know, that, "I will do this for them," you know.

■

LJA: Do you think he doesn't respect you because of that [that you're not
   middle class]?
Doris: Probably. Also the fact that we're women. Women, we're lower
   class or poverty, and what good do we do really in his eyes. In his
   eyes, we give him aggravation, right? We give him aggravation.
   Isn't that what we do to him? . . . He looks at our parents as, "Who
   are these women?" mostly [women], I mean. You know. "Who are
   these women—who half of them have quit high school—to sit in
   here and try to tell me what to do when I'm the Executive Director!?"

   If this executive director is a particularly misogynist man, he nevertheless only exaggerates existing assumptions in Head Start. Women
are supposed to need to be taken care of, by one man or by the male
state (Sapiro 1990; Smith 1984). Local Head Start administrators
simply acted on this view, supported by the whole history of American welfare policy.

   As these descriptions of the executive director also make clear, it is difficult, empirically, to distinguish patronization and condescension based on class from that based on gender. There are, indeed, conceptual distinctions that are important to the theoretical analysis of class and gender intersections. However, women's identities and daily experiences are not separated in that way. Naples, after examining the lives of activist women of color, argues: "Just as the community workers did not separate their identities as women from their class background or racial-ethnic communities, so must sociological theorists resist fragmenting social life into artificially disconnected areas of analysis" (1992: 460).

The women (and we) recognized that both class and gender were involved, but where one stopped and the other began is unclear. In lived lives, the assumptions are bound up together, empirically inextricable. The *set* of assumptions, in any case, dictated that these women needed to be taken care of, and that's what administrators set out to do.

Nancy (staff): I think [the executive director] sees himself as being—and this is just me—being a good person because he's helping all these poor people. You know. It's like he's cleansing his soul because he's giving so much to these families.

■

Carla (staff): And the mission statement talks about helping people out of poverty, and we were asked to write down what we think we're doing right or what we think we should be doing to achieve that. Well, I don't think that we're helping people out of poverty with the general run of things. If you give people food, that will help for a week. If you give them HEAP, that will help for a month, but it's not showing them how not to need that HEAP next year or how not to need the food.

■

Patty (parent): The community action philosophy and the Head Start philosophy butt heads. Head Start's philosophy is to get parents empowered and move on. [CAP] gets funding to help low-income people. They need more low-income—. I mean they *need* low-income people in order to fund them[selves]. So they wanna *keep* you there. That's where I think they butt heads.

■

Evelyn (former parent on staff): We have a mission statement, and I can't quote it exactly, that says, "Our mission in Head Start is to help families to learn, how to solve—, how to educate themselves, and how to change their lives." [CAP's] mission statement says, "We're going to move people out of poverty." And that's subtle. It's a real subtle difference, but it, to me, it's the core of the thing. If you move somebody, you haven't done anything for them. If you have the right answers, and you tell them this is the way you do it. "I know, big, fancy, smart me, with my degree and my nice salary and everything, knows how to do it." I've only put you down. I haven't empowered you. If I say, "I'm going to listen to you, and I'm going to give value to your ideas; you have good ideas; you can use your brain. Use it. And you have a right, this program gives you a right to do it." Then you've built me up and it's so subtle, but it's such a core. It's so important. And I don't understand why people miss it all the time.

Yet, administrators did miss it, much if not all the time.

CEREMONY: ADMINISTRATING CONSENT

The deck seems to be stacked against parents' exercise of real power, for reasons both of class and gender. Parents, though, seem to take quite seriously the promise of the Policy Council. Despite her condescension, the HHS trainer was right that this is a new treat for the women. Mothers are astonished at how promising—and forbidding—the PC is.

Janna: [The family worker] called me up one day and she's like, "We need somebody for Policy Council," and I was like "Okay, okay." Then I realized how much it involved, you know, and I was like oh, my God.

■

Clara: Well, they [the PC] have a lot of say in what goes on in the Head Start and everything, which I didn't realize. I thought it was just something, meeting of people. I didn't know that you could have so much say as you can.

The front-line staff knows how difficult the PC can be for mothers, but are there to encourage and support their involvement, because the staff, too, believes in the potential power of the PC. Louise explains:

And that can be quite daunting, our Policy Council. That's a big challenge, to be on a board, you know? I mean, first they laugh, it sounds very alarming. "Oh, I couldn't do that." But with support and help, they can. And they can find that they do have a voice. . . . They go in and it's bewildering. I will say even when I've been on boards, myself, when you go in and you look at the budget, you know, and you're supposed to make some intelligent comments about this budget that you've only just seen. You don't know what on earth it's about. All these things that people are discussing, it doesn't make any sense to you. Later on, you begin to get the feel of it.

As Louise points out, it takes some time for people to figure out what's going on. That was one of the first problems we noticed. This learning period can mean that PC parents remain powerless for a time. Annie, a full-time mother of three, told us, "It seems like it took me most of the year to figure out what was going on. In meetings, it's so confusing at first."

Clara and Abbey, both parents, note that many important decisions are made during this time of confusion. Some of these decisions would likely not have been the same later in the term.

Clara: See, when we first started, I don't know if you were there the very first part in September when we first went, and they wanted them to vote on something. They did the same with us last year but we voted, and we didn't even know what we were voting on. After the year went on, we realized we shouldn't have done it. And we said [to the new PC], don't do this. Find out what you're voting on. But I mean, we just took for granted, well, this is the way it's run.

■

Abbey: Actually, I think that's really peculiar that you have a new group of people coming in the beginning of November and that budget has to be in. So the first meeting that you go to, they throw the budget with a bunch of numbers to these people. I've been on boards before, so this wasn't new to me, but a lot of people on Policy Council, this is their first time they've ever served in any capacity where they've had the right to make choices. . . . Because you shouldn't expect people to walk in the door and pass something that they've never seen before. And saying to that group of people, "It was discussed last year," just to help us. We weren't there. And maybe we want to change it, but we have a right to know what was discussed. Why this was decided on, why that was decided on. Especially if it's going to affect us this year.

Even later in the term, though, parents remained at a disadvantage in terms of information. Administrators were careful, in our observation, to control the agenda as much as possible. This is in spite of the clear warnings against the ceremonial role of the PC in 70.2:

> It may not be easy for Head Start directors and professional staff to share responsibility when decisions must be made. Even when they are committed to involving parents, the Head Start staff must take care to avoid dominating meetings by force of their greater training and experience in the process of decision making. At these meetings, professionals may be tempted to do most of the talking. (Head Start Performance Standards 1970: 3)

In fact, it was not easy for the staff not to do most of the deciding and most of the substantive arguing. (This was true, too, for the board, in which case the executive director seemed to be in firm control.)

One story is especially illustrative: In 1992–93, the administration went to the PC for a decision on how to meet a very large budget shortfall. Rather than brainstorming with the parents to arrive at solutions, management showed up with seven well-developed proposals for meeting the emergency. Several PC and committee meetings were held over six days and feelings ran very high over some of the proposals, particularly staff layoffs and the canceling of field trips. During the course of those meetings, seven additional proposals were presented by PC members, ranging from cutting back on supplies to better use of volunteers. The Head Start Director patiently explained why these added proposals would not produce the revenues needed. In the end, six of the seven management-proposed measures were enacted without major modification; none of the PC-proposed measures was enacted or ever mentioned again. The administration's plan seemed to be the only possibility.

Not only were the prepackaged proposals the only options seriously considered, but not even fully engaged was any question about the reason for the shortfall in the first place. The problem was caused by the CAP's insistence on hiring a lawyer to negotiate with the staff's new union (see Chapter Nine). This shortfall was $30,000—a lot of money. Several PC members did ask why a lawyer was needed at all, and why the money should have to come from Head Start program funds. The administration simply asserted that he (the lawyer was always assumed to be a "he") was really necessary and that, of course, the money had to come from the Head Start budget. No one, not even the professional-level community representatives, was prepared to rebut the assertion. The PC would have been well within its powers to refuse to spend that money at all or that much money. Yet, the administration controlled the debate and kept it focused on which among its proposals would be approved.

There are lesser examples, too. For instance, when parents had questions about fact or policy, they would turn to the Head Start administrators present at the meetings. Sometimes the questions would be answered thoroughly and straight-forwardly. Sometimes long-winded, complicated, round-about, even misleading answers were offered, confusing the parents (and us) and/or turning them off to the process. Sometimes, administrators would claim ignorance and promise to look up the answer and get back to the PC at next month's meeting—sometimes that happened; often it did not. We watched several times, too, when administrators would simply ignore a question. That is, a general question would be asked, "I want to know why we have to do this in this way?" No one would answer. No one thought to ask the question directly of the administrator, and she was not forthcoming. After the embarrassed silence that followed, the matter was usually just dropped.

In these and many other ways, administrators controlled the information and options available to the PC and thereby controlled the kinds of topics that were treated in depth. In addition to their "greater training and experience," administrators spent forty hours a week on Head Start. The parents had many fewer hours to spend and had more difficulty arranging even that time. For low-income parents, transportation, schedules, work commitments, child care, and other family obligations are predictably difficult to manage and plan. Not only are there monthly meetings of the whole council, there are also regular committee meetings.

What tended to happen, then, is that PC meetings were mostly taken up with trivial issues: approving resignations for people who had already left, hirings for people who had already started, budgets they had not had sufficient time or training to evaluate. The major decisions had been made by administrators before the PC knew about the issue. For the longest time observing the PC, we viewed very little in the way of substantive decision making at PC meetings. We were becoming, in fact, quite distressed at the routine, after-the-fact, boring nature of the agenda. So were some parents:

LJA: How about for you? You're both on Policy Council. Why? I mean, what made you want to be Policy Council?

Carol: We were bribed.

Eileen: We were forced into it. Honest to God, we were.

Carol: I didn't want to do it. Eileen had told [the family worker] if she needed something, she'd be on it, and then they had some other lady that was going to be on it, and she ended up moving, so then the day of the first Policy Council where they had the training, [the family worker] would say, she goes, "Carol." I said, "All right."

LJA: What good things can come of your being on Policy Council?

Carol: Well, you find out a lot of information about things that shouldn't be done and things that are being done.

Eileen: That you don't have no concept of.

Carol: Yes.

LJA: Like what kinds of things have you found important?

Carol: I don't know. It's just monotonous. . . . Just the meetings go on for a long time up there. The only thing you learn is when you go to Policy Council, you make sure there's nothing else for the rest of that day. You never know when you're getting out of there.

LJA: Do you think the Policy Council has some control over the program? Has some say?

Eileen: Do you think so, Carol? Honestly?

Carol: To be honest?

Eileen: I don't.

Carol: No, I do not.

LJA: Should it?

Carol: Yes, I think it should. I don't feel that [we have a say], because we can okay it, and then the CAP can turn it down, and then you have to redo it again to their likings, and basically, they have to do it the right way or else you don't—.

Eileen: I was told right from the beginning that Policy Council was a step for your child, that you're going to have a lot of say and a lot of pull, a lot of this and a lot of that. You know, to me, you're there just for show then that's it.

It seemed to us, as it did to Carol, that PC decisions were sometimes ignored, and often the PC was asked to reconsider issues, as if they had never made a decision. This was perhaps part of the administrators' tactics to smooth over potential disagreements between the board and PC. It may well have been part of the administrators' bid for control, too. In any case, it caused a good deal of resentment—the parents were not fooled.

LJA: How much—. What does being on Policy Council do for you? or your child? or the program?
Genine: Hardly anything at all.
Dick (Genine's husband): Hardly anything at all.
LJA: Then why do it?
Dick: Because Policy Council, when we first heard Policy Council, we figured it would be decisions that would be made on kids' education and stuff.
Genine: That would affect the children directly.
Dick: And 90 percent of it, 99 percent of it was just, how can we say this?
Genine: Horse hockey.
Dick: Horse hockey.
Genine: I enjoyed my year so far on Policy Council. But then again, it's very obnoxious. There's really no sense in it.

This nonsubstantive, "horse-hockey" quality is, in part, a direct consequence of the remedial assumptions being made by the administration: The parents were only being educated in the process; they were deemed, as yet, incapable of wielding genuine power. Many parents, like Janna, found this an exercise in futility and withdrew, largely without a fight:

I have bit my tongue a lot of times. I wanted to say a lot of stuff to somebody, but well. . . . It's just when I get interrupted—. I'm trying to say something and I get interrupted, it irritates me. . . . It's very frustrating, you know. I try to get my point of view out, and then I

get interrupted and it's like, forget it. I ain't going to say it. I ain't
going to try. To hell with it, you know.

Parents want to spend their time in fruitful and enjoyable ways,
like most of us. As Eileen says: "Let me put it this way. Instead of
going to Policy Council, I'd rather be here at school with the kids
than go to Policy Council."

When parents withdraw from active participation as decision
makers, when they do not expect to be able to genuinely influence
policy, the administration keeps power by default. Parents do not
consider this acceptable, though. There is a distinct difference, they
believe, between the way administrators think and the way parents
think. Abbey tells us, "We think like parents, and they think like administrators, you know." Lois says much the same thing:

Lois: So, in the Policy Council, I guess they did change a couple of things.
LJA: Do you think that what the parents decide would be different from
     what the administrators decide? Why?
Lois: Because they are just that. They are administrators. I don't know how
     to explain it, but high up is high up.
LJA: Do they care about the kids?
Lois: Yeah, they care. But they have their priorities jumbled up—
     paperwork, bureaucracy.

Administrators, with their jumbled priorities, are not in touch
with the people they serve. Nancy, a long-time staffer, says, "[The
executive director] doesn't understand what the community is going through," and therefore cannot make appropriate decisions.
Janet, a former mother who now holds a professional job, agrees:

LJA: Well, here's another alternative. Just get rid of the Policy Council.
Janet: I wouldn't do that. I wouldn't do that for a reason. I like the concept
     of the Policy Council. Because it serves a purpose. I think everyone
     needs oversight, and I don't necessarily think confrontation is bad.

> . . . If you don't have a Policy Council, who is going to be
> overseeing the administration agency besides the Fed?
>
> *LJA:* Who are stretched.
>
> *Janet:* Right. They don't know the needs of my community like I know the
> needs of my community, and my kids or your kids or whatever. You
> know as well as I do, when you're at that level you lose sight of—
> you've never been in the field. Because, you don't even know what
> low-income means anymore. Or what it's like to live hand-to-mouth,
> to live in a facility that doesn't have a bathroom or living room.

Much of what happens at the Policy Council is controlled by the full-time staff. Some of this is due to the tendency, common to all organizations, of staff to know more than board members. Much of it is due to the assumptions built into Head Start about the deficiencies of poor women. However, there was another dynamic present in the Lake County Head Start, a dynamic that exacerbated those other tendencies. Head Start programs in general are under great pressures to become more "accountable," to tighten their management practices, to become more bureaucratic. Responses to these pressures even more gravely endanger the promise of power for mothers.

❖7❖

The Bureaucratization of
North Country Head Start

*And nobody's doing nothing about it, you know, it seems like—
I know it's bureaucratic red tape and things take time, but!*

*We're treating [the CAP] much more like a business these days.
Which it is. We should run it like a business.*

*And Head Start staff people are not like that. We're people
people. We don't work in a business world.*

The systems that control the lives of poor women are many:
banks, social services, the economy, schools, Child Protective Services, and so on and on. Women have very little control over, or even influence on, these systems. In fact, poor people
have learned to distrust these systems and have learned not to make
too many waves, given the sometimes severe consequences of doing so (Calabrese 1990; Gowdy and Pearlmutter 1994; Horowitz
1995). Encountering and being dominated, even battered by such
systems is everyday business.

Suddenly, in Head Start, parents are told they can have an influence, can even have *control* over the way the program is run. They are
often not sure what this means and are hesitant to believe it. When
they do believe the promise, many parents accept with gusto the challenge to help structure their children's futures—and their own.

Democracy is messy. It is unpredictable. When a group of parents, the composition of which is constantly changing, is asked to democratically make policy, the policy made is necessarily sometimes disjointed and inconsistent from year to year, sometimes from month to month. Different groups of people make different decisions. Of course, when policy is jointly made by two groups with very different interests (e.g., working-class parents and the middle-class board of the CAP agency), the two groups may often end up in conflict.

The conflict, though, can be productive, stimulating thoughtful discussions and challenging unexamined assumptions. The give-and-take of coming to decisions collectively can bring members of a group closer, and can bring different groups together. However, such conflict is often seen as dysfunctional, a symptom of a "breakdown of communication," rather than as a positive concomitant to democracy.

In the last chapter, we detailed some ways in which the administration, because of demeaning views of poor women *and* because they were like any other administration, kept the PC policymaking process tidy, not messy. There is more to this story, though. In our time in the field, we saw the increase in tidiness accelerate. That acceleration concerns us greatly. Empowerment cannot be tidy.

BACK TO BUSINESS

When CAP agencies were instituted, there was considerable fear, especially among local governments, that they would act as revolutionary change agents. Yet, almost immediately, the potential for that kind of CAP was lost (Kramer 1969; Greenberg 1990 [1969]; Moynihan 1970). Changes were made to the Economic Opportunities Act (EOA) to prevent CAPs from forming as extra-, not to mention anti-, governmental agencies. Further, more and more programs for the poor came "prepackaged" for the CAPs to simply administer; there was less and less opportunity for the CAPs to develop innovative service programs, not to mention innovative political movements (Kramer 1969). Only a few years after their institution, Kramer could write, "[T]he CAP appears destined to succumb to more local government sponsorship and control and become increasingly 'deradicalized' and institutionalized as it evolves into another social service bureaucracy with which the poor must contend" (1969: 269).

In more recent times, greater and greater emphasis is being put on tight fiscal management and responsibility. This is a change noted for social service agencies nationally, with increasingly centralized policies and methods of cost control (Sosin 1986). According to the National Association for Community Action Agencies, a "large-scale effort to strengthen the role and management systems" of CAPs was begun in the late 1970s. For Head Start in particular, Skerry (1983) notes that this effort was a result of the Westinghouse report of 1969, which brought the benefits of Head Start into question—a question Head Start has never quite shaken. There are now federal legislative initiatives to create closer accountability and "better" management of Head Start programs (Takanishi and DeLeon 1994).

A U.S. Health and Human Services' report, *Creating a 21st Century Head Start*, emphasizes strengthening "management practices at the local level." A major recommendation of this report is "increasing the emphasis placed on the *business practices* of the Head Start program, including the development of performance standards in the area of fiscal management" and "requiring minimal competencies for *staff* involved in financial and management related *jobs*" (pg. 30, emphasis added). Much farther down the list was "reinforcing the role of parents in the decision making process." There is no connection made between the two sets of recommendations, that is, no recommendation to increase the competencies of *parents* making financial policy decisions as well as *staff* competencies. This is not accidental.

Head Start grantee agencies (such as CAPs in the North Country) are now being expected to run much tighter financial ships, with the stimulus coming from the federal government, their funding source. This national trend seems not unreasonable on the surface. There are currently too few dollars to serve all the children eligible for Head Start (Health and Human Services 1993). Efficiency seems necessary to make inadequate funds go farther. Yet, this emphasis will also serve to finish the deradicalizing institutionalization process Kramer described twenty-five years ago.

Just since 1993, we have witnessed a major movement toward bureaucracy and business-like management in North Country Head Start, in all *three* counties. This change has considerable consequence for the possibility of parents exercising real power over Head Start—tight, centralized management and messy democratic oversight are quite incompatible. The changes, small and large, may seem perfectly reasonable on the surface. They have ostensibly been aimed at greater efficiency, cutting waste, and greater accountability—all laudable aims.

Yet, as we've said, what these changes have done and will do is move North Country Head Start farther and farther away from the radical potential of Great Society participation. Moreover, even the empowerment we described in the last section may be jeopardized. In order to empower women, the deficit-based programs must be delivered with respect, allowing the women to transform the services into entities of their crafting. The more the Head Start program becomes just "another social service bureaucracy with which the poor must contend," the less that will be possible.

We consider the changes toward greater bureaucratization in North Country Head Start, then, to be quite perilous.

THE WAY WE WERE

Since the changes toward greater accountability and bureaucratization began before we entered the field—they seem to have begun in earnest in the late 1980s—we are dependent on our respondents' memories for much of this section. Some of the changes reported we *can* vouch for; all of the changes we describe here have been reported to us more than once in independent interviews. Though we recognize that memory can romanticize the good old days, the version of the past we report is, in any case, the version that operates to guide our respondents' actions, their resistance.

In general, the long-time staff and former parents remember the Head Start operation as loose, creative, and caring—a memory that is consistent with the literature on Head Start. Skerry, for instance, refers to Head Start as a "haven of informality" in a bureaucratic world (1983: 37). Histories of other local programs are compatible, too, with our respondents' memories (Greenberg 1990 [1969]; Kuntz 1995).

Louise remembers especially the freedom the staff had to take care of families and experiment with teaching children.

JE: Earlier in the program, like in the seventies, did you feel the program was different?

Louise: Yes.

JE: In what way?

Louise: Now look. I'm only talking about Lake County, because every place is different, you know. . . . We had a lot of training, every Friday. We would have workshops and training and people were doing CDA [Child Development Associate, a certification program in the fundamentals of child development] and going to college, and almost all the staff were doing this. All summer we were going to school. So, that was very exciting, too. There was a lot of stimulating thinking going on, and challenging, and that was an exciting time, and people did get their master's degree and did stay on with the master's degree.

∎

Then we had one family worker per center, and now it's one for every two. And yes, you can deal with thirty-six families [at two centers]. You can, but you're doing more paperwork. Whereas when there were seventeen [families per family worker] . . . then if there was a family need, a family worker could go and could spend time. It's very different now. As I say, yes, you could do seventy families, you know, because you would just have the names in the books and you would make a phone call, whereas [before] like I said, you would make a home visit and spend some time talking with the person or inviting them to bring them into school and bring them in with the babies and things like that. There was much more of that. And so I think that has changed.

We used to have, also, more emphasis on field trips and things. We used to, when I was in Douglas Town, we would have swimming at the Y once a week. We'd have a field trip once a week, and then Val would come in and do nutrition. We just were very busy crews of people. And the parents came and brought their children, and Valerie would keep going through all these little ones, and I didn't mind having them in the classroom, you know, so that has made a difference.

■

So we had such freedom. If we couldn't go on a field trip that was planned because of the weather or something, I could call Pete [the HS director] the following week and say, "Pete, it's a lovely day today, can we go to the park or something," and Pete would say, "yes." So there was a different kind of freedom. And we would make a trip. We would be in town, and I could call and say, "We want to drive along the lake," and I would let the children see the lake before the frost and then the lake and the ice. Much more, there was more freedom. We felt that.

One of the most intriguing stories we heard about the old days was when, in the late 1960s, a mother and a former mother on the staff decided that another center was needed in a village at the edge of the county. They simply insisted that it be started and worked steadily toward that outcome. They generated interest and money, all on their own. This event, the two mothers tell us, could happen because of the trust and the flexibility of the program.

JE: I've heard you tell the story about getting the Douglas Town Center started.

Lila: Oh yes.

JE: Can you put that on the record?

Lila: That was interesting. This was a long time—I don't even remember what year that was, but Evelyn K. had one of her sons in the program here in Lake City, and Evelyn was the chairman of the Policy Council. And her and I got to be quite close, and she was moving to Douglas Town, so she did move to Douglas Town, and I got a call from her. And she said, "Oh, Lila. We need a Head Start center here in Douglas Town." So I approached Pete, who was our director, and I said, "Pete, you know, Evelyn is saying they need a program in Douglas Town." He said, "Yes, I know, I'm sure they do."

So we brought Policy Council in. We had an emergency meeting, and we were going to sit down and decide how are we going to do this. So, all we could think of was to have a walk-a-thon to Douglas Town [about fifteen or so miles]. And so we went out and we got sponsors, and I don't even know how many of us were in the walk-a-thon, but we walked to Douglas Town, and out of that I think we raised over three thousand dollars, enough for Summer Head Start.

In a separate conversation, we asked Evelyn about her memory of those times:

Evelyn: I lived in Douglas Town. I had moved. We moved around a lot. And we were living in Douglas Town in a trailer park. And I looked around that trailer park, and there were people who were in lots worse shape than I was. I mean, we had kids stealing food out of garbage cans and really bad situations, lots of them in this particular trailer park. And I came to Policy Council, and I said, "You know, I think we need a Head Start program in Douglas Town." And they said, "We have all the programs we can have, but we'll talk to the [Health and Human Services] program specialist [in the New York City HHS Regional Office]."

So they talked to the program specialist, and he said no, they weren't ready to open another program. They weren't sure they had need. But because Lila and some of those people encouraged me, particularly Lila, that, well, maybe we ought to look into it. And they didn't say "No, that's a stupid idea, we can't do it." Pete Cooney was the director at that time, and he said, "Well, you know, New York said no." But Lila would keep saying, "Well, how many people are there?" "What ages?" and "What do you think?" And finally I said, "Well, could we run a summer program?" Well, there would be this problem and there would be that problem, and there wouldn't be teachers and there wouldn't be—and we didn't have enough money. Basically it was coming down to there wasn't enough money.

So I can remember sitting there and thinking, well, you know, we keep talking about the need, and these are all neat people who might be willing to. I said "Well, I don't, I can't teach class. I don't have those skills. But I'd be willing to volunteer my time at a summer program. And I'll bet somebody else would be willing to volunteer to cook. Can't we do it with a lot of volunteers?" And idealist that I was, I figured we're going to get these teachers, yeah, we'll get everyone else to come in. Well, lo and behold, we got a lot of volunteers. And then Pete picked up on it and said, "Well, how much money would we absolutely need to pay the things, to buy the food, and do this?" And in the office they picked up on it. And we figured out how much money we'd need.

And then I happened to have visited my sister in Connecticut, and they were doing a crop walk in her church to raise money. And I came back. I talked to the lady after church about how. Now you have got to see, this is somebody who's grown a lot to be able to go to my sister's friend and say, how do I run a walk-a-thon? And I kind of—. And then they said, fine, go ahead, organize it. Well, I wasn't sure that was something I could do, but they were there and

they helped it, and helped me whenever I needed it, and
encouraged me.

And we organized a walk-a-thon, and I think all the Head Start
staff, and a lot of parents, and a lot of kids, went out and got
pledges. And we walked from Lake City to Douglas Town. And the
idea was we were bringing the program to Douglas Town.

LJA: A long trip.

Evelyn: Fifteen miles. It took me all day to walk it, and I was in bed for two
days afterwards. But there was no way when I had organized it, I
wasn't going to walk the whole thing. Because I was not in very
good physical condition. And we got the money, and we ran a
Head Start program with that money, and the volunteers that we
had that people picked up on. And New York then said, "Well, I
guess they really want a program there. And they need one." And
they funded a program the next year in Douglas Town.

And so that was like, you know, for all of us who were involved
in that, they do listen to the parents. They do listen to the community
that says, "Hey, we need this." And that, I mean, that was such a
thing for me as the little person.

That was in the late 1960s, very soon after Head Start had been
conceived and had come to the North Country. Twenty-five years
later, things have changed:

LJA: Do you think you could start a new center like you did in Douglas Town
or Northville? Do you think that would happen, those kinds of things?

Lila: Do I think it would happen now? Nowadays? I don't really think it
would.

CHANGES

Why would it be unlikely to happen now? The answer is not necessarily less capable administrators or less enthusiastic staff or parents. The answer primarily is the changing structure of authority

within the CAP and thus in Head Start. That new authority structure is due largely to a new administrative philosophy and new management "style," all originating with and validated by national-level policies.

Over the years, Lake County Head Start and the Lake County CAP had been administered by a series of social service providers who were intimately involved in the delivery of services as well as the management of them. In the late 1980s, there was a concern among CAP board members that administration of the agency had been lax and that the fiscal house was not in order. When a new executive director of the CAP was needed at about that time, that emerging concern led to a search for a business-oriented manager. This new executive director had no background in the front-line delivery of social services, but did have experience with business administration. The new executive director took it to be his responsibility to establish fiscal and administrative discipline on the overall agency and on each program. Indeed, in his first several years, he pleased the board greatly by doing just that: "We're treating [the CAP] much more like a business these days. Which it is. We should run it like a business" (written comment from a board member).

But the staff and parents who were involved with the program before saw things differently. To them, the changes were not in the right direction:

Doris: And Head Start staff people are not like that. We're people people. We don't work in a business world. . . . It's been part of the North Country for all these years, and we're not used to dealing with people like this. You know what I'm saying? We're not used to dealing with people that are not human service people. . . . We are not used to dealing with people that come from a business background or a business world who want to save money, get money. You know, you don't get money from a program that's federally funded for children.

■

Nancy: And I think that's partly why it's so hard on the staff is because for the most part, I mean, there's new staff, but the staff that have been around for awhile, you know, we were part of that, where you were part of the decision making. It wasn't an authoritative, "you do as I say" kind of thing.

New Quarters

One major administrative change made by the new executive director was to move the offices of Head Start staff. In an effort to both contain overhead costs and keep control over the program, the executive director moved the Head Start administrative staff into a newly acquired central office of the CAP agency. Prior to that event, they had been physically located in a separate building, miles from the executive director's office. Most of our respondents argued that the change had a decidedly negative effect on Head Start. The building itself came to symbolize the larger changes in administrative style.

Mary, a former parent and current staffer, says, "I think it was a bad idea when we merged into the same building, because we had separate buildings. We didn't have these problems when we were separate." Doris, too, objects to much about the new building:

Doris: The head office wasn't as fancy as it is now. I don't know. It's not them. It's not home. It's more official. This would be more home to them than down there.
LJA: This office [at the college]?
Doris: Yeah, we've got old chairs. It's not that I'm saying you have—.
LJA: We have tacky furniture. It's true.
Doris: These people live this way. They don't live that leather, in the leather world. [The new offices were furnished in red leather and rich wood.] . . . I don't even myself, personally—. I'll say this personally because I don't know how other staff members feel, but I

don't feel welcome down at that office.

LJA: Oh really? As a staff member?

Doris: As a staff member. I don't even feel welcome walking in there. . . .
It's like *our* office, and I'll be dipped. I'll say that until the day I die.
. . . We wanted to hang pictures that the children made? When
there were no pictures in it at all. You know, blank walls. He didn't
want the pictures hanging that the children made. I don't know. It's
very—. So how do you feel welcome?

Doris (and Lila below) refers to the fact that Head Start is the
CAP program with the largest budget for overhead. There was considerable feeling among Lake County *and* Kent County staff and
parents that Head Start was little more than a cash cow for the CAP,
allowing the executive director to have organizational trappings
(such as the fancy office) that would be otherwise impossible—"It's
like *our* [Head Start's] office." The feeling was that the executive
director thereby misused Head Start funds.

Lila: It's supposed to be an agency for low-income people, but it's got a
different facade. It doesn't present itself in that respect. When you
enter those doors, it's not warm. It's not appealing. You have to go
to a receptionist before you can go anywhere, and they don't want
you there if you're dirty, and they don't want you there certainly if
you have lice. It's just different. You know, you go in, and used to
[be] you came into the Head Start office or [the CAP] and you sat
on an old rickety chair and in Head Start you sat on folding chairs.
That's all we could afford. Now they go in and they sit in these
stuffed chairs where there's not even a magazine for them to look
at. . . . There are no pictures. I mean, we can't even have a picture
out in the hall that says, "You're now with Head Start." So, it's just
not appealing. It looks more like you're walking into GE [General
Electric] or something.

JE: I was just thinking that.

Lila: There's nothing there. There's absolutely not a thing there that is appealing to somebody poor. And to me, that says a whole lot. Everybody's in their little offices, and you have to be buzzed and sometimes people have come in, and I would tell [the receptionist] I'm in my office. I would hate that when the phone would ring and if she'd tell someone I'm not there, and I was down in the bathroom, you know. And that happened to us a lot of times, and I would say, "Don't tell people that." Say, "I'll be right back." You know. "Well, I didn't know where you were." Well, that's baloney. You know, when you're in the building, you're there. And the fact that [CAP] doesn't even have a sign that says Head Start outside, I think, is a slap in the face for Head Start. Brings all the money in, but can't have its name on the wall. It's not warm; it's not welcoming; it's not appealing. It's cold, it looks sterilized.

JE: It wasn't like that when you were over at Regal Street?

Lila: No, it wasn't like that, gratefully not. No, at Regal Street when they were there, you walked in and it was just a big old drafty, cruddy building, but you could go in there and get whatever you wanted, you know. The people were all at your fingertips and it made—. It was just a different place. Not the same, and if they don't want you there [at the new building], they make damn sure you know you're not supposed to be there.

JE: I don't always feel very comfortable there. I hadn't thought of it, but you're right. That setup is very off-putting.

Lila: Yeah. And I think when you're a human services program, you can't be all business. You darn well had better be people business, or else you are in no business being in that business, right?

LJA: Do you think the parents know that there's something different?

Lila: Absolutely. The parents say, "We don't go down there," you know.

No one deserves tacky furniture or "cruddy buildings"—not college professors or Head Start parents. If it had still been true that "people were all at your fingertips," Lila and the parents may well have welcomed the new, posh furniture. However, the coldness of the office did not emanate only from the furniture. It was indeed a new attitude toward both the staff and the recipients of services that generated people's discomfort, an attitude only symbolized by the fancy new quarters.

Tightening Up the Reins

That new attitude was soon made clear in new administrative policies and a new strictness in policy adherence, as well as in the new furniture. Under previous directors, apparently, Head Start had been very autonomous from the CAP. Nancy remembers, "We were part of [the CAP] but it was like I feel they were the bankers. You know." There was little day-to-day supervision or intrusion. Other staff, like Seraphina, agree:

> We were never really a part of CAP. When we were over at Regal Street, we had our office and we had their office, and we had to go down there occasionally to get purchase orders or maybe to get our paycheck on certain occasions, but for the most part, everything was handled within Head Start. The [CAP] director was there. The director of the CAP was never really a big part of our program.

Then, Head Start had had its own set of personnel policies, for example, which had been developed by the administration in conjunction with the Policy Council. These personnel policies were flexible and enforcement was lax. Nancy explains:

> He [Pete] was director, very, very strong director in that he did whatever he had to do for Head Start. He backed the staff; he backed the families. He had worked in the classroom, so he knew what the teachers were going through. There was more trust in—. Example. I had worked [on a new grant], and the grant had just come in, we had just gotten started. My mother-in-law died, and they live in [a Midwest state]. This was about—we got started in like October; this was the week before Thanksgiving in November. Pete says, "Go.

When you're back, you're back. We'll take care of it." And I went, and we took care of it, and we came back. And I mean, that was the kind of man he was, you know. He knew we were putting extra time, extra hours, and whereas you wouldn't necessarily get paid for it, if something—family emergency or whatever, or if it was a Friday, and everybody was tired, and it had been a hard week, and he knew it, it was like, we'll see you Monday.

It was not just Nancy who had benefited from loose enforcement of personnel policies. Seraphina told us:

I was in the program two weeks and my grand parents died. One died, and then the other one died like nine days apart, and like I said, you know, from two weeks, and they said, "Take whatever time you need." I mean, don't overdo it. I mean, I only took a day or so. But "take whatever time you need, and we'll make it up later," you know.

The new executive director, though, was hired to take greater control over the running of CAP programs, including Head Start personnel policies—"flexible" is often a special target for "accountable." The Head Start policies were quite different from those in force for the staff of other programs administered by the CAP. When Head Start moved into the same building as the other programs, the differences became apparent to the executive director. As we will see in the next two chapters, the executive director caused himself no end of grief when he unilaterally decided that these personnel policies had to be standardized across agencies. The parent Policy Council fought him on changes; the staff unionized in large part because of the changes. Nevertheless, in the end, the new, standard policies did give the administration much greater control over Head Start—and that, after all, had been the aim.

One of the most obvious differences between Head Start policies and the rest of the CAP was in terms of snow days. Head Start centers were routinely occasionally closed because of adverse weather—the children were not subjected to the danger of two bus rides during winter storms. These snow days were *paid* days off, since weather was not the fault of the staff. Administrative staff *also* got snow days off, not just center staff. So, other CAP staff (including the executive director) were walking past empty offices during bad weather. This, the executive director decided, would cause dissension among the whole of the CAP staff.

New, standardized policies were written. Among other provisions, when center classes were canceled for snow, center staff and administrative staff were nevertheless required to show up for work. Further, these new policies were neither flexible nor to have lax enforcement. The staff felt that keenly.

Carla: Everybody bent all the way around [before]. But all of a sudden, it was like really important to be at a certain place at a certain time. And the rules were having to be followed.

■

Seraphina: I just feel like everything's so—. Might as well have a time clock. You know. Got to punch in, punch out. Everything's so—. It's scary now.

Nancy has a very specific example, one that shows emphasis on the letter of the policies even while losing the spirit of Head Start:

What happened was, with trying to get the initial home visits done and get the classroom going and everything, I worked over a half hour and there was no one to ask [for permission]. I put down the time I worked, and was told [later] it was not approved. So, since you're supposed to make up the time over, within the same period, then Friday, we got out of a staff meeting at three-thirty, so rather than putting four o'clock, I did put three-thirty because I figured there was seven and a half hours on Thursday, so on Friday, there was the six and a half hours that made the same out to me. They docked me an hour because I did not work that half hour on Friday, and I worked a half hour that wasn't approved.

Many staff members note that some of the changes had merit:

LJA: What caused these changes? What was behind these changes?
Louise: Different things. Sometimes it's finances. Sometimes it's—. Well, now the bus drivers have to have a permit, a special permit, whereas before, anyone—if you had your license, you could drive the small buses, not the big ones. So anyone could do it. And we didn't have to have all the same rules and regulations, and some of them—. Just things, when we think what we used to do. My goodness.

We would put, sometimes for some reason, we were going somewhere, we could put all the children in the back of the station wagon and off we would go, you know. Well, we know now you can't even do this in your own car, so. But we used to. That was just great. We could do all kinds of things. So some of those reasons are very legitimate ones, you know, very reasonable ones, that we do have bus drivers who have better training.

Nevertheless, many of them wish for the days of greater spontaneity. But, as Nancy demonstrates, spontaneity and firm fiscal control are not compatible:

Nancy: [I went elsewhere for a couple of years], all of a sudden, there wasn't money for supplies. And it was like, wait a minute. Head Start, I mean, it didn't matter what you want, how much you wanted, it was there. Where you wanted to take the kids, do it. I mean, within reason. You know. We could take the kids to [a local restaurant] for lunch, just to experience Mexican food. Anything. You know. Do it. And now it's like, well, we'll have to see. And then, by the time they approve it, or disapprove it, or make a decision, or whatever they're going to do, most of the time it's gone.

You know, the kids have forgotten all about whatever, you know. Whereas before it was like if the kids really got into trains, you know, and you're thinking, gee, let's take them on a train ride, you know, go, and have a ball. And it's not like that anymore.

LJA: Because you had to follow procedures?

Nancy: Well, not only follow procedures. We had to follow procedures, too. I mean, we had to put in the field trip request, but now it takes them so long to make a decision. I mean, you might not find out for a month or more that it's okay to do it, or it's not okay to do it.

Doris, another staffer, echoes the feeling of giving lesser service due to stricter rules:

We used to have food at the old building. We had our own food in the back. Where we could go and get food and take it [to Head Start families]. You can't do that anymore. We used to have things like toothpaste, toilet paper, those kinds of things that they can't get with food stamps. Can't do that anymore. You have to go through all the Outreach [programs]. More control.

Lila, of course, has known Head Start and its service since the year it began.

JE: Are you saying that you don't have that flexibility to provide them special times, like for the woman who thought she was going to kill her baby?

Lila: Oh, that wouldn't happen. No, I don't—. No.

JE: I don't get that. Would they do something unusual or—.

Lila: In the past, the Head Start employees gave two hundred percent. You didn't get near the wages that you're getting today, but everybody knew the importance of their job. Today, it's like you're working in a fish bowl. You're under a microscope, and all you worry about is doing what it is that they want you to do and getting the hell out and go home.

Bureaucracy

So, while some of the small changes were reasonable, perhaps, the overall effect was to make it more difficult to run an innovative, exciting, flourishing program. The staff felt inhibited and constricted. As we will see in Chapter Nine, they also felt endangered, and fought back by unionizing. (Ironically though, in the process of unionizing, they likely *increased* the level of bureaucratization with which they had to deal.)

One of the costs of increasing managerial accountability, then, was a decrease in the vibrancy of Lake County Head Start. The changes in the CAP organization were also marked by some of the dysfunctions well-noted in the study of bureaucracy (Fischer and Sirianni 1984; Rothschild and Whitt 1986). Controlling information, for example, became a compulsion for the administration. Carla's story is a case in point:

> So I did have a question because in the old building, when the mail came in, it would go to the secretary. If she was busy, she just handed it unopened right to the person it went to. If she was not busy, then she opened it if it was something that didn't say personal and confidential, and it just made that much less work for the other person when they had it, and so when we got into this building [new offices shared with all of the CAP], we had some concerns because we were getting very little mail. Nothing was showing up. I mean, a couple of things a day compared to fifteen things a day, and where was it going? And I wasn't trying to be accusatory when I asked him, but I just said, "I have a question" because I have a question. "I would like to know why the mail has to go through the channels it does when it gets here?" And he asked what I meant. And I said, "Well, mail that normally would go directly to us, and some of our things are very confidential. Parents are expecting that the only person that's going to see it is [the addressee]." I said, "The secretary sees it, then I understand that it goes to you?" I said, "I'm

not sure, can you tell me the channel?" . . . I just said I had concerns about why that was necessary since we never had to do that in the old office. And he said, "Well, that's the way it's going to be done here." And finally I said, "Well, you know, what's the point of it? Is it, you know—." And he said, "Well I have legal and fiscal responsibility." . . . He said, "I'm not saying that I have to read every single thing, but it gives me an idea of the kind of things that are coming through here."

The Policy Council president, Hannah, was also incensed that her mail was opened. Often, she complained, she would receive mail addressed to her a week or more after it had been posted. Some things, she claimed, she never received. She insisted the executive director had no right to open mail addressed to her. This was a clear point of friction.

Another event shows the lengths to which the new administration went in order to "CYA" ("cover your ass"), as the staff put it. They seemed nearly desperate to prevent bad news from reaching HHS. Apparently, a group of parents (not the PC) wrote a letter to the HHS regional office, complaining about the playground facilities at their center. The executive director and the Head Start director directed the center staff to instruct the parents not to do so again.

Seraphina: We had to call a meeting. They sent letters out to all the parents. They made us all meet at our center, and we had to meet a half an hour before the parents got there, and we were told, you have to tell them, the parents—.

Nancy: That they did wrong.

Seraphina: That they were wrong. I said, "Excuse me?" . . . I said, "You're saying that what they did was wrong?" And [the executive director] said, "No." [The Head Start director] said, "No. We're saying that they didn't go through the proper channels, chain of command."

Nancy: "Chain of command," right.

Seraphina: And I said, "So what you're telling me is they're wrong. They are wrong, and we're supposed to tell them they're wrong in writing to the regional office." And [the executive director] said, "Yes." He said, "They were wrong."

Nancy: I said, "But they did—."

Seraphina: They weren't.

Nancy: They did go to [the Head Start director]; they did go to Policy Council. The playground still isn't up.

■

LJA: I heard he made you yell at them.

Doris: He wanted me to yell at them. Yes, he did.

LJA: Did you?

Doris: No, I didn't. Staff was told to be there a half hour early, and I was there, and [the Head Start director] called me in the office, and she said I was to tell the parents they did wrong, and I said, "They didn't do wrong." And she said to me, "They didn't follow proper protocol." I said, "Oh, well." I said, "If I wanted to write to the president of the United States without going through the governors and the senators and all that, I could do that." That is a human United States right. And I said [to the administrators], "I told them [the parents] proper protocol." I said, "I did. I told them. But if they chose not to use that, then, oh well." They didn't do wrong. They just took it a couple of steps further.

LJA: They don't work for [the CAP].

Doris: No. They were the parents and New York [City HHS] is their home office.

Clearly, the administration did not like the untidiness of democracy, preferring the control of a rigid "chain of command." Increasingly, problems were kept quiet, even among the staff. This meant, of course, that problems were not solved.

Nancy: This is just me, but it's almost like sexual abuse. You know, like it's happening, but don't talk about it. Keep it quiet. Just, you know, there's these bad things going on within the program, but don't let anybody on the outside know about it. You know? And it's like, "Hey, wait a minute."

■

Carla: One of the problems that we do run into with our whole situation, too, I don't know how to explain it to you. It's a feeling that I have, and it's a feeling that a few other people have said that they have, is that [the administration] wants everything to look positive. We aren't allowed to use words that even sound negative. There's nothing wrong with saying that there is a problem and then finding a solution.

LJA: Right.

Carla: But we're not allowed to do that. Everything has to be so up, so cheerful. Well, it's a denial. It's a form of denial, and it's an unhealthy way to look at things, and if you're going to run a program, I'm scared when I can't look at what the problems are.

LJA: Because it's just going to get worse.

Carla: Yeah, and that's what I see happening is that we're denying that there are problems. Not we, but management is basically denying that there are problems. They are thrilled about the praise that they get, which we all would be from, you know, the regional office and the federal government and wherever it may be coming from, and I understand that. But to deny that there are problems isn't going to stop them. They're just going to compound. So.

■

Holly: We wanted the public to be aware of what's going on because [the executive director] tries to cover up everything and [the Head Start director] goes around like "Gidget's Going to New York," and everything's well and everything's good, and you know it's not, but—. You know.

So, the negative, dysfunctional aspects of bureaucracy were entering the picture, along with the greater levels of accountability and control desired by federal and local administrators. As Skerry noted, the former "catch-as-catch-can feature of local programs makes Head Start an administrative nightmare. But, it also contributes to its enduring success" (1983: 30). With less of a nightmare, there is also less likelihood of enduring successes.

COMMON SCENARIOS

We most closely observed this bureaucratization in Lake County. However, very similar things occurred in the other two counties we studied. The account below, as told by Evelyn, is from *Kent* County, not Lake County, though the parallels first struck us as too, too eerie.

> I guess the agency, the CAP agency, hadn't had their personnel policies done for a long time, so she [the CAP director] rewrote the policies, and she decided that, for a long time, Head Start was just going to be absorbed. And it was going to be, I mean, she really has resented that we were kind of different and a separate entity. And we had to move into their building a couple of years ago . . . primarily because they could not afford—. She was buying a building for the CAP agency and couldn't afford it without Head Start. Moved in, we made all the renovations, and we had very nice offices, I have to admit. . . . Well anyway, the personnel policies, all of a sudden, showed up. And we had to have these personnel policies. And instead of looking at what Head Start needed in their personnel policies, she just wrote these policies without consulting anyone from Head Start, without anyone from Policy Council, and the whole agency; they were going to cover the whole Agency.

The stories we tell in the next two chapters also were previewed in Kent County. The parents there fought the CAP director's bid for total control over Head Start; the staff unionized.

In River County, the third county we studied, the CAP administration seems to be beginning the process of wresting control over

Head Start away from the long-time Head Start staff and parents. The front-line staff is considering unionizing. As Yogi Berra reportedly once said, "It's like déjà vu all over again!"

Further, parents and staff members, like Evelyn, report that this is not a phenomenon limited to the North Country:

> I tell you, if I knew how to get a hold of Geraldo [the talk-show host] or somebody. It just seems to me that it would make a real good investigative thing for somebody, because it's not just Kent County. When I talk to people—, and it's not just Kent and Lake County. When I talk to people at conferences, there's a whole lot of this kind of thing that you hear from other parent involvement coordinators, that the CAP agencies, basically, people have the attitude that these people [the parents] all shouldn't have anything to say. . . . Obviously, if you're trying to run an agency that has fifteen programs under it, you want everything. You want to be able to go, "Yeah." I said that to [the CAP executive director]. "I understand it's a lot easier to come in and you make the decisions and not have to deal with the Policy Council. But you're missing the boat."

If Evelyn saw parallels in talking with staff at conferences, parents were also talking with other programs' parents and finding commonalties.

LJA: You know, when we first started this research, everything we heard about Head Start was positive: It's good for kids; it's good for parents.
Patty: It's great for parents.
LJA: The staff loved it; the staff really like their jobs. And then all of a sudden—.
Patty: All hell broke loose.
LJA: What's goin' on? Obviously that happened in Kent. That happened in Lake. I think it's happening in River.
Patty: All right let me tell you. Gonna go back a little bit. When Kent

County was going through their [problems], there was a group in Massachusetts that had the same thing happen. And I got in touch with this woman [a mother in the program there]. And she said at the time that it was happening to them, she knew it was happening to somebody in New York state. That she was trying so hard to find out who she could get in touch with to let us know [it was happening in different places].

Parents and staff believe that this bid for bureaucratic control is common among Head Start programs nationwide. In Janet's words:

And I think, to some degree, that the umbrella agencies [CAPs] don't necessarily want to give up the autonomy. . . . And I think they just feel sometimes that, you know, Policy Council is there as an advisory without—. They'd like to see them as an advisory without real power. The Policy Council sees themselves as a power agency, you know.

Parents (some of them, anyway) continued to believe in the legitimacy of the power they had been granted. They fought back against the control exercised by the administration, fought back against both the inherently demeaning notions of policy-council-as-compensatory-education and against the increasing "accountability" of the local administration.

❖8❖

Defiance . . .
and Withdrawal

You're darned right, Policy Council makes a difference!

Seventy-point-two is not a guideline. It's the law. They have to listen to us!

What difference does it make what we do? They just do what they want anyway! Why should we bother?

So, the parents on Policy Council are up against a number of hurdles in their efforts to exercise authority over their children's education in Head Start. They are unfamiliar with power; the administrators of the program seem to consider them child-like and quite deficient in important respects; grantee agencies are under pressure to increase efficiency and administrative control over the program. Parents were quite aware of these hurdles and the implications for their own power.

Some few parents accepted their ceremonial role and played along with administration efforts to "reform" them. Some parents were immediately turned off and withdrew from participation, even if they continued to attend meetings. Other parents insisted on exercising genuine power. When the latter happened in Lake County, the parents met with administrative intransigence—because of the pressure for greater accountability, because of wide-spread disrespect for poor people, because of patriarchal presumptions. That intransigence had the effect of discouraging additional parents, but also had the opposite effect of energizing a few of them to greater defiance.

Given the Lake County administration's strong bid for greater program accountability, for absolute control, though, in the end virtually all the parents gave in to withdrawal. Efficiency comes at great cost.

POLICY COUNCIL WINS!

In our time observing the PC, we noted a few, small, gradual changes that, in the end, made big differences in how much control the administration had over the mothers. Our time there, remember, spanned three school terms. Mothers are members usually for a single term. They would not be aware of these changes.

For instance, Lila, the parents' advocate, used to be the Head Start staff member in charge of arranging the PC meetings and answering parent questions (about process and substance) in the meetings. Suddenly, we realized that Lila had not attended the meetings in a while, and that, instead, the Head Start director was there, answering questions. Also, the CAP executive director had begun attending meetings and often had much to say. We cannot say for sure that the administrators' control over the meetings increased through these moves; we just know that the administrators were strongly vying for control by the time we realized the shift.

Notwithstanding this control, the administration was, on occasion, seriously challenged by parents. In fact, parents experienced some victories.

During the 1992–93 year, the PC was asked to approve updated job descriptions prepared by the Head Start director and her staff. At one meeting, descriptions were to be approved for two positions, cook and assistant cook. The descriptions were included in the PC packets distributed at the beginning of the meeting. The parents had had no time to review the drafts or to talk about them. There was no discussion of the cook's description and it was approved, ceremonially. However, when the assistant cook's draft description required a high school diploma or GED, Martha, a mother, objected: "I cook for eight kids, and I work in a restaurant. I know I'm a good cook, and I don't have a diploma." Other parents agreed. All agreed with the director, though, that Head Start should encourage all its employees to get a GED. Parents insisted the requirements be amended to accept applicants who were willing to begin work on a GED. The amended job description then passed. It is not clear, however, that the change ever affected any actual hire.

On the agenda of the first meeting of the 1993–94 PC was an issue which seemed quite routine, but which turned out to be of critical interest to parents. As explained in the last chapter, the CAP had recently consolidated office space, moving all programs into a new building. At that point, the CAP executive director had asked the board to approve standardized personnel policies. After approval by the CAP Board, these new policies had been in effect for some months, pending the legally required PC approval. The previous year's PC had approved these policies in committee, though the matter had not come before the full group.

The policies were now being brought before the full PC. The issue was presented by the PC chair, Hannah, who noted that the previous year's personnel committee had thoroughly reviewed the policies and approved them. A newly elected mother raised her hand and asked to read the policies before she voted on them.

The administration present was reluctant to distribute the policies, since there was some concern with keeping them confidential—to be sure an odd concern, since they were in effect. Further, as the executive director of the CAP agency (who was attending the meeting as a guest) made clear, the policies were already in force: "You don't understand. These are already in place. The board has approved them." The strong implication of his comments was that it did not matter what the parents thought, these were to be the policies. The PC, moreover, needed to approve them, and approve them without comment—ceremonially, as a rubber stamp. He was simply matter-of-fact, not particularly condescending or arrogant—at least in tone.

Nevertheless, several parents demanded to see the policies. Genine, for example, said, "I don't think we should be asked to vote on it before we had a chance to read it." And Abbey declared, "I'm not gonna approve it if I can't see it."

These arguments appealed strongly to reason and procedure, guaranteed by 70.2. They were thus effective. After raising reasonable objections about voting on policies they had not read, copies of the policies were distributed. The demand could not be reasonably refused given the statutory authority of the PC.

While PC members were thumbing through the lengthy policies, Genine spoke up:

> I just want to clarify something. The committee that approved these was the old committee right? And they were recommending to the old group right? Well we have a new group and a new personnel committee now. Shouldn't we get a recommendation first from that committee? Isn't that how it should work?

Again, a reasonable request, given the rules of decision making for this body. After some discussion, including some reservations about lost time from the CAP executive director, there was this:

> *Genine:* I motion that we send this back to have the personnel committee give us recommendations.
> *Iris:* I second.

Given the rules of the meeting—*Robert's* Rules, not "Roger's Rules"—there was then no choice but to vote on the motion from the floor. The executive director could not raise reasonable objections or prohibit the vote to table the issue. He did not try. When there was no discussion, the motion was carried resoundingly.

The tabling gave the parents time to thoroughly discuss the matter (in committee and in private) and decide how their interests were served or not. In fact, they later strongly objected to some of the provisions, which were deemed unfair to *mothers* on the staff. In time, the new personnel committee met with some of the board and was able to work out a compromise. The compromise allowed the staff to use some of their sick leave for family emergencies—an issue critical to caretakers of children.

There were other small victories in 1993–94. Apparently, there had never been a formal mechanism for resolving differences between the board's decisions and the PC's. The two bodies were *both* responsible for running the program. It seems nearly inevitable that there would be disagreement on occasion, and such a resolution policy would be needed. It seems, though, that the PC had heretofore always either immediately gone along with recommendations by the board, or had come around to its way of thinking quickly. (Remember from Chapter Six that Carol had referred to having to redecide issues if the CAP did not agree.) This is significant evidence that the PC had been functioning as a rubber stamp, as a ceremonial power only.

The board, for immediate reasons that remain unclear, proposed a formal mechanism for an event that had not yet occurred. This proposal was a straight-forward mechanism for conflict resolution: Each side would elect one member to a resolution team, and those two would then select a neutral third member. Those three people would resolve the issue in a binding manner. This is a very ordinary mechanism, well-used in a variety of settings.

However, the parents balked. They wanted to know, before they voted on it, who would constitute a neutral third party. Administrators and some community representatives on the PC were annoyed about this, noting (in undertones to Lynda during the meeting) that this procedure was so ordinary, why didn't the parents know this? What was their problem?

Part of their "problem" was probably unfamiliarity with such procedures. However, there was something more compelling, too. The North Country is very much a small town, in the sense that the human services community is tiny. The members have connections with business people, with clergy, with much of the educated population. In short, administrators and the board are likely to know or have some connection to most of the people who would be nominated as "neutral." Poor mothers are not so well-connected. From their perspective, then, how neutral could this person be? Parents were becoming very wary, in general, of the administration's requests.

The PC tabled this issue. The board was annoyed. The administration was annoyed. Even some community representatives on the PC were annoyed. The issue was not resolved until two things happened. First, the PC received from the staff written assurances of true neutrality. The Head Start director actually copied a page out of the dictionary, showing them what "neutral" meant. The parents let this condescension pass unremarked (although they noted it well) in light of the second event. Simply, there was an issue that the PC wanted resolved, an issue the board would have let go indefinitely. So, before the PC could push for resolution of this issue, there had to be a mechanism in place.

When it suited their interests to do so, the PC passed the policy. The issue, by the way, was this research project. Recall from Chapter One that the board refused to grant us "permission" to do this study. The parents wanted this book written. Both they and we much preferred to have the board "approve" it, though we all recognized that approval was not necessary. We're convinced that the board approved the research primarily because the PC was evidently ready to push for resolution through the new mechanism.

Clearly, these victories were minor in terms of policy affected and quite equivocal. Under 70.2, the PC has the power, for instance, to approve personnel policies for Head Start and to design and approve any set of policies it wished, in theory. There was no need, from the view of the parents or Head Start staff, for any standardization of policies with other programs. The standardization was desired by the CAP director, not the PC, not Head Start. Even with the changes made by the PC, the new rules were much more restrictive than the old ones had been. Further, as we shall see in Chapter Nine, the strict application of the new rules negatively affected the staff.

The PC "won" in changing a detail of the policies, but never really engaged the larger battle, the battle over keeping Head Start distinct from other CAP programs. As with paying the lawyer, the administration never allowed the larger issue to be seen as a battle at all, presenting the already-formulated policies to be voted up or down. The administration still set the agenda, administrating consent.

That notwithstanding, these small victories were important. A number of parents were empowered, emboldened to seek greater and more genuine power. They learned, in these little victories, what the rules and tools are. The victories were important, if only as training. The administration, in its turn, was prodded by these victories to exercise even greater control over the PC.

UNDERMINING POLICY COUNCIL

During the three years we were in the field, there were a number of times that PC mothers did fight back, seeking to exercise power, especially in 1993–94 and 1994–95. At first, women were excited, if unsure, about this "Christmas present" they had to open. When they were met with disdain from the administration—which they generally were—more women simply withdrew, but others were invigorated. Most of the women clearly recognized who, as Ed Sadlowski put it, was "screwing them"—demonstrating an understanding of the immediate power *structure* in Head Start. Those few who fought back began to develop a more profound understanding of systemic domination *and* of ways to fight against it collectively. However, over and over, the struggle was seemingly in vain. Again and again, administrators simply outlasted, outpowered, the mothers. More and more individual women withdrew, surrendering empowerment.

We will illustrate this process with several accounts.

Resistance: For Lila

One incident that particularly angered 1993–94 PC parents concerned Lila, who had requested an unpaid leave to travel south for two weeks during the winter. In the past, the staff tells us, such requests were routinely granted. Lila's request came to the PC for approval, as 70.2 requires. At the PC meeting, parents noted Lila's long and dedicated service and moaned about the very cold, very snowy winter that the North Country was having. Her leave was approved unanimously and the parents wished her a happy vacation in the sunshine.

However, some time *after* the PC approval, the Head Start director denied Lila the time to take the leave. Outside of meetings, PC parents were outraged at this move by the administration for two reasons. The first was that they felt Lila deserved a break and that management was being punitive in denying it to her; the second was that they felt the administration had no authority to override a PC decision. Several parents were eager to confront the administration over this issue and demand that their decision be honored. However, one of the parents reported that Lila did not wish them to have such a confrontation over this event; she wanted to avoid further trouble with her superiors. The PC parents decided to honor Lila's request that they let the matter slide. Nevertheless, anger and resentment remained.

Soon thereafter, Lila took an extended disability leave, a leave from which she would never return. Among parents, the general belief was that Lila was suffering from stress related to being hounded by the administration. In a PC meeting that had been declared closed to the administration, a parent reported that Lila's recent performance appraisal had been negative and included such criticisms as "she was too friendly with parents." Another parent stated that Lila had been "written up" for using her sick time for family emergencies, which was against personnel policies. (Ironically, it was this very provision to which the PC would *later* successfully negotiate a change.)

When the administration tried to advertise to fill Lila's job, the PC objected that the position was not vacant, that Lila was entitled to return to it from her leave. The mothers took action, making phone calls to the regional office of HHS and to the state Workers' Compensation Board, seeking information, strategies, and support. They solicited the help of various board members. They demanded meetings with the executive director.

At one PC meeting, people showed up wearing black ribbons with tiny red roses sewn on. These ribbons symbolized support for Lila and the desire to have her back. Parents wore these symbols defiantly. In Chapter One, we noted that Lynda attended a meeting with the executive director and board chair to discuss the study. Hannah, the only parent amid professionals, came to that meeting wearing the ribbon and rose. Though everyone surely noticed, not a word was said about it.

These were actions *not* typical of the individual women, at least not before their Head Start involvement. Several reported to us that they had never before made such demands of officials. They had never before taken part in a symbolic protest, such as wearing the ribbons. Their aim was to keep Lila's position open *and* to make enough changes to the conditions in the office to allow her to return without further trauma. In this fight, the women were determined not be steamrolled. The initial conflict with the administration gave them energy and purpose; they used their anger to fight back.

But Lila never came back. And a PC member nonetheless sat on the committee selecting her replacement, as though this was a routine job search. The full PC later approved the hire without significant protest.

Resistance: For Nancy

Some months later, another long-time Head Start staff member, Nancy, resigned in large measure because she had not received a raise the PC had approved more than a year earlier. Nancy had worked for a long time at Head Start, then left for a different job, and then returned. Her pay upon returning did not reflect her earlier service, and the raise would have corrected that. Until the resignation, the PC was unaware that the raise had not been granted. When questioned, the administration claimed that the increase had been held up due to the advent of union negotiations that would affect Nancy. The parents felt that their authority had again been ignored. Again, they were angry, particularly since the resignation was not delivered through regular channels by the administration.

According to 70.2, the PC must approve all resignations, as well as other personnel actions. The normal procedure for these votes is that the administration forwards resignation letters to the PC chair who reads them and asks for a motion for approval from the floor. In this case, the administration did not forward the letter. Nancy herself, though, had given a copy of her letter to one of the community representatives, who handed the letter to the PC chair, Hannah, at the beginning of the meeting.

At the end of an acrimonious discussion, the PC voted *not* to accept the resignation. The parents made plans to consult both with the union and Nancy to ascertain what hurdles had been in the way of the approved increase, and to report back to the full PC. PC members were adamant that they needed to and would hold someone accountable for this failure to carry out the PC's decision.

And yet, Nancy did quit—she had already stopped working when the PC voted not to accept her resignation.

Resistance: The Union

During the period we were in the field, the unionization of the staff was a major event for parents on the PC. For quite some time, though, parents' sole source of information about the union and the negotiations with the administration came from the staff, in informal conversations at the centers. The administration continued to tell the PC that things were going well and would "soon" be resolved. It was clear to parents, though, that things were not going well at all.

The negotiations dragged on and on. For the first several months, negotiations were conducted by the thirty-thousand-dollar-shortfall lawyer and the CAP executive director. No one else from administration sat at the table. Parents at PC meetings often discussed the lack of progress in the negotiations, and often expressed frustration that they could not find out more about why it was taking so long. From their conversations with the staff, the parents grew concerned either that there would be a strike, interrupting services to the kids, or that the CAP would succeed in delaying the contract—and the union itself—to death. The parents were instinctively in the corner of the staff on this issue, noting well how little the staff was paid and how devoted the staff was to serving their families.

The parents called a special, all-day meeting of the PC at which no staff member would be present. Here, they were able to discuss a number of issues completely and without intimidation or interruption from the administration. To this meeting, they invited the union organizer, who briefed them on the purpose of the union and the union's demands in negotiation. From the administration, though, the parents could still get no satisfactory answer.

The parents finally got fed up. After discussing the matter with other parents, Hannah, the PC chair, proposed to both the union and to the CAP that she attend the negotiations as an observer. The argument was that the PC would be required to approve the contract and should have first-hand knowledge of the negotiations. The union was keen on the idea; the CAP Board was not.

The chair took steps to assure herself a place at the negotiations table. She called HHS—she was now on a first-name basis with several members of the regional staff—to ascertain the PC's rights in such circumstances. She met with the CAP executive director repeatedly, wearing him down, until she was officially designated as part of the management negotiating team—though she had to promise to remain silent during actual negotiations.

Whether coincidentally or not, the log-jam in negotiations was broken shortly after this parent began attending sessions and reporting on its content to other parents. There was no strike and the union won a contract.

Hannah was able to bring detailed information about the newly proposed contract back to the PC. A committee of parents was formed to go over the various provisions in detail before an approval vote was called. Indeed, the parents had a number of issues with specific clauses, thinking them too restrictive on the staff who were themselves parents. Staff members who had been active in the union drive were asked to appear before the PC and give their views on the contract. The CAP executive director was also thoroughly questioned by the PC. He was asked to verify in writing that the contract would be administered in full accordance with 70.2, so that parents could assure themselves of their full role.

In other words, the parents took seriously their authority to run the program and forced the administration to do so as well—at least in this one instance.

WITHDRAWAL, AGAIN

These three event histories illustrate how parents attempted to exercise the power they believed due them in the face of recalcitrance by the administration. The administration, though, by and large simply moved along with actions they considered necessary, regardless of the PC. When parents became aware that they were being ignored despite their proactive stance, again there were two reactions, withdrawal and renewed defiance.

For instance, though the PC voted not to accept Nancy's resignation, that very afternoon the administration issued a posting for her job, deemed by them to be vacant. Hannah, who saw the posting that day, expressed considerable exasperation: "What difference does it make what we do? They just do what they want anyway! Why should we bother? I'm just so frustrated."

Over the year this group was on the PC, we indeed observed the administration exercising and demanding more and more control. PC members—parents and community representatives— clearly felt deluded by the administration. This was true for even the parents seemingly most "empowered" during the year. Jody, if you remember, had told us she "was like a vacuum lately, sucking up information," but she recognized powerlessness, too. She says, "We aren't told a lot of things. They don't want us to know about a lot." Other mothers recognized it, as well, and did not like it.

> *LJA:* Does that happen a lot, where the Policy Council decides something and then it gets overruled by [the administration]?
>
> *Camille:* I found out so far about four or five different things. They do what they want to do. They have a mind of their own. They're gonna do it anyway. . . . I think they don't listen to parents because they figure that some of them are low economically, and who cares, gives a damn, what they feel like. You know, "We have run this program for years and we're not going to listen to them. We'll just listen to them to pacify them, but we'll do what we want to." . . . It seems like they make up new rules once you make a decision on something else, it's like, let's make up another rule. . . . You know, like whatever they want us to know. Little stuff, little stuff. They let all of us take that and let them run with it for a while. "Keep them busy over here, so we can do this over here." I mean, I think a lot of stuff is just shuffled. You know, "well, let's let Policy Council know this, but let's keep this going over here." That's the way I feel.

Abbey had been outspoken about process from the first day when she helped table the personnel policy vote. She is highly critical of administrators.

Abbey: Administration could care less. And being in Policy Council just showed me that. Seeing them bicker they way they do.

LJA: Administration?

Abbey: Yeah, administration. And taking all the values we teach our children about not lying, about being truthful, about trying to come to a reasonable conclusion, and they take all those and they threw them right out the window, because they're adults and they lied to us as a group, because they figured we didn't have enough sense to figure out what was going on. . . . When they need us, we're important, then they flip the coin. . . . It's "go by the book," but when they need to, they change the book and you're not supposed to be smart enough to read it.

Such negative sentiments were echoed by professionals serving on the PC as community representatives:

Margot: It may be because I'm new, but I always get the feeling there's a hidden agenda, that I'm not being told everything.

■

Geri: There's a lot of things I should hear about but I don't. I hear them from the staff, not at Policy Council. That's not right.

■

Val: When you get to know something about the program, they take you off [the PC].

For parents, this behavior is especially disheartening. The parents involved in Head Start are, by definition, economically disadvantaged. They are used to losing battles with employers, banks, social services, schools, and so on (Calabrese 1990; McAtee n.d.). At the time they begin Head Start involvement, they typically report their self-confidence to be low (Parker, Piotrkowski, and Peay 1987; Reiner, List, and LaFrenier 1983; our Chapter Three). Their confidence in themselves as capable administrators is virtually nonexistent. When their efforts to exercise their statutory control over the program are met with paternalism, with disrespect, with disdain, it seems to mothers to be just business as usual (Fruchter 1984; Rosier and Corsaro 1993; Ackelsberg 1988). As Jody tells us, "I don't think we make any real difference. They don't really listen to us. They don't have to."

KNOWING WHO'S SCREWING YOU

Empowerment does, necessarily, require some understanding of how to fix what's wrong. We argued in Chapter Three that empowerment involves women seeing avenues open to them to make changes in their lives, or creating those avenues. In the events we've described, an avenue for power that was shown to them—participating in decision making on the PC—was deliberately closed and blocked. Women needed to understand who and what was the cause of the blockage.

As the following reveals, there was often deep hostility aimed at individual administrators perceived to have patronizing attitudes (to protect the respondents, these quotes will not be attributed, even to pseudonyms):

PC Community Rep: [Administrator] is an a—hole.
PC Parent: [Administrator] is a puppet.
Non-PC Parent: They only care about their own salary.
PC Parent: They want to look good. But they don't care about helping low-income people get back on their feet.
PC Parent: Somebody said [administrator] is like a cult-leader. He can talk people into anything. He'd be dangerous as a cult-leader.

This focused hostility allows the parents to withdraw only partially. They maintain their loyalty to Head Start by drawing distinctions between center staff and programs on the one hand, and administrators on the other. They can continue to receive some of the benefits of participation, and continue to be trained in lifestyles and values deemed appropriate by the staff. They may thus nevertheless become better cooks, learn better (or at least different) disciplinary styles, and develop friendship networks. We believe some of these changes are useful to the women in making their lives somewhat easier (see Chapter Three). Certainly the women tell us that is the case.

Under such circumstances, women often withdrew from illusory power and returned to their immediate, validated interests in their children's well-being. Carol says, "It's here [at the center with the kids] that I want to be. Here's where I matter." And, Janna's distinction is even stronger: "I love being with the kids. PC makes me crazy."

Structural Solutions

And yet, many parents, such as Patty, also knew that there was something more systemic at work here, and that they needed to keep fighting:

> My sister gets so mad at me. She says, "Why don't you just give up?" I said, "Because this is how the system works." If you work hard enough, may take you ten years; but if you don't have people like us working, then nothing ever gets changed in this country. I says, "Maybe I like that dent in the brick wall" [where I pound my head]. Hah! It just makes me more determined!

While particular administrators came in for direct denunciation, the mothers understood that getting rid of the individuals would not solve their problems.

LJA: Do you think if you got rid of those two people [administrators], things would be fixed?
Camille: No, because they'd probably hire two of the same. You know what I'm saying? They're looking for that certain type of person.

Staff members, like Doris, knew this, too:

> That's why I asked Hannah what her main goal was at that meeting. I wanted to know what her main goal was. If her main goal was to get rid of [the HS director] and get rid of [the CAP executive director], so what. We could get two other people ten times worse. But her main goal is to be freestanding and that is what my main goal is.

Fewer and fewer parents remained actively involved in efforts to resist the administration's domination. By the summer of 1994, only a handful of parents continued the fight against the administration—and they did consider it a fight. In one meeting, for instance, the parents had decided to eject the administrators and other staff. They wanted to discuss the issues on their own, without any of the controlling interference we have discussed. The CAP executive director launched into an eloquent plea for "better communication" and "trust"—meaning not closing the meeting to administrators. Hannah looked down at her watch and interrupted him. "You've got three minutes, and then you'll have to leave." He left, very slowly, but he left.

The fight became harder for the remaining parents to sustain because they knew that a new PC would be formed in the fall, when school began again. They knew that the administrators could—and were prepared to—simply wait them out and deal with the new group. A fight by parents in New York City public schools resulted in the use of similar tactics by that administration (Lurie 1970; see also Arnstein [1971] for these tactics in a more general discussion of citizen participation). Parents hypothesized, in fact, that the administration was stalling on a number of issues (such as Nancy's resignation) for this reason. A new PC would not know the background and might do as the administration asked, without question. Remember the concerns raised by Clara and Abbey in Chapter Six that many things get passed early in the term, before parents learned the ropes.

The parents began talking specifically about how to leave some institutional memory, the background they individually had on various issues, for the next PC. This was an explicit attempt to change the structure of power. Abbey spoke again about how hard it was for them to have been plunked down into roles of authority:

> What happens is that Policy Council comes in November, and they kind of like flounder around for three months. Just about the time you start to build up a head of steam, school's out. So what needs to happen, and that's why I keep pushing this annual report thing, and not because it's my idea, but I think it's a good idea. And I don't want a flowery—like we had a raffle and all that stuff. I want Policy Council, when they come in in November, hopefully there'll be enough of us left from last year, from this year, I want them to know from the beginning that these are the problems that we encountered. We were unable to decide on this, so this is a priority. I want them to know that they don't have to take a lot of things just because administration says that's the way it goes.

The parents on the PC had agreed that the training session for new PC members, given at the beginning of the year, had been inadequate in the past, but was the proper vehicle by which to pass on to new parents the knowledge and insights the current PC members had gained through their hard work and their battles. They began developing training materials that would, among other things, inform new PC members what the contentious issues had been, so that the administration could not "pull a fast one" and get approval on something the new parents knew nothing about.

The parents thus tried to take steps to assure that the administration had to treat the PC, as an institution, with respect. They were attempting to preserve an aspect of Head Start they deemed both important and due them.

But there were, in the end, too few of the parents left, and no one left with enough energy, to put the new training materials to-

gether and deliver them, especially against the wishes of the administration. There was no institutional memory, no annual report,
flowery or not, left to the new PC. The administration had waited
the parents out.

Becoming Freestanding

Through 1993–94, parents and staff became increasingly convinced that the answer did not lie in tinkering with the existing structure of Lake County Head Start. They decided that a more radical
change was necessary. They began investigating the possibility of becoming a freestanding program, one that was its own grantee agency.
They had determined that being free of the CAP and its business-like
practices was necessary. Patty, who had experience in Kent County
and was now on the PC in Lake County, puts it this way:

> You know what my basic goal is right now? Head Start has
> outgrown CAP agencies. Head Start should be on its own. That's my
> goal. Because, I understand the need for them way back when. But
> we have gotten so big now that we don't need anybody else. We
> could do it ourselves. And I think it would be less complicated.

Parents made phone calls to HHS in New York City and in
Washington, D.C., for information about de-funding the Lake
County CAP. They called parents in other counties and states who
had become freestanding, asking for advice and strategies.

This particular battle is still raging as we write and will not be resolved soon. Our point here is primarily that parents did understand
the structural causes and the structural solutions to their powerlessness in Head Start.

However, they remained relatively powerless. The PC parents
collected reams of documents showing how the PC's decisions had
been ignored and overridden illegally by the CAP administration.
They presented these documents to the CAP Board. Some board

members seemed outraged at the administrators' behavior; most seemed bored and somewhat annoyed. The parents sent the documentation to the New York City HHS regional office. But nothing happened.

Though Kent County parents had been working on this issue much longer, had had much more contact with program administrators at HHS, not much had happened there, either. Patty talks about her earlier experience:

> The executive director did everything she could to get rid of our management team, to take our Policy Council and just ignore us. Because [the management team] are very, very strong believers in Head Start, and they followed 70.2 to the letter. And, as they trained the Policy Council in 70.2. The executive director did not *want* that. . . . The issue that I think it is, it's money. That's it. . . . She will not follow 70.2. [She claims], "70.2 is nothing but a guideline. It is not a law; it is a guideline." They succeeded in getting rid of the management team. And I blame that on the—. I don't even blame the CAP agency. It's regional office's fault. New York City. They sold us out. I don't know what they're doin'. We always wanted it to go to court because once the judge found out what was goin' on, regional office would've been in trouble 'cause they should've stepped in three years ago and didn't do it.
>
> ■
>
> At the beginning, she [the executive director] was just circumventing PC. She would do what she wanted. We said, "Unh-unh. You can't do that. This is our money." She said that the CAP agency, they're responsible for the funding so they didn't have to come to PC for approval. And, no matter what you said to her, and showed her the law, and what ever, she knew it was unenforceable.
>
> ■
>
> We had that [HHS regional office person] up here. He sat there and was very, very rude. Told us he couldn't even believe we had outhouses up here and, you know, just that kind of an attitude. I'm

so sick of that attitude. Well he's from New York City and then he tried to say, well New York City has all these Head Starts. You know. We're back on the list somewhere. We're just, you know, in the boonies up here. That type of attitude, and I thought, well.

■

I told somebody at the regional office, I said, "Don't you dare. I'm so upset. To empower me is a great thing. But to empower me to slam my head against a brick wall is nonproductive. Why are you doing this to us?"

Now the CAP agencies have a lawyer. Regional office has themselves. They're supposed to be our backing, and they're not. So here we are, parents, fighting this fight. Washington is running like hell from us. They don't even want to hear from us, and I had everybody's name. Like [the HHS administrator]. She hears my voice on the phone, and she's immediately not available. You know. Why are they doing this?

Other Kent County mothers, like Penny, have similar accounts:

You know they [the administration] would call parents up to see how they're gonna vote. And then when I call the regional office, and say, "You know, I believe that's unethical." "Yeah, so what do you want me to do about it? So she's unethical." Like, oh my God. A million times that's it. We got to the point where we didn't even think they would take our phone calls. 'Cause like every time we'd call they'd hear our names and wouldn't call us back. And when you can't get support from your regional office, which is, you know—they got upset with us because we went over their heads— "But hey, we're not getting anywhere with you." You know. "You're telling us all this stuff and nothing is happening." You know, we need to see some results of some kind.

As more time went by, parents in both Kent and Lake Counties gave up, lost interest, had to divert their time and energies to more immediate concerns in their lives. In the end, parents were dependent on other powerful people to back them up in their exercise of statutory authority—but that backup did not come. As Ackelsberg wrote: "If the activities I undertake in the larger political context are ignored, or their political significance denied, my frustration may well end in resignation and the process of the production of consent" (1988: 299). When those powerful potential allies either ignored the parents or sided with the administration, there was no other avenue open to mothers. It seemed they had lost.

DEFIANCE LOST

In these incidents, there were two reactions to disrespect and roadblocks from the administration. One was to fight back, harder; the other to withdraw from the battle. In fighting back, parents had had to dedicate significant energy and time to the process of retaining the PC's authority. Sometimes real differences in policy were effected; other times proper respect for the PC was restored, if only for a time. However, in the end, administrators retained considerable, if not absolute, control over the program. In the end, the parents' champion, Lila, did leave, and Nancy did quit. The personnel policies came to include a more generous sick-leave provision, but were still not as generous or flexible as the original policies had been. In the end, the new PC did approve a number of actions about which the new members knew little.

Every time parents discovered that their efforts had *not* made a difference, had been ignored, even the fighters edged closer to resigned defeat and withdrawal. As their own children moved on to the public school system, their own compelling interest in Head Start also waned. In the public school system, moreover, they would again be reminded of how little power they held in the world (Calabrese 1990; Fruchter 1984; Skerry 1983; Garfunkel 1986).

We have watched many women withdraw from involvement in the PC, in frustration or hopelessness. For these parents, Policy

Council work is more exhausting and dispiriting than it is empowering. A sense of having been demeaned, co-opted, or tricked reduced their participation. Their withdrawal not only keeps their voices from being part of Lake County Head Start program development and any larger discussion of poverty programming, it may also help cement the socially constructed characteristics of the poor. Apathy, for example, is taken to be a prime reason for poverty, but was clearly produced and reinforced in this case by the administration's actions.

Further, in our (albeit limited) experience, these women are not the ones who seek to return to school or who seek employment within the program—avenues of empowerment taken by Hannah and Lila. We know that the withdrawers stop believing in themselves as *powerful* participants; they tell us so, and we have watched the changes. As Hannah says, "I know I told you that Head Start gave me self-esteem. But now I can't justify that, with what you've seen. I mean. It's so different now. They *try* to make me feel stupid. I feel so bad for all the new parents. And the kids."

The withdrawers withdraw from using power, and they no longer make claims for dignity from Head Start administrators. Again, their withdrawal may serve to collude with existing stereotypes of poor women (Ackelsberg 1988). They are not empowered.

And this is troubling.

❖9❖

Devotion, Social Class, and the Union

[If the executive director could], people that had been active in the union would be fired as sure as the grass is green, you know.

But do you know when we went for that union vote, it was like thirty-nine staff then. We got thirty-eight to one. We got it thirty-eight yes to one no. One was contested. So that's how bad people wanted this union in there.

The administration, seeking to establish fiscal and procedural discipline in Head Start, soon had a battle on two fronts. Parents battled against the demeaning and disempowering actions taken by the administration. The front-line Head Start staff also fought back, strongly.

When we began this project, we initially treated the unionizing process as just one of several issues over which the PC and administration differed and clashed. However, we came to see the staff's fight as integral to the changes Head Start, as an institution in various communities, is undergoing. The issues raised in this chapter are the issues raised in this book: the empowerment of poor women.

In the first place, the program has hired many parents, giving them work they find meaningful and important, empowering them. It is, in large part, former mothers' stories we are telling in writing about the union. Even more critically, though, it is the workers who make Head Start empowering for anyone. We wrote in Chapter Three that women in Head Start found avenues to take control over their everyday lives, in Chapter Four that some women found avenues for upward mobility. The women made very clear to us that the reason they were able to take advantage of the program at all was respect and encouragement from the staff. That Head Start had not yet become "another social service bureaucracy" (Kramer 1969: 269; Skerry 1983) was due to the devotion shown by front-line staff.

The staff of Head Start unionized, in large part, to try and maintain the kind of Head Start they had found useful for themselves and for the women they served. The changes we noted in Chapter Seven endanger the way Head Start workers work, forcing them to work in a much more bureaucratic and synthetic way, a much less self- or other-empowering way. The workers wanted to preserve a more holistic, humanistic, familial way of working with "their" families. This is the kind of Head Start that *can* be empowering. Under the circumstances, there was little choice, we agree, but to turn to unions.

However, we will argue, too, that the coming of the union may also have the effect of increasing the bureaucratization of Lake County Head Start. U.S. unions and union tactics are based on an industrial, economistic model where class lines are clear and increased wages and improved working conditions are the primary goals (Cobble 1993; Milkman 1985). But in the Head Start setting, as we will see, class lines are not at all clear, and increased wages are nice, to be sure, but not nearly all of what the workers want most.

At the time of our writing, unionizing seemed, at best, a delaying tactic, though a necessary one. Committed staff members and parents were seeking structural solutions to their problems, a search that would take time and energy, and lots of both. The administration was fighting them and winning, partly by attrition, mostly because of their superior position of power. The union would not give the workers what they and the parents wanted in the long run, but it was a way of challenging the administration, forcing it to deal with the workers on a more equal footing for the time being.

Despite our seeming pessimism about the union's long-term utility and efficacy, the unionizing process is instructive for our analysis of empowerment. The tale provides another view of class and gender, and the mechanisms by which poor women can fight back. Unions have been key institutions for working-class women's resistance (though they have not been uniformly welcoming).

We should note here, if it's not already clear, that the majority of Head Start staff is female. There are several men, primarily bus drivers, but the teachers, teachers' aides, cooks, and family workers are women. Some of the men were instrumental in the union fight. Yet, the nature of the work as *women's* work is key in understanding the union drive and the reaction thereto by the administration. Again, this is primarily a women's story.

NEEDING A UNION

In Chapter Seven, we detailed recent changes in Lake County Head Start. The new executive director had not been a social service professional, but instead had a background in business. The board wanted him to establish a sound fiscal operation, and he had taken steps to do that and to exert more administrative control over the entire operation. In exerting control, he began to alarm the staff.

LJA: So what made you all start thinking about the union?
Emma: They started talking, [the executive director] started talking about putting us on unemployment during our holidays—break. And just, just taking, you know, things like that away from us.

■

LJA: So why the union? Tell me about that.
Nancy: I think what was happening is that [the CAP], [the executive director], kept taking back, kept pulling tighter and tighter and

becoming more authoritative, in that, "you will this," you know, and people getting reprimanded. . . . And I think what was happening is that the staff was getting scared because things were getting a lot tighter. There was less flexibility. People getting called in the office and being reprimanded. They were talking about taking away the unemployment during the summer, and it was just a way for the staff to feel they still had some power, still had some control.

Because center staff was on payroll only during the school year while the children were actually in Head Start classrooms, they collected unemployment during the summer when they were considered to be "laid off." Staff salaries are very low, nationally and in Lake County (Granger and Marx 1990; Pennsylvania Association for the Education of Young Children 1992); it is not possible for most of the workers to live for twelve months on their nine-month Head Start pay. The unemployment benefits during the summer are necessary to their financial survival. If the administration planned to deny them those benefits in order to save the CAP's contribution to the unemployment fund, it would be devastating to the workers and their families. An alternative fear (Emma's) was that staff would be officially laid off and not paid by Head Start during shorter school breaks, such as at Christmas. This would mean applying for unemployment for short time periods, and there would be a lag for benefits during which they would receive no wages. Either scenario was worrisome for these low-paid workers.

In sharing stories, the staff realized that many of them were being harassed in subtle and not-so-subtle ways. Long-time workers were being "written-up" for myriad trivial concerns, including working too many hours, even if the time was not billed on a timesheet. A twenty-seven-year veteran was given her first-ever negative review for what were widely believed to be trumped-up reasons. Though Head Start policy requires that qualified current staff members be promoted before a job is posted publicly, several highly qualified long-time staff members seemed to have been deliberately passed over, and outside people hired. People who were laid off during a staff reduction were not brought back when new openings occurred. As Doris tells us, the staff only gradually became aware of the extent of the harrassment:

> And it was like he didn't want us to sit together to talk or discuss because then we'd find out what he was doing to all these other places. We don't know what's going on in [the other centers]. We just know what's going on within our center, and when you get to talk to these people, you find out how much more is going on and the things he's doing.

The staff felt vulnerable and abused. But the question of control over the program was also key.

Seraphina: Unemployment was a big issue [in voting for the union]. And I think because we felt that [the CAP] was trying to take over Head Start.

LJA: And what difference would that have made?

Seraphina: Their policies are different than ours. They don't have the same philosophies as we do.

■

Holly: We don't get paid very well, but we wear a lot of hats—but we're there for the families that we serve and the children. But the management is in there for totally different reasons. They treat it like a business more than they treat it for what we're really supposed to be all about, and ever since [the CAP executive director] got in there and [the HS director] came in behind him, the contest totally changed. We lost—we lost Head Start somehow. We're under [the CAP] and we're lost. It's just like we're under their umbrella and we just lost ourselves.

There were, then, two sets of reasons for seeking a union. The first was a standard reason: protection against a punitive and tight-fisted management. The second was less standard: trying to save a *program,* not just individual workers, from "efficiency" and "professionalism." The staff feared changes to a program they loved. They did not want the program run as a business. Many of them had put years and years into Head Start at pitifully low wages and had done so because they loved the work.

This is not an unusual phenomenon for women's work. There is a long tradition of sacrifice among women doing "good work." There are strong cultural expectations that people (or at least female people) working with the poor or sick, working with children are doing what they do out of love, not out of pecuniary interest (Armstrong 1993; Finkelstein 1988; Johnson 1984; Zinsser 1986; Trolander 1987; Modigliani 1986; Steinberg and Jacobs 1994; Naples 1992). Joan Smith (1984) argues that such jobs could not exist if women were not available to do them at low wages.

The staff of North Country Head Start was clearly not working for the money alone. The sacrifice in wages had been tolerable, though, given that they viewed the program as so important in helping low-income people. Nancy, who quit Head Start even though the Policy Council fought to keep her, said, "[Head Start] was like your family, and that was the hardest thing for me as far as quitting. I felt like I was deserting my family." This, as Carla says, is a common sentiment among the staff:

Oh, we love the job. [It's] the only job I know . . . where you work with the total person, almost holistically. And the total family, I should say. . . . [Other social service programs] you know, you put a Band-Aid approach on some of these things. But you don't really get to the bottom of, gee, "What's your goal? How do you feel about life? What is it that you've always wanted to do? Have you got a dream?" These are the kind of things that we can help people to discover themselves and then move on. . . . And that's satisfying.

That satisfaction led to extraordinary dedication. Doris describes her dedication:

I would have went in with a headache or with the flu or—. I've gone to work driving school bus with the flu just to get the kids in because there was nobody to take my place. But I mean, where do you find dedication like that? I mean. And all of our staff. . . . I mean. We don't make big money. We're there because we want to be there. Because it's part of the North Country.

Doris seemed to be right. "All of our staff" showed willingness to work for however long it took. Diana told us, "I would come in early, stay late. I wanted to do this work!" And parents, such as Jody, noticed this dedication:

The teachers there really care. I think the teachers in [public] school, they teach. There's not—. There's some I've seen that care, that really care. But the teachers that are in Head Start, they care. They're not there because they're making thirty thousand a year. They're not there because they're getting major benefits. They're there because that's where they want to be.

But the dedication to Head Start was in jeopardy.

LJA: Would you recommend that parents do that, apply for a job at Head Start?

Emma: (pause) Yeah.

LJA: OK. Why the hesitation?

Emma: Um. Well, just because of the problems that are going on now. Yes I would. I think it's a great opportunity. . . . We used to get comp time for working late hours. I lost over a hundred hours comp time the first year I worked. But I loved what I was doing. And what I was doing, was helping my parents. And they wanted GED classes. So I set that all up, and I took 'em to it. . . . And, most of the [staff] that have been parents in Head Start are dedicated to the program. And they stay. Right now, it's kinda hard to do that, but. . . . I know what we're feeling is a lot of pressure.

The staff *was* afraid of what the CAP would do. They believed that one of the tactics being used by the CAP to take over was getting rid of the old-timers.

LJA: What were you most afraid of at that time?

Doris: Most afraid? Don't laugh at me. I was afraid that he was going to take away what everybody had fought for for years. Take away the staff and the program that everybody had fought for for years, and I am talking . . . the old timers. And I'll be dipped to see him destroy it, and in my eyes, he is slowly destroying this program.

■

Nancy: When I went in to give her my resignation, I told her that when we voted for the union, it was not a vote against her. It was a vote against [the CAP] taking over more and more control.

■

LJA: What would he take away from the program?

Doris: What would he take away from the program? All the services, number one, I would say he would take away. He is getting rid of, slowly but surely, the experienced so-called higher-paid help and sticking people in there that don't know anything, and that way he can have more control.

■

Holly: They really started on her, saying that she wasn't doing her job effectively. The woman's been there twenty-some-odd years, knows more than [the Head Start director] and [CAP executive director] put together. Because anybody that knows more is a threat to them, so they want them out of there, which would be Lila, which is Nancy, Louise. They've got twenty-some-odd years there. They know how Head Start's supposed to be run inside and out. These people pose a threat to them. They want them out of there.

LJA: So anybody who knows what Head Start used to be.

Holly: The old regime. Yup. You got Louise, you got Nancy, you got Lila. Well, I've only been there for four years. But I'm telling you, these people have been there anywhere from fourteen to twenty-some-

odd years, they know. They know the seventy-point-two. They know
Policy Council and what the guidelines are, how things are
supposed to be run more than [the Head Start director] and [CAP
executive director]. They want them out of there. And they do little
things to ensure that that will happen. Like they drove Lila
completely to where she's so stressed out, she doesn't feel she can
come back.

LJA: That's a loss to the program.

Holly: Yes. That's a big loss. Lila used to train Policy Council. Train them
the right way. Because right now, the way they want the Policy
Council is so they can be able to pull the wool over their eyes and
say, "Yes, let's vote this in. This will be good for us." Show them two
different, three, four budget sheets that they don't even know what
they're voting on. And you got new parents that come in every
year. They don't know. The wool gets pulled over their eyes, and
they do exactly what [the CAP executive director] wants.

Like the PC parents who planned to develop training material for
new PC parents, the staff was convinced that the administration
wanted full control. This would *not* be in the best interests of the
program to which they were devoted.

THE UNION DRIVE

Staff members knew they needed protection and knew there was
something going on with the program that they did not like. However, the union drive was not particularly comfortable for many of
them.

LJA: So who first started talking about a union?

Doris: Who first started? I think it was Louise. Louise went to a meeting in
River County, and then they came. We had a meeting and this was
all new to me, too. This was a whole new world to me, too.

LJA: Union.

Doris: Union, right. I felt like a Ku Klux Klan member. These meetings were all secretive. We weren't told until the day or what time or where they were going to be held so nobody could crash them, and oh, man, I was like, oh, jeezum, this is like Ku Klux member here, you know.

■

LJA: So how did you start thinking about a union? How did that come up?

Nancy: The union approached us.

Seraphina: One of the other counties had been approached by the union, and one of the employees who had worked with us—. Well, she had worked in River County and then worked with us for a year and then went back to River County. Called Louise and told Louise about it, so Louise brought it to our attention and we met with them.

LJA: What were your first impressions?

Nancy: They just wanted a piece of the pie.

Seraphina: I was nervous. I had been down in New York City or Albany. I was in Albany, so I asked a lot of questions about them because we were advocating for child care at the Capitol Building and there was a lot of [union members]. I know they were down there, and there was a lot of groups of unions, and I asked a lot of questions and I asked a lot of people. And they said, just be very careful about a union because they demand—you know, they'll demand your program of money, and if they don't have the money, they're going to suck your program dry, and you're going to lose your program.

And, but then again, I had other people telling me that it was a good thing, and that they can pull from resources in your community to get the money, and you know, that you can do it that way, too. And they said it's not a bad thing, but just be careful how it's done. So I had asked a lot of questions.

But we were all a little bit nervous about it. We were thinking that they wanted exactly that, a piece of the pie.

The workers decided, though, that the union presented them with an important chance, perhaps their only chance to save Head Start.

Holly: But do you know when we went for that union vote, it was like thirty-nine staff then. We got thirty-eight to one. We got it thirty-eight yes to one no. One was contested. So that's how bad people wanted this union in there.

■

Emma: We took a vote, and then [the executive director] didn't agree with that vote. So we had to take *another* one. If I'm right it was like thirty-seven to one? Thirty-seven yeses to one no. So I mean that should've told him something to start with. But it didn't.

CREATING BOUNDARIES

One of the first tasks of the union was to define who was potential union staff and who was management. In most organizations, this may be a relatively straight-forward task. In North Country Head Start, it was not. For one thing, in this rural area, social classes are not separated geographically (Duncan and Lamborghini 1994). Management and staff live near each other, attend the same churches, shop at the same stores. Indeed, some staff members are related to some management, and there are many family and community ties crossing class lines.

There is also a more fundamental problem, one related to empowerment.

Excluding Family

In Head Start, the philosophy and practice from the program's War on Poverty beginning was to employ, as much as possible, parents of children enrolled or graduated from the program. Nationally, up to one third of Head Start staff are parents of Head Start graduates (Zigler and Styfco 1994). Among our formal respondents, about half have had children enrolled in the program. For some of these parents, getting a job in Head Start has required them to complete a GED after having dropped out of high school; oth-

ers have learned the skills involved in driving a school bus or cooking for a class of twenty preschoolers; others have obtained college
degrees and work in professional-level positions (see chapters Three
and Four). This employment and consequent individual upward
mobility is one of the major successes of the Head Start project.

In Lake County Head Start, the Head Start director reported to
the CAP executive director and (in theory) to the parent Policy
Council. There were then five "coordinators," managing various aspects of the local centers. One of these coordinators was Lila, whose
story we told in Chapter Four. A former mother, Lila had been an
inspiration to many of the professionals and mothers in the program. Indeed, she had nurtured a number of the current staff.

Yet, due to her supervisory position as coordinator, the union
considered her management, ineligible for union membership. The
staff was not happy about Lila's exclusion, noting that many of the
gains in the contract ought to be due Lila, too. Moreover, Lila had
been a primary target for the administration, and has since been
forced out of the program. The staff wanted to be able to protect
Lila in the same way they themselves would now be protected.

Though the inclusive sentiment may not have applied fully to
other individuals on the "management team," as the coordinators
were called, the staff counted on the philosophy of employing parents and promoting in-house. The staff expected that they would
be in line for coordinator positions, and expected that coordinators
in general would share the same devotion to Head Start as they did.
As Holly stated, "our main plan at the beginning was to get the
union in and then vote our coordinators in[to the union]. . . . We
wanted our coordinators in there." They wanted to consider coordinators family, not adversary.

Policy Council: How Deep an Alliance?

There was a second, more problematic complication in drawing
boundaries between management and union staff. Given the over-

sight authority specified in 70.2, the Policy Council was clearly part of the management structure. Indeed, their approval was necessary to make the contract official from the management side. However, for the mothers on the PC, being considered management was completely foreign and unwelcome. They were, after all, the same people who were likely to be hired onto the staff, drawn largely from the same economic and social background.

The negotiations were being conducted by the CAP executive director and "his" lawyer. Even the Head Start director was not permitted to be in the room during negotiating sessions, though she was expected to be nearby. No one from the CAP Board of Directors attended the sessions, and no one from the PC.

As we detailed in the last chapter, negotiations were dragging on and on and on. The union organizer/rep came to a special PC meeting to tell the parents about the union, its demands, and the negotiating process. The rep encouraged the PC to get involved in the negotiations—they were management; they should be there. This was obviously an attempt to forge alliances with the also unhappy PC. There were many less formal attempts to do so, as well. The PC held informal meetings with individual staff and groups of staff. Staff members quietly kept parents informed about issues when they saw them at the centers. The belief among the staff and parents was that they had a common interest in protecting the program from the administration; and that the union contract was one piece of that protection.

Parents *also* supported the economistic union demands:

Jody: We're watching our teachers do their best to give our kids something that's important to them. And we're watching them, basically, being fought all the way. What they're asking for [in negotiations], I don't think is that wonderful that they shouldn't get it. And you look at incomes from other people in the program [families being served] and you look at the teachers' incomes, it's, you know. Our teachers shouldn't be eligible for Medicaid.

That's what I think, you know. It should be above that, just a bit, so. I mean, that's such a kick in the head for trying to do something for children, for going into a category where they really want to help children, to an area where it's very—it's really needed. And then just getting slapped in the face with a low-paying job.

■

Abbey: So probably a lot of us don't understand why there's such a hullabaloo over teachers' negotiations. Why, if there is X amount of dollars set aside. . . . A lot of parents are under the impression that that money goes to Head Start [for staff salaries]. . . . Our job [at PC] should be to make sure that that doesn't happen to anybody else. Anybody else that has put any amount of time and dedication into this program should not be stepped on the way Lila was. . . . And somewhere along the line this has got to—something has got to stop. . . . Anything that they [the union] can be asking for can't be that outrageous. I mean, they don't have a whole lot right now.

■

LJA: Are you in favor of the union?
Betsy: Oh yeah. I am.
LJA: Why is [the CAP] fighting it so hard?
Betsy: Because they don't want to pay the teachers what they deserve, and they don't want to pay the help what they deserve.

Recall that the PC chair began demanding a seat at the bargaining table. She pushed the issue with the executive director, the board, and HHS until she was granted that seat, and, shortly thereafter, the contract was finalized. Clearly, the pushing from the PC was making it difficult for the executive director to stall the contract. It was an important alliance between the staff and PC, that is, between staff and an element of management.

The PC would ask for the favor back, though, and the union hierarchy (though not the rank-and-file) would balk at returning it.

As we noted earlier, in Lake County and in Kent County, the PC became determined to remove the local CAP as the grantee for Head Start funds. They wanted a freestanding program, independent of CAP interference.

The Lake County staff was enthusiastic about that possibility. At a clandestine meeting among staff and the PC, it was a staff member who first broached the subject. All staff present expressed support for such a move by the parents.

Doris: But her main goal is to be freestanding and that's what my main goal is. . . . I think the staff really supports being freestanding, yeah.

■

Holly: It's just like we're under their umbrella and we just lost ourselves. We'd be better out on our own.
LJA: Would you like to see that happen?
Holly: Yeah, I would.

In Kent County, plans were much further along. At one point, the federal funding agency *did* pull the grant from the CAP and give it (on an interim basis) to another county's CAP. One of the conditions of that change, though, was that the union not come with the program. The staff was divided on the move and the union's new role—or lack of role. In any case, the move lasted only a very short time. The grant was returned to the original CAP and the union remained certified.

Some of the staff and parents in the North Country believe that the union hierarchy joined with the original Kent County CAP in efforts to keep the program where it was, *against* the efforts of the parents. Some parents and some staff felt betrayed.

LJA: What do you think of the union's role in Kent County?
Patty: Well when it first came about, the Policy Council was behind the staff to unionize. Because we as Policy Council were supposed to be

able to protect them, and we couldn't protect them anymore, and
they needed it. Then. As far as I—this is just my own opinion—the
union and CAP got into bed with each other. Hey. That union isn't
gonna do didly squat for those people. They just want their money.
And it split the staff.

■

LJA: Are the parents happy with the union?
Penny: Well when the union first came, a lot of Policy Council felt that the
union was, you know, in bed with [the administrator]. . . . And at
one point, the staff got together and wrote the union a letter and
said, "Listen. You have no right, you know, [to threaten PC]." . . .
The staff has stuck by Policy Council. . . . no matter how hard it's
gotten, and for a while there, they weren't working either. You
know. They have stuck by us. They stuck by Policy Council.

The union rep is clear, though, that she could not actively support the parents' attempts to move the grant—there was a valid
contract with the CAP, and she had to enforce that contract.
While alliances over contract issues could be made with a more
amenable element of management (the PC), the union per se
could not ignore or deliberately work to eliminate the more in-
tractable element (the executive director of each county): "You
know, these are the guys I have to negotiate with. Doesn't matter
if I like 'em or not. I can't demand there be someone else! These
are the guys."

In Lake County Head Start, such a seemingly reasonable move
by the union, though, if it came would cause a serious rift between
parents and union, and perhaps between union rank-and-file and
union hierarchy. Parents and staff members described themselves as
fighting for the life of Head Start. That required not just protection
from the executive director, but his elimination *and* the elimination
of the prospect of getting another director "ten times worse." Parents and the staff were clear on that and would not appreciate interference from union hierarchy.

ADMINISTRATION'S RESPONSE

While devotion to the program was one impetus for the union drive, and the basis for a critical strategic alliance with parents, devotion was also used, on the other hand, by the administration in its attempt to fight the union. In a federally funded program serving low-income families, higher wages would come, not out of company profits, but out of program money that otherwise would be used for supplies or field trips or children's lunches. Management played on those trade-offs, trying to sow dissension among the staff and trouble between staff and parents. (See Levitt [1993] for a frightening tale of union-busting tactics used elsewhere, told by a former practitioner of those tactics.)

Recall that the administration required the PC to cut thirty thousand dollars out of the program budget to pay for a lawyer to negotiate the contract. The cut resulted in staff layoffs and the cancellation of some popular field trips. This was explicitly cast by the administration as a tragedy for the children caused by the union and its demands. The administration also used the union as an excuse for not implementing the PC's decision to give a raise to Nancy.

The administration became punitive in its approach to staff members and working conditions. That reaction and the union's advice to workers increased the regimentation of daily practices.

Nancy: [There used to be] that kind of give and take [between staff and administration].
LJA: And that wouldn't happen now?
Nancy: Never. Never. You're accountable for every five minutes.

■

Seraphina: So they're going to follow it [procedures] right to the tee. This is their way of saying, okay, you want your union. We're going to hold you to it, step by step, and I was warned of that.

■

Doris: I used to take all kinds of extra work home. The work I couldn't get done at the end of the day. I would take it home and do it.

LJA: And now?

Doris: No way. I left a pile of work sitting on my desk. I could have taken it home tonight. . . . I'll get to it tomorrow, maybe. Why take it home and work another hour at home? Why do that? That's one thing that the union made me open my eyes to.

LJA: That you shouldn't do that?

Doris: Right. Shouldn't do that kind of stuff. Because that's the kind of stuff they bank on, so why do it?

PROTECTION

The staff had been initially unsure of what unions could do for them, though they had embraced the union resoundingly in their certification vote. They found that the union offered them needed protection from the kinds of "tightening" and harassment they had faced in the previous years.

Holly: And I'm not going to be penalized if I take a sick day, you know, you feel like you got a voice. There's a voice out there. You're not all alone. You've got a voice, and it's our union together, and then if something happens to one of us, it's affecting all of us, and it affects the way the program is run, and we're going to do something about it. And we'll do something about it together. . . . So that's why I say the union—. They can't do the underhanded things they've been doing anymore, you know.

■

Nancy: [If the executive director could], people that had been active in the union would be fired as sure as the grass is green, you know.

■

Doris: We needed something and there is nothing else. He probably would have had us all gone and all going on unemployment in between times and no snow days and all this and that, and it hasn't happened yet, and I don't think it will happen with the union here.

■

Carla: And if there was no union, I would be gone [fired].

■

LJA: You said you thought the union was great. What does it do for you.
Emma: At this point it has kept us with our paid vacation time and, you
know. Otherwise I don't think we would have been able to fight
[for] it like we have, and to keep it. I think people would just
complain about it. And some people have a hard time fighting.
They need, you know, stronger people fighting for them. And if we
wouldn't have had the union I don't think that would happen.
People would've just quit. . . . Otherwise I don't think we'd've stuck
together. I think we would've tried. I don't think it would've worked.
Because we wouldn't've really had the power behind us. It seems
like power. I mean they're giving us the ability to sit at the table and
say, "This is what we want," and negotiate it till there's a happy
medium. And otherwise, that wouldn't've happened. I think he
would've probably just fired us all.

In addition to protecting individuals, the union helped provide
a cover from which the staff could launch other fights. One of their
primary goals was to protect the program, per se, and they needed
help to do so. They felt they needed to publicize the goings-on of
the program to gather that kind of support. Without the union,
generating that kind of publicity could be individually very costly,
if not lethal. With the union, it was possible, though not necessarily without cost.

One Saturday morning, the staff gathered in front of the CAP
offices with placards. There was a smattering of parents and children. The placards drew attention to some of the problems the staff
saw in the program. For instance, they claimed that centers were not
fully staffed and that the children were thereby endangered. The
putative reason for understaffing was to save money. What the staff
wanted was to alert board members and the public about serious
deficiencies so that something would be done.

A newspaper reporter came after a couple of hours and took pho-
tos. The story appeared the next morning on page three, with a
large picture of the demonstrating staff.

Carla: Saturday. That's the end. That's the climax of many things. And it's
really not the climax because it's now the beginning of a new era,
that's not really the word. It's the first time we've come out and
really voiced our feelings and there may have been other ways. . . .
So this was the way to do it, team effort, and it might have been
what some people would call radical. I think we kept it as
organized as we could, as professional as we could. . . . But, why
did we do it? I guess we did it because when different staff members
have continuously gone to management and said this is our
problem, this is our problem, this is our problem, they are told,
"We'll do what we can." . . . And the final word often is, "Well, we
know you can handle it." Well, that's not helping.

■

Seraphina: Well we need to stand up for our rights, and we had every
right to do what we did on Saturday. And we don't have any right
to feel ashamed about it. . . . Well, everybody was really worried,
you know, about this demonstration on Saturday. And of course, it
took me almost an hour to get my butt out there. [She had been
standing on the sidelines, reluctant to pick up a sign and march.]
But there you are, in the [newspaper]; I got to hear that from some
of the people who demonstrated all afternoon. "You picked up that
sign for twenty minutes, and you got your picture in the paper." I
said, "Hey, I didn't ask for it, believe me." And my [classroom]
assistant wasn't too thrilled to have her face right front and center.

The Monday after the demonstration, the shop steward was
called into the office. She immediately got on the phone to the
union rep, who called the executive director and told him, "This
better not be a disciplinary action." The union and the staff had
been careful to call the demonstration an "informational picket"

and not to use the union's name as sponsor. The picket was legal and the executive director had no legal right to punish participants.

The executive director was angry. Though he had been warned against retaliation, he called the staff together the next Friday. (The children are not in class on Fridays.) At that meeting, he sang the praises of the Head Start management team and Head Start in general. He sang some of his own praises, too. He told the staff who had demonstrated that they should be ashamed of themselves for talking "trash" about the program. He was very intimidating and bellicose.

The union *was* able to protect the demonstrators from overt retaliation—a significant benefit, to be sure. It was not able to make the demonstration a success, though.

The demonstration had been directed at the public, but particularly at the CAP Board members. At the regular board meeting shortly after that demonstration, the CAP executive director orchestrated his own demonstration. He had members of the Head Start management team report on the wonderful things accomplished by the program over the last years. He thereby short-circuited any real discussion of "problems" in Head Start. Board members (with two or three exceptions) were not sympathetic to the claims made at the Saturday demonstration. (This is the same board that was generally disrespectful of the PC and overly suspicious of this research.)

Further, though the union could protect workers from outright reprisals, it could not protect them from petty harassment. That harassment reportedly continued against targeted individuals, primarily long-timers. At the time of this writing, Lila had left the program; Nancy had quit; Louise had retired in frustration; Carla had found another job. In our last conversation with Doris, she said she was wearing her sneakers to work so that she could "walk," meaning could walk out of her job, quit. Seraphina, too, was seeking another job. These were women who had absolutely loved their work with Head Start.

FEARS FOR THE FUTURE

As detailed earlier in this chapter, workers felt that the administration was seeking to get rid of long-time workers who knew what it had been like before the movement toward greater administrative accountability and bureaucracy. They also believed that union members and the union itself were targeted.

Holly: Yeah. We don't force people to be union. [They don't have a closed shop.]

LJA: So if he just fills positions with people who won't choose to go union—.

Holly: Exactly, he's going to get nonunionized people in there. I think that's his objective, because he does not like this union.

■

Carla: And if there was no union, I would be gone. And boy, they'll find a way now because of [Saturday's picket]. It won't be because I did that. Because that would have struck my civil rights, but they will find a way. . . . They don't want the union anymore, and if they get enough of these people [new and less pro-union] and can get rid of enough of us, it will weaken us, and so then eventually the union here would be done away with.

That would take away an important voice, one that spoke not only for the workers themselves, but respectfully for the needs of the parents and children. One concern among staff members and for us is that the process will mean that new Head Start workers, whether unionized and consequently regimented, or nonunionized and powerless, will not be the same kind of workers. If, as Lila fears, workers will simply think about doing "what it is that they want you to do and getting the hell out and go home," there will not be the same kind of devotion to the work that currently exists.

LJA: So for your families, one of the things he's taken away is your ability to serve them?

Doris: Definitely that, because there are days when I don't feel like working. I mean, let's put it this way. Just everyday stresses. I mean, who would feel like going into work and giving it a hundred percent? Nobody.

■

LJA: Why are they raising the qualifications [for Head Start positions], do you think?

Emma: I'm not sure. I don't have no idea why they're doing that.

LJA: Do you think they're better workers? With degrees?

Emma: No I don't. I mean they have a lot more information, but I mean, in training we could get that information. You know. But they're not dedicated. They're not happy. You know, they got degrees, and, you know, this is only, only till they can get something better. And usually, that's not long. You know. If they stay a whole school year, you're lucky.

If there is no devotion, will there be respect for parents and children? If there is no respect, can there be empowerment?

UNIONIZING HEAD START

The union has been a positive event, here in the near term, allowing the staff some security and the program some reprieve from the onslaughts of "efficient" administration. However, the long-term picture is less clearly positive. One problem is that unions are not now well-suited to handling the boundary dilemmas sketched above, having evolved from a male, industrial model where sides and class-based interests are clear and issues can be limited to wages and working conditions (Cobble 1993; Johnson 1984; Milkman 1985).

Another problem is the general movement of Head Start administrations toward a much more industrial-like management style, also not well-suited to managing a staff devoted to the program as they see it. It seems that the combination is likely to result in a net loss to the staff and the program—it must become more industrial-like itself. There will no longer be the likelihood of developing deeply gratifying devotion: both union and management will require highly rule-bound work, the major payoff of which will be wages, not satisfaction. Unfortunately, the wages are likely to remain low, given the nature of the work (women's work serving the poor) and the relatively low power of a union of women workers serving the poor (Modigliani 1986). With neither good wages nor uniquely gratifying work, Head Start itself will seem less an option for parents' employment and upward mobility.

In the end, what the workers want—the return to a family-like and fluid Head Start program—cannot be achieved through the union process as it currently exists. In order for anything like that to occur, there is a need for a completely transformed movement of workers, a movement that can achieve not just stability in wages and benefits, but effective control over the work itself, control held by the workers and the community they serve (Robinson 1993; Briskin and McDermott 1993; Kessler-Harris 1985; Herzenberg 1993).

Yet, the workers *have* developed much stronger relationships among themselves during the union fight. Their centers are scattered over an entire rural county, some an hour's drive away from the central office, and up to an hour and a half from each other, one-way. The union meetings and informal get-togethers have provided opportunities for discussing their work, the good and the bad, away from the watchful eyes of management. This provides some hope. Only where there is a collectivity is there room for collective action.

❖10❖

The Limits on/of Empowerment:
What Is to Be Done?

This is how the system works. If you work hard enough, may take you ten years, but if you don't have people like us working, then nothing ever gets changed in this country.

The problem is, in fact, you can't move on. Because this is not finished.

We have said that this research was not a dispassionate exercise for us. We set out to document, indeed to celebrate, the ways in which some poor women had made important changes in their lives after their involvement with the Head Start program. We intended that this documentation would help make it possible for more women to do the same. In the course of systematic inquiry, we discovered that many of the changes women make are not necessarily "important" in any conventional sense; certainly most would not be called stunning by policymakers. We discovered, too, that the change-facilitating process seems to be in jeopardy of being lost altogether because of a national-level stress on administrative accountability. This national drift and its local embodiment seem to be insurmountable. This is not what we had planned, and certainly not what we wanted, to find.

Given our actual findings and our interest in the facilitation of poor women's empowerment, we are left with two policy-related questions. First, are the empowerments we have presented enough to make the structures of Head Start worth emulating in other governmental and community programs? Second, what is to be done to ensure that those structures remain able to facilitate empowerment in the face of the quest for accountability?

These questions of public policy bring us back to the questions and dilemmas presented in Chapter One:

1. Why are poor people poor—individual character deficiencies or the social structures of monopoly capitalism, institutional racism, and patriarchy?

2. What are the purposes of public poverty policy—to change the poor? change the economy? or to make the poor as comfortable as possible in their inevitable poverty?

3. What constitutes empowerment? For what are the poor to be empowered?

We'll spend this chapter reexamining those questions in light of all our data, and examining the policy implications of the answers.

POVERTY

In Chapter Five, we documented women's orientation to the American Dream. The women with whom we have spent the last three years are hard workers. Their dreams for their children involve solid education and good jobs. Some of them dream such dreams for themselves, as well as for their children. These dreams are not rare; a number of studies have documented the work ethic of poor people (Rank 1994; Horowitz 1995; Harris 1993; Rosier and Corsaro 1993; see also the review in Burton 1992).

Yet, the national verbal contest—we hesitate to call it a debate—on poverty discounts the very possibility that the poor, especially poor women, desire to work hard and improve their life chances. Some analyses, academic as well as journalistic, purport to show that current welfare programs "coddle" the poor and actually perpetuate poverty. Many provisions of the "new welfare" are thus harsh and bullying: Teenage mothers must live with their parents to receive aid; or, teenagers are denied aid altogether, regardless of where they live; children born while mothers are living on AFDC will not be considered for additional aid; mothers of truant children will see their benefits cut; mothers of even very young children must take a job, any job, or their benefits will be cut off.

The push to get mothers into the paid labor market denies the legitimacy and hard work of raising children. Instead, poor mothers are assumed to need outside motivation, if not outright compulsion, to enter the paid-labor force and to encourage their children to do so when they grow up. There is no recognition that even class-privileged women can have severe economic and emotional stress from combining employment and child rearing, and that these stresses are increased geometrically for women without resources.

However, it is clear that working for wages, in itself, may not end any individual's poverty. We know that the numbers of *working* poor are increasing, especially in rural areas (Fitchen 1992; Lichter, Johnston, and McLaughlin 1994; Gorham 1992; LeCompte and Dworkin 1988; Rodgers and Weiher 1989). As the gap between the rich and working classes in this country grows wider, so too does the gap between the economic resources of rural and urban areas, with rural places growing sharply poorer (Rural Sociological Society 1993). Wages too low to lift families out of poverty are an especial problem for rural women working in underpaid female-dominated jobs (Cautley and Slesinger 1989; Bayes 1988; Rural Sociological Society 1993). Mothers who are working for pay may not have access to quality child care, and the child care they do have is expensive, further eroding their wages. Regardless of the level of human capital, regardless of attachment to the labor force, there are millions of employed *workers* and their families who remain poor. We have seen this among our respondents—Jody, Abbey, Lois, Carol, Jamie, Mickey, Dorothy, Betsy, and others. These women and their partners have worked, but remained poor.

Poverty will not be lessened, then, by correcting presumed deficits in the area of the work ethic: The work ethic already exists; paid work itself will not necessarily end poverty.

And yet, we also documented that, for a number of women—Lila, Evelyn, Mary, Celeste, Helen, and others—movement into a particular labor force, a particular occupation *did* enhance their economic stability. These success stories show that where there is opportunity, genuine opportunity, poor women will take advantage of it. We have argued that many of the success stories we told involved women taking paths that revolve around socially approved motherhood, that allow them to help their children and others, as well as themselves. This work gave some women a calling, gave them work they found personally satisfying. Such economic and personal achievement *was* one of the original expectations of maximum feasible participation.

However, there are very few such positions available. Though there are many, many anecdotes of mobility for Head Start mothers, *most* women with children enrolled in Head Start do not move up economically, whatever their work ethic. Further, most poor women are not even served by Head Start at all. There are too many poor women to be employed in the satisfying human service jobs that exist, and these human service and education jobs are the very ones most targeted by recent cutbacks in public spending—soon, there will be even fewer. In any case, we would argue for a broader range of work deemed "acceptable" for women and mothers, and an enrichment of many jobs to provide more satisfying work to all women—and men.

Most jobs being created in the United States and in the North Country are those on the bottom of the service sector, complete with low pay, low satisfaction, low advancement opportunity (New York State Department of Labor n.d.; Fitchen 1992). The majority of these jobs do not offer a living wage, much less a calling. Such jobs contribute to the widening gap between rich and poor, to the growing number of employed poor, and to the growing number of poor, employed women. Smith argues that the increase in these jobs and the increase in the number of women who must work are related. The jobs could not exist without the availability of female labor, assumed to be "properly considered a cheaper and more dispensable labor force" (1984: 139). North Country Head Start women know well that working for wages often only sets them back, making it necessary to purchase dependable, independent transportation, and making them ineligible for assistance with medical care or home heating. Most paid work does not provide them with economic stability and it takes time away from child rearing.

Clearly, the solution to poverty in the North Country does not lie in simply reforming women, in giving them a work ethic or even work skills. There are serious structural impediments to achieving the American Dream. Though upward mobility has been important for some women—a significant success of the program, to be sure—Head Start's reform-minded, deficit-based programs cannot solve this structural aspect of poverty.

ANTIPOVERTY POLICY

Most of America's policies that address poverty have not taken the view that reforms in the social structure are necessary to end poverty. Most have, instead, trumpeted the successes and opportunities of capitalism and declared that the poor need to be reformed, their character and human capital deficits corrected. Some programs seem geared only toward making life a bit easier for the unfortunate, deficient poor, who are assumed to be, however lamentably, always with us. There has been a plethora of job training programs (for jobs that do not always exist and usually for traditionally sex-segregated work), programs training people to write resumes and be interviewed, parenting-skills programs, programs that punish poor women for being full-time mothers instead of "working", programs trying to instill a work ethic. There are in-kind and cash assistance programs that ensure (or try to ensure) that the poor do not starve in the streets and are minimally "comfortable."

In the North Country, as in rural areas in general, even these welfare programs may be harder to come by and less effective than in urban areas (Cautley and Slesinger 1989; Rodgers and Weiher 1989). Recall that at least one of our respondents had not known that the food stamp program existed. Many poor rural women cannot meet application requirements due simply to a lack of regular transportation to the social service office. Further, though welfare programs everywhere in the country are demeaning, there is often a particular stigma attached to receiving welfare in small towns and villages (Fitchen 1992). Our respondents were keenly aware of negative and insulting attitudes about poor people using public assistance programs.

Moreover, much of the welfare structure in the United States is aimed at children, not mothers. The needs of children and the needs of women are not the same (Miller 1990; Gordon 1994; Hutchinson 1994). In this country's welfare policies, the needs of women—for autonomy, for meaningful work, for community—have been subordinated to the presumed needs of children. Mothers are seen only as (deficient) caretakers of children, children for whom there may still be some hope. Welfare policies do not seek to foster women's *self*-sufficiency, seeking instead only to prevent them from "ruining" their children.

Existing welfare programs are clearly inadequate to meet the needs of the women of the North Country, whether for reform or comfort, and are certainly inadequate for changing the structures of poverty.

Some of the programs in the War on Poverty—or, at least, some of the poverty warriors—had additional aims. In the first place, there was the clear understanding that the economy had to remain vibrant to provide jobs for the (perhaps newly reformed) poor—it has not. Though it seems more than obvious that an adequate number of adequately paying jobs is a necessary condition for the absence of poverty, this understanding seems to have been lost in recent years (Rodgers 1988; Danziger, Sandefur, and Weinberg 1994). Very little official attention has been paid to creating well-paid jobs in rural areas (Rural Sociological Society 1993). A simple increase in the minimum wage would do more for North Country women than more of the usual welfare programs (Cautley and Slesinger 1989), but that need is also rarely mentioned in policy discussions.

The other key aim of some poverty warriors in the 1960s was the empowerment of the poor through the vehicle of maximum feasible participation. Though community action was disappointing overall in this respect, in Mississippi (Greenberg 1990 [1969]), in Newark (Quadagno 1994), in Syracuse (Moynihan 1970), in Philadelphia and New York City (Naples 1991), in other cities and towns in the United States, poor people had, in fact, begun the empowerment process, had begun to challenge some structures of society that affected them negatively. One measure of the potential success of that process was the swiftness with which community action was attacked and defunded by the existing powers. As a colleague at our college put it (regarding a much less consequential change), "When the bad guys get pissed off, you know you've done something good." There *was* the potential for fundamental changes in the exercise of community power, and that annoyed and angered those benefiting from the existing structures.

Today, there is very little discussion about the social structures of poverty. Most proposals to reform welfare for the poor focus solely on the presumed deficits of poor people and how to "correct" them—usually with punitive and just plain mean policies. The poor are accused of adopting a "victim" posture to garner sympathy and benefits (Rank 1994). Beginning in the 1980s, there was a new paternalism in welfare policies (Heclo 1994), denying again the ability of the poor to manage their own affairs. Conservatives today propose to eliminate all "welfare" under the premise that indolence and dependence are fostered by such programs. The governor of New York recently declared that his policies had "emancipated" many people from welfare, assuming that poor people are enslaved rather than fed and housed by public assistance. (The racial implications in such a statement are clear, as well.)

When "empowerment" is discussed at all, it is in terms of *forcing* the poor to take "responsibility" for their actions. The talk today is never about finding avenues for the poor to change existing institutions of power as they see fit. Structural interpretations of poverty are virtually absent from the public imagination and public policy. The American public, anxious and bitter about declining economies, has instead been incited to rage at the very idea of welfare. Scapegoating of the poor, nonwhites, immigrants, and of the War on Poverty itself threatens all social programs.

And yet, again, it is only through structural changes that poverty can be completely and finally addressed.

EMPOWERMENTS

The last vestige of community action, as envisioned in the 1960s, lies in Head Start's 70.2. In Lake County, the provisions of 70.2 allowed parents the space to challenge the edicts of professionals concerning their own and their children's needs. Mothers learned to use power, albeit limited power. In Head Start, women (whether on the Policy Council or not) began to change their lives for the better. In chapters Three and Four, we presented women's views of how much their lives had improved, in small and large ways. The mothers considered that they had been empowered through these changes.

The question remains, is this sort of empowerment enough to make Head Start worth emulating? Head Start participation has not led to changes in social structure and has not led to a reduction in poverty levels. So, is the sort of empowerment we have observed worth emulating? Is it enough?

These are not new questions. Many social movements have wrestled with the issue of limited reform. For example, as the women's movement flowered anew in the 1960s and 1970s, women with a radical analysis of the various oppressions affecting us sought systemic, societal change—in the long term. However, in the short term, the changes that seemed possible were often dismissed as mere "reform." Charlotte Bunch (1981 [1974]) noted that many radicals were afraid that working on reforms would dilute the more revolutionary work to be done, would take energy away from the more fundamental changes. There were fears of being coopted by the system and of thereby strengthening, rather than weakening, the existing systems of oppression.

Bunch argued, however, that reforms could not be rejected out of hand, rejected because they were merely reforms. The movement had no specific program as yet to achieve revolution; the movement had very little with which to replace reform work; the movement would be paralyzed. Instead, Bunch argued that reforms be analyzed for their potential to lead to revolutionary work, in the long term. We should see, she insisted, the radical nature of "re-forming" institutions.

There are similar cooptation fears with Head Start's deficit-based reforms. These women already have strong beliefs in the American Dream. If they are made more comfortable in their poverty (through social services, through developing friendship networks), they may never come to question the assumptions of that dream. If they see evidence of women like themselves succeeding in conventional ways (evidence such as Lila's story or Hannah's), they may come to devalue themselves if they cannot do the same. The systems oppressing them then become stronger.

And yet, taking seriously the challenge to analyze reforms for revolutionary potential, we must see that the women themselves consider such changes in their lives to be empowering. What the changes have given these women is some respite from immediate and consuming demands on their time and energy and other, limited resources. This is critical for their ability to act in any broader way. Even more dramatically, almost to a woman, there are reports of changes in self-esteem and self-reliance. Through their participation in Head Start, women came to believe in themselves and trust their abilities. This is a very difficult task, quite an accomplishment in a world where poor people are scorned, women devalued, and poor women despised. It seems a required step if women are to make deep changes in society (Collins 1991; Naples 1992).

Further, we showed that Head Start structures give women the space and mechanisms to come together, to act together, in noncritical ways (such as raising money for a needier family) and in more directly political ways (such as battling the bureaucratic administration). This coming together was often in spite of, as well as because of, Head Start structures—women transformed services into those they needed. Of course, there can be no collective action, no revolution, without collectivities of actors. So any reform that provides for the formation of those collectivities holds some promise. These collectivities can then become, in Fantasia's words, cultures of solidarity, "practical attempt[s] to restructure, or reorder, human relations" (1988: 11).

So, Head Start's empowering processes *are* worth emulating because of demonstrated successes in giving women control of everyday life and a new vision of themselves, and worth emulating because of the potential of collective action. Yet, is it enough? This question really boils down to: Is the potential for transformative collective action great enough? Our answer must be, no, not quite. Even with their other accomplishments, it is true that women in the North Country have not developed a broad structural view of their powerlessness with regard to class or gender, not to mention the combination. Though they are empowered to battle the immediate power structure of one organization, they will not likely begin struggling against patriarchy or capitalism, certainly not racism. These, though, are the roots of their problems. Naples notes similarly that women's inability to make these broader connections "interfered with [their] ability to challenge the established political system" (1991: 479; see also Plotkin and Scheuerman 1990).

And yet, that potential remains. There *has* been some political education; perhaps there could be more. Maybe it's not enough yet, but maybe it could be.

POLICY IMPLICATIONS

Head Start's policies regarding participation and democratic control are worth emulating in other governmental welfare policies and in a variety of community programs and organizations—including, for instance, college classrooms. There are, I think, two key aspects to the success women have had with Head Start, and to the endangering of that success. First is the simple and demonstrated respect for women, poor women, at all levels of the Head Start organization, endangered now by changes in staffing policies. Second is respect for democracy, messy as it is, at all levels of the organization, endangered by increasing administrative control.

Letting Head Start Be Head Start

Skerry (1983) has argued that one reason for Head Start's "enduring success" is its nonbureaucratic, "catch-as-catch-can" character. This is both a cause and a consequence of extensive parental involvement in service delivery and in policymaking. That is, since Head Start is deliberately underfunded—typically covering only 80 percent of costs (Skerry 1983)—parent involvement is key simply to running the program day-to-day. This quality has meant that administrators cannot plan as precisely, as bureaucratically, as they might like. Moreover, as we showed in Chapter Eight, parent policymakers can undo the best-laid bureaucratic plans. On the other hand, Head Start has been a "'permeable institution,' one that raises relatively few bureaucratic or professional barriers against parents and neighbors who wish to be part of it" (Skerry 1983: 36). This makes Head Start a friendly and secure place for parent involvement, and so, people participate.

Yet, as Kramer noted in 1969, as Skerry noted in 1983, and as we have noted here, there are ever-increasing efforts to more fully bureaucratize Head Start. The implications of our data are that this is a mistake for the effectiveness of Head Start, effectiveness in both reforming and empowering women. Instead, the "administrative nightmare" (Skerry 1983: 30) needs to continue and, in fact, increase. That is, the "extremely loose administration" is fundamental to the success of Head Start (Skerry 1983: 26), certainly for the parents' success in the program. Without it, parents will not feel able to participate and, indeed, will be prevented from participating genuinely.

However, this does not mean that the government need abandon attempts to improve quality at low-quality sites. Rather, it means that evaluators must learn to recognize that quality can come in a variety of forms and that quality can best be judged by locally defined needs. Allowing—better yet, encouraging—the "nightmare" requires a faith in and respect for democracy, including acceptance of "bad" decisions. As Cahn and Cahn (1971) argue, there is a right to be wrong, particularly when the consequences of the decision are borne by the decision makers. This, though, requires that professionals give up some of their control over programs and people. As 70.2 language recognized in 1970, professionals find it more than difficult to do this. Giving up control may mean relinquishing claim to the title of professional (Powell 1982) and is thoroughly resisted by many social service providers (Funiciello 1993; Gordon 1994; Hagen 1994; Horowitz 1995; Garfunkel 1986).

This is not an issue unique to Head Start. In general, democratically run organizations experience difficulties with professional hierarchies and differential access to knowledge (Cornforth 1989; Ames 1995). This need not be fatal to parent participation. If, for example, management skills need to be upgraded (as HHS in its *Creating a 21st Century Head Start* asserts), those skills can be taught to parents as well as to paid administrators. Early Head Start programs recognized that they would need parents competent in early childhood education to staff the classrooms. Head Start took the initiative to develop specific training programs to give parents that competence in child-development issues (Benson and Peters 1988). It is long-past time to extend such training to policymaking and administrative competencies as well. Good management need not exclude parents.

Indeed, "paid" staff need not exclude parents. Working on the Policy Council takes up an incredible amount of time and energy. Head Start could, perhaps should, pay a stipend to PC officers, allowing them a little more flexibility in terms of paid employment and validating their hard work. At the very least, significant work on the PC should "count" as employment for the purposes of social service eligibility: Any demands to engage in a job search or job training, for instance, as a requirement for receiving public assistance should be deemed met by PC work.

Cornforth (1989) also asserts that democratic organizations (such as a parent-led Policy Council) need institutional support. Even in this presumably democratic society, most organizations do not function at all democratically. Those that do, then, are alone, without support for their processes or their decisions. That isolation makes continuing democracy difficult. In the case of this federally funded program, there must be very emphatic support for parental decision making, starting at the top of HHS, and it must be firmly enforced at each level. When parents are thwarted by a local administration and seek help from HHS (as happened in Lake and Kent Counties), HHS must seek to resolve the difficulties in a way that preserves parents' legitimate authority (which did not happen in either Lake or Kent). Without that emphatic enforcement, the trend toward greater administrative control and only-ceremonial power for parents will continue.

Moreover, this support from the top must come without the existing assumptions of parents as deficient (Swap 1990). Clearly, the reason women of the North Country were empowered on a day-today level was the respect, and consequent self-respect, offered them by the front-line staff. That respect needs to be reflected in HHS administrative activities as well. Parents cannot be treated as children with new scissors or a Christmas present. Just as clearly, this is a tall order. Professionals at HHS are no less jealous of their status, turf, and expertise than local professional staffs.

A less-tall order, but one that would increase the likelihood of respect for parents and democracy at the local level is to revitalize the practice of hiring parents into the program and promoting them. As we have shown, former parents working in the program serve as role models and advocates for current mothers. The advocacy would help provide a system of checks and balances to counter the professional tendency to guard turf and control agendas (Garfunkel 1986). Parents should be offered specific training and general schooling so that they will qualify for jobs, including professional jobs within local Head Start programs.

Yet, in Lake County, such workers came to be devalued—or at least many parents and staff members felt strongly that they were not valued, even that they were specifically targeted for elimination. There was a general feeling that parents would not be hired in or trained for or promoted to *responsible* positions. That feeling would mean that fewer mothers would aspire to such positions and thus that fewer would make the dramatic changes in their economic stability we documented in Chapter Four. Any reality underlying that feeling of devaluation, any real devaluation, would mean that the Head Start administration would become further and further removed from the people it serves; fewer and fewer administrators would come from low-income backgrounds. Head Start would no longer be seen as a permeable institution, loved by those it serves, would no longer provide a safe space for participation.

One possible route to preserving Head Start's "catch-as-catch-can" and permeable character is to give the parents and front-line staff of Kent and Lake Counties (and elsewhere) their wish—to make Head Start freestanding. This would take away one key level of

entrenched, bureaucratic, professional power—the CAP agency itself. This may also be a way to return to Head Start's roots in au-
thentic community action, allowing poor parents to run the program
according to the needs of the community and individuals being
served. In this case, we might actually see genuinely revolutionary
re-forming, such as happened with the activities of the Child Development Group of Mississippi (CDGM) (Greenberg 1990 [1969]).
As the members of CDGM did, parents could then teach themselves
about the structures that constrain their life chances. What's more,
they could teach their children.

Parents leading the fight for a freestanding Head Start in the
North Country did not presume that they could take over administration of the program without help. They fully recognized that
expertise in finances and managing, for example, would be needed.
Such expertise, though, could be gained from community representatives on their Policy Council, from HHS consultants and training, and from managers hired—and fired—by the Policy Council.

Of course, there are many difficulties in increasing parent involvement or employment in the program besides professionals' recalcitrance. One critical issue is that there has been a major change
in employment patterns since the 1960s. Full-time, stay-at-home
mothers have become more rare. Mothers and fathers in the paid-
labor force are currently virtually shut out of participation in the
program (Washington and Bailey 1995; Miller 1990). The sched-
uling of parent and Policy Council meetings must take work schedules of parents into explicit account, else many, perhaps most, parents will be excluded from significant levels of participation. Again,
this may make for some administrative headaches and imprecision,
but that is a small price for the benefits of participation.

A related concern is that Head Start was not designed as a child-
care institution, which has penalized employed parents from the
beginning. Many of the front-line staff we talked with were vehe-
ment in drawing distinctions between day care and Head Start,
considering the former to consist of merely warehousing children.

However, for parents who work in the paid-labor force, a Head Start program that ran for a full work day would be very valuable indeed (Polokow 1993; Sherman 1994). There is not necessarily a contradiction in providing quality preschool to children and quality day care to parents.

Head Start has given much to many parents and has the capacity to give much more to many more. We are concerned that the program is losing its ability and its *mission* to do so. Seeking to ensure that ability and that mission in the ways indicated will not always be easy, surely, but the rewards to individual parents and children, and to our society in general seem well worth the effort.

Let Head Start be Head Start.

Maximum Feasible Participation, Again

Polly Greenberg asserts (1990) that the notion of client participation in War on Poverty programs was born with Project Head Start. The professionals on the original taskforce sought to emulate the kind of mothers' participation typical of the middle-class child-care cooperatives in which their own children were enrolled. The participation encouraged in Head Start may now be unique among federal social service programs, but it was not new. Indeed, the model of participatory, consumer cooperatives has been and is well-used in many settings (Rothschild and Whitt 1986; Krimerman and Lindenfeld 1992). It is a model to be copied.

We would like to argue here that a policy of maximum feasible participation needs to be reconsidered and could usefully be introduced into existing federal and local "welfare" programs. Such reconsideration would not necessarily mean reactivation of full-scale community action—we would like that, actually, and think it useful in achieving the full benefit of participation, but recognize the political improbability. Instead, such participation might build on even conservative politicians' demands for "responsibility" among the poor.

For example, Jack Kemp, when he was in the Reagan cabinet, advocated selling public housing to the people who lived in the projects. The rationale seemed to be that residents would take better care of the buildings if they were the owners. That logic makes some negative assumptions about the residents, I think, including that the primary reason for the decay of urban housing projects is resident apathy. Again, structural issues of rampant unemployment, political graft, and police brutality, among others, are ignored. Nevertheless, if residents were indeed given collective control over the running of the buildings—and mere individual ownership is not necessarily control—there is every reason to expect that the buildings would be run in a manner more helpful to the residents' collective lives. Residents' control over costs, repairs and upkeep, security arrangements—preferably even over the *design* of housing—would be critical to their *empowerment*, but that is not necessarily subsumed under ownership of individual units. Under conditions of democratic control, Kemp's is a proposition to be seriously considered.

Job training programs have long been criticized as irrelevant and demeaning (Quadagno and Fobes 1995; Hagen 1994). However, when these services are presented in a respectful manner, women can gain much from the program—though, as in our study here, not necessarily what policymakers had in mind (Horowitz 1995). Where recipients of services are themselves in charge of the services, programs can become focused more exactly on what the women actually need (Gowdy and Pearlmutter 1994). Gowdy and Pearlmutter, particularly, but also Horowitz (1995), show that job training and remedial education programs delivered with respect and flexibility can function much like North Country Head Start did, providing for community building among women and for the development of self-esteem.

Further, any such program—whether job training or building ownership or some other—can seek to employ the people being served. In doing so, the programs, like Head Start, can provide financial stability and satisfying work for some, as well as important models for upward mobility. That employment, too, may help keep the programs working for the people intended to be served, rather than for professionals' career aspirations—the former clients can serve as advocates for current clients and reality checks for professionals.

Aside from social services, an obvious arena where there is great potential for democratic participation by parents-as-consumers is in the public schools. This is the site of high (though now decreasing) levels of public spending. There have been sporadic calls for greater parent involvement there for many years. Yet, it has been clear, also for many years, that administrators and teachers do not really want to give up control or to so fully open their classrooms and offices to lay scrutiny (Lurie 1970; Caliguri 1970). Parents naturally stay away in such an unwelcoming atmosphere (Calabrese 1990; Fruchter 1984), but then are blamed for being apathetic. The power of participation (Winters 1993) has therefore rarely been realized in the public schools.

We have seen, though, that in North Country Head Start, parents who were *welcomed* did come to the school and did participate at many levels. Not only does such participation stand to benefit the parents (as we have documented), it may well have deeper ramifications. Fitchen (1981) argues specifically that rural school teachers and administrators have low expectations for poor children, which results in artificially low performance for those children, which contributes to the reproduction of class inequality. Garfunkel argues, too, that "the domination of public education by professionals is intertwined with substantial inequities in education. One way to begin to deal with these inequities is to involve those who have been the victims and to place appropriate checks and balances on those who have been responsible for developing or maintaining discriminatory practices" (1986: 19).

The implication here is that if more parents, more poor parents, were to actively participate in the public schools, the expectations of teachers (and the consequences thereof) could be changed. Head

Start's welcoming atmosphere and inclusive structures—the parent room and the Policy Council, for example—could serve as a model for public schools (rural and otherwise) truly interested in parent participation. However, as in Head Start, parent involvement that is empowering, that acts as a genuine system of checks and balances, requires a transfer of genuine power.

These speculations are intended to suggest that democratic participation by consumers of public services is possible and may well be beneficial. We do not, though, discount the difficulty, political and practical, of implementing that democracy.

Structural Changes

Short-term changes in women—reforms, perhaps—are clearly facilitated by giving them control over programs affecting their lives. This was a major aim of the War on Poverty's maximum feasible participation and has been a remarkable achievement of Head Start, in the North Country as elsewhere. What such limited control has not done is to change—or even to address—the structure of the labor market or of the housing market or of inequality itself, which was the other, long-term aim of community action.

As we said in Chapter Three, we agree with other scholars that systemic change is necessary to truly make a difference in the lives of poor women in general and over the long term. We don't agree, though, that the onus to make those changes is on those women. We endorse calls for common-sense political and macroeconomic policies to alleviate poverty (Rural Sociological Society 1993; Danziger, Sandefur, and Weinberg 1994; Greenstein and Shapiro 1992): a higher minimum wage; universal health care; quality public education at all levels; affordable day care; more equitable tax policies; all efforts to strengthen the economy and create meaningful, well-paid jobs with security. We have also advocated here for a different sort of labor movement, one that would provide not only higher wages but greater control over work and workplaces. We must transform, too, relations between work and home (Smith 1987), giving women real alternatives in their lives. These are proposals for structural changes, changes that would enhance the life chances of the women in this book.

CONCLUSION

In many ways, this book has been about respect. In earlier chapters, we introduced women who have come to respect themselves through their work with Head Start. We have argued that the way the women live their lives and see their world deserves our respect, even if that view differs from our own. We argue emphatically that decisions made by the women collectively—democracy, after all—need to be respected by administrators and professional "experts." Our analysis of policy options, too, calls for respect—though very little in the way of respectful dialogue can be heard from policymakers.

But the book is also fundamentally about power and changes in structures of power. Giving women respect, individually and collectively, personally and institutionally, gives women power and gives them the space to take power and transform it and themselves—and maybe someday transform society. Given respect, women reformed can be women empowered.

REFERENCES

Abramovitz, Mimi. 1988. *Regulating the Lives of Women: Social Welfare Policy from Colonial Times to the Present.* Boston: South End Press.

Ackelsberg, Martha A. 1988. "Communities, Resistance, and Women's Activism: Some Implications for a Democratic Polity." In A. Bookman and S. Morgen, eds., *Women and the Politics of Empowerment.* Philadelphia: Temple University Press.

Alinsky, Saul D. 1946. *Reveille for Radicals.* Chicago: University of Chicago Press.

Ames, Lynda J. 1995. "When Sense Is Not Common: Alternatives to Hierarchy at Work." *Economic and Industrial Democracy* 16(4): 553–76.

Armstrong, Pat. 1993. "Professions, Unions, or What?: Learning from Nurses." In L. Briskin and P. McDermott, eds., *Women Challenging Unions: Feminism, Democracy, and Militancy.* Toronto: University of Toronto Press.

Arnstein, Sherry R. 1971. "Eight Rungs on the Ladder of Citizen Participation." In E. Cahn and B. Passett, eds., *Citizen Participation: Effecting Community Change.* New York: Praeger.

Arroyo, Carmen G., and Edward Zigler. 1993. "America's Title I/Chapter I Programs: Why the Promise Has Not Been Met." In E. Zigler and S. Styfco, eds., *Head Start and Beyond: A National Plan for Extended Childhood Intervention.* New Haven: Yale University Press.

Bayes, Jane. 1988. "Labor Markets and the Feminization of Poverty." In H. Rodgers, ed., *Beyond Welfare: New Approaches to the Problem of Poverty in America.* Armonk, N.Y.: M. E. Sharpe, Inc.

Bee, Helen L., Lawrence F. VanEgeren, Ann Pytkowicz Streissguth, Barry A. Nyman, and Maxine S. Leckie. 1969. "Social Class Differences in Maternal Teaching Strategies and Speech Patterns." *Developmental Psychology* 1(6): 726–34.

Benson, Margaret S., and Donald L. Peters. 1988. "The Child Development Associate: Competence, Training, and Professionalism." *Early Child Development and Care* 38: 57–68.

Bloom, Benjamin S., Allison Davis, Robert Hess, and Susan B. Silverman. 1965. *Compensatory Education for Cultural Deprivation.* New York: Holt, Rineholt, and Winston.

Bookman, Ann. 1988. "Unionization in an Electronics Factory: The Interplay of Gender, Ethnicity, and Class." In A. Bookman and S. Morgen, eds., *Women and the Politics of Empowerment.* Philadelphia: Temple University Press.

Briskin, Linda, and Patricia McDermott. 1993. "The Feminist Challenge to the Unions." In L. Briskin and P. McDermott, eds., *Women Challenging Unions: Feminism, Democracy, and Militancy.* Toronto: University of Toronto Press.

Brophy, Julia. 1994. "Parent Management Committees and Preschool Playgroups: The Partnership Mode and Future Management Policy." *Journal of Social Policy* 23(2): 161–94.

Bryson, Lois. 1992. *Welfare and the State.* New York: St. Martin's Press.

Bunch, Charlotte. 1981 [1974]. "The Reform Tool Kit." *Building Feminist Theory: Essays from Quest.* New York: Longman.

Burton, C. Emory. 1992. *The Poverty Debate: Politics and the Poor in America.* Westport, Conn.: Praeger.

Cahn, Edgar S., and Jean Camper Cahn. 1971. "Maximum Feasible Participation: A General Overview." In E. Cahn and B. Passett, eds., *Citizen Participation: Effecting Community Change.* New York: Praeger.

Calabrese, Raymond L. 1990. "The Public School: A Source of Alienation for Minority Parents." *Journal of Negro Education* 59: 148–54.

Calhoun, John A., and Raymond C. Collins. 1981. "From One Decade to Another: A Positive View of Early Childhood Programs." *Theory into Practice* 20: 135–40.

Caliguri, Joseph P. 1970. "Will Parents Take Over Head Start Programs?" *Urban Education* (April): 53–64.

Cautley, Eleanor, and Doris P. Slesinger. 1989. "Labor Force Participation and Poverty Status among Rural and Urban Women Who Head Families." In H. Rodgers and G. Weiher, eds., *Rural Poverty: Special Causes and Policy Reforms.* Westport, Conn.: Greenwood Press.

Chambers, C. A. 1974. "An Historical Perspective on Political Action vs. Individualized Treatment." In P. Weinberger, ed., *Perspectives on Social Welfare.* New York: MacMillan.

Clark, Kenneth B., and Jeannette Hopkins. 1968. *A Relevant War against Poverty: A Study of Community Action Programs and Observable Social Change.* New York: Harper and Row.

Cobble, Dorothy Sue. 1993. "Introduction: Remaking Unions for the New Majority." In D. Cobble, ed., *Women and Unions: Forging a Partnership.* Ithaca, N.Y.: ILR Press.

Collins, Patricia Hill. 1991. *Black Feminist Thought.* New York: Routledge.

Cooke, Robert E. 1979. "Introduction." In E. Zigler and J. Valentine, eds., *Project Head Start: A Legacy of the War on Poverty.* New York: The Free Press.

Cornforth, Chris. 1989. "The Role of Support Organizations in Developing Worker Cooperatives: A Model for Promoting Economic and Industrial Democracy." In B. Szell and C. Cornforth, eds., *The State, Trade Unions, and Self-Management: Issues of Competence and Control.* Berlin: Walter de Gruyter.

Costello, Cynthia. 1987. "Working Women's Consciousness: Traditional or Oppositional?" In C. Groneman and M. B. Norton, eds., *"To Toil the Livelong Day": America's Women at Work.* Ithaca: Cornell University Press.

———. 1991. *We're Worth It!: Women and Collective Action in the Insurance Workplace.* Ithaca: Cornell University Press.

Cravens, Hamilton. 1993. *Before Head Start: The Iowa Station and America's Children.* Chapel Hill: University of North Carolina Press.

Croteau, David. 1995. *Politics and the Class Divide: Working People and Middle-Class Left.* Philadelphia: Temple University Press.

Danziger, Sheldon. 1988. "The Economy, Public Policy, and the Poor." In H. Rodgers, ed., *Beyond Welfare: New Approaches to the Problem of Poverty in America.* Armonk, N.Y.: M. E. Sharpe, Inc.

Danziger, Sheldon, Robert Haveman, and Robert Plotnick. 1986. "Antipoverty Policy: Effects on the Poor and the Nonpoor." In S. Danziger and D. Weinberg, eds., *Fighting Poverty.* Cambridge, Mass.: Harvard University Press.

Danziger, Sheldon, Gary D. Sandefur, and Daniel H. Weinberg. 1994. "Introduction." In S. Danziger, G. Sandefur, and D. Weinberg, eds., *Confronting Poverty: Prescriptions for Change.* Cambridge, Mass.: Harvard University Press.

Danziger, Sheldon, and Daniel H. Weinberg. 1994. "The Historical Record: Trends in Family Income, Inequality, and Poverty." In S. Danziger, G. Sandefur, and D. Weinberg, eds., *Confronting Poverty: Prescriptions for Change.* Cambridge, Mass.: Harvard University Press.

Datta, Lois-Ellin. 1970. "Head Start's Influence on Community Change." *Children* 17(5): 193–96.

Davens, Edward. 1979. "Remarks." In E. Zigler and J. Valentine, eds., *Project Head Start: A Legacy of the War on Poverty.* New York: The Free Press.

Delgado-Gaitan, Concha. 1990. *Literacy for Empowerment.* London: Falmer Press.

Donovan, John C. 1967. *The Politics of Poverty.* New York: Pegasus.

Duncan, Cynthia, and Nita Lamborghini. 1994. "Poverty and Social Context in Remote Rural Communities." *Rural Sociology* 59: 437–61.

Edelsky, Carole, and Chris Boyd. 1993. "Collaborative Research: More Questions than Answers." In S. Hudelson and J. Lindfors, eds., *Delicate Balances.* Urbana, Ill.: National Council of Teachers of English.

Eisenstein, Sarah. 1983. *Give Us Bread but Give Us Roses.* Boston: Routledge and Kegan Paul.

Ellsworth, Jeanne. 1992. *Women, Children, and Charity in Migrant Labor Camps, 1919–1939.* Unpublished dissertation, University at Buffalo, Department of Educational Organization, Administration, and Policy.

Ellwood, David. T. 1989. "Conclusion." In P. Cottingham and D. Ellwood, eds., *Welfare Policy for the 1990s.*

Fantasia, Rick. 1988. *Cultures of Solidarity: Consciousness, Action, and Contemporary American Workers.* Berkeley, Calif.: University of California Press.

Finkelstein, Barbara. 1988. "The Revolt against Selfishness: Women and the Dilemmas of Professionalism in Early Childhood Education." In B. Spodeck, O. Savacho, and D. Peters, eds., *Professionalism and the Early Child Practitioner.* New York: Teachers' College Press.

Fischer, Frank, and Carmen Sirianni, eds. 1984. *Critical Studies in Organization and Bureaucracy.* Philadelphia: Temple University Press.

• Fitchen, Janet M. 1991. *Endangered Spaces, Enduring Places: Change, Identity, and Survival in Rural America.* Boulder, Colo.: Westview Press.

———. 1992. "Rural Poverty in the Northeast: The Case of Upstate New York." In C. Duncan, ed., *Rural Poverty in America.* New York: Auburn House.

Fraser, Nancy. 1989. *Unruly Practices: Power, Discourse, and Gender in Contemporary Social Theory.* Minneapolis: University of Minnesota Press.

• Fruchter, Norm. 1984. "The Role of Parent Participation." *Social Policy* (Fall): 32–36

Funiciello, Theresa. 1993. *Tyranny of Kindness: Dismantling the Welfare System to End Poverty in America.* New York: The Atlantic Monthly Press.

Garfunkel, Frank. 1986. "Parents and Schools: Partnership or Politics." *IRE Report No. 11.* Boston: Institute for Responsive Education.

Gelfland, Mark I. 1986. "Elevating or Ignoring the Underclass." In R. Bremner, G. Reichard, and R. Hopkins, eds., *American Choices: Social Dilemmas and Public Policy since 1960.* Columbus: Ohio State University Press.

Gilbert, Neil. 1970. *Clients or Constituents: Community Action in the War on Poverty.* San Francisco: Jossey-Bass, Inc.

Ginsburg, Herbert. 1972. *The Myth of the Deprived Child: Poor Children's Intellect and Education.* Englewood Cliffs, N.J.: Prentice-Hall, Inc.

• Gorham, Lucy. 1992. "The Growing Problem of Low Earnings in Rural Areas." In C. Duncan, ed., *Rural Poverty in America.* New York: Auburn House.

Gordon, Linda. 1990. "The New Feminist Scholarship on the Welfare State." In L. Gordon, ed., *Women, the State, and Welfare.* Madison: The University of Wisconsin Press.

———. 1994. *Pitied but Not Entitled: Single Mothers and the History of Welfare 1890–1935.* New York: The Free Press.

Gorelick, Sherry. 1991. "Contradictions of Feminist Methodology." *Gender and Society* 5(4): 459–77.

Gowdy, Elizabeth, and Susan R. Pearlmutter. 1994. "Economic Self-Sufficiency Is the Road I'm On." In L. Davis, ed., *Building on Women's Strengths: A Social Work Agenda for the Twenty-First Century*. New York: The Haworth Press.

Gowens, Pat. 1993. "Welfare Warriors." *Equal Means* (Winter): 33.

Granger, Robert C. 1989. "The Staffing Crisis in Early Childhood Education." *Phi Delta Kappa* (October): 130–34.

Granger, Robert C., and Elisabeth Marx. 1990. "The Policy Implications of Compensation and Working Conditions in Three Publicly Funded Early Childhood Systems." *Early Childhood Research Quarterly* 5: 181–98.

Greenberg, Polly. 1990 [1969]. *The Devil Has Slippery Shoes: A Biased Biography of the Child Development Group of Mississippi*. Washington, D.C.: Youth Policy Institute.

———. 1990. "Before the Beginning: A Participant's View." *Young Children* 45: 41–52.

Greenstein, Robert, and Isaac Shapiro. 1992. "Policies to Alleviate Rural Poverty." In C. Duncan, ed., *Rural Poverty in America*. New York: Auburn House.

Gruber, Judith, and Edison J. Trickett. 1987. "Can We Empower Others? The Paradox of Empowerment in the Governing of an Alternative Public School." *American Journal of Community Psychology* 15(3): 353–71.

Hagen, Jan. 1994. "Public Welfare and Social Work: New Opportunities." In L. Davis, ed., *Building on Women's Strengths: A Social Work Agenda for the Twenty-First Century*. New York: The Haworth Press.

Harris, Kathleen Mullan. 1993. "Work and Welfare among Single Mothers in Poverty." *American Journal of Sociology* 99: 317–52.

Head Start Performance Standards. 1970. U.S. Department of Health and Human Services.

———. 1984. U.S. Department of Health and Human Services.

Health and Human Services, U.S. Department of. 1993. *Creating a 21st Century Head Start: Final Report of the Advisory Committee on Head Start Quality and Expansion*. Washington, D.C.: Health and Human Services.

Heclo, Hugh. 1994. "Poverty Politics." In S. Danziger, G. Sandefur, and D. Weinberg, eds., *Confronting Poverty: Prescriptions for Change*. Cambridge, Mass.: Harvard University Press.

Herzenberg, Steven. 1993. "Whither Social Unionism?: Labor and Restructuring in the U.S. Auto Industry." In J. Jenson and R. Mahon, eds., *The Challenge of Restructuring: North American Labor Movements Respond*. Philadelphia: Temple University Press.

Horowitz, Ruth. 1995. *Teen Mothers: Citizens or Dependents?* Chicago: The University of Chicago Press.

Hubbell, Ruth. 1983. *A Review of Head Start Research since 1970*. Washington, D.C.: CSR, Inc.

Hunt, J. M. 1969. *The Challenge of Incompetence and Poverty*. Urbana: University of Illinois Press.

Hutchinson, Elizabeth D. 1994. "Child Welfare: A Woman's Issue." In L. Davis, ed., *Building on Women's Strengths: A Social Work Agenda for the Twenty-First Century*. New York: The Haworth Press.

Iannello, Kathleen P. 1992. *Decisions without Hierarchy: Feminist Interventions in Organization Theory and Practice*. New York: Routledge.

Joffe, Carol E. 1977. *Friendly Intruders: Child Care Professionals and Family Life*. Berkeley: University of California Press.

Johnson, Susan Moore. 1984. *Teacher Unions in Schools*. Philadelphia: Temple University Press.

Katz, Michael B. 1986. *In the Shadow of the Poorhouse: A Social History of Welfare in America*. New York: Basic Books.

———. 1989. *The Undeserving Poor: From the War on Poverty to the War on Welfare*. New York: Pantheon Books.

Kessler-Harris, Alice. 1985. "The Debate over Equality for Women in the Work Place: Recognizing Differences." In L. Larwood, A. Stromberg, and B. Gutek, eds., *Women and Work: An Annual Review*. Newbury Park: Sage Publications.

Kramer, Ralph M. 1969. *Participation of the Poor: Comparative Case Studies in the War on Poverty*. Englewood Cliffs, N.J.: Prentice-Hall, Inc.

Krimerman, Len, and Frank Lindenfeld, eds. 1992. *When Workers Decide: Workplace Democracy Takes Root in North America*. Philadelphia: New Society Publishers.

Kuntz, Kathryn R. 1995. *Aiming for the Children: A History of Head Start, 1965–1972*. Unpublished Master's Thesis, University of Wisconsin, Department of History.

Leacock, E. B. 1971. *The Culture of Poverty: A Critique*. New York: Simon and Schuster.

LeCompte, Margaret D., and Anthony Gary Dworkin. 1988. "Educational Programs: Indirect Linkages and Unfulfilled Expectations." In H. Rodgers, ed., *Beyond Welfare: New Approaches to the Problem of Poverty in America*. Armonk, N.Y.: M. E. Sharpe, Inc.

Lehman, Jeffrey S. 1994. "Updating Urban Policy." In S. Danziger, G. Sandefur, and D. Weinberg, eds., *Confronting Poverty: Prescriptions for Change*. Cambridge, Mass.: Harvard University Press.

Leik, Robert K., Mary Anne Chalkley, and Nancy J. Peterson. 1991. "Policy Implications of Involving Parents in Head Start." In E. Anderson and R. Hula, eds., *The Reconstruction of Family Policy*. New York: Greenwood Press.

Levitan, Sar A. 1969. *The Great Society's Poor Law: A New Approach to Poverty*. Baltimore: Johns Hopkins Press.

Levitan, Sar A., and C. M. Johnson. 1984. *Beyond the Safety Net: Reviving the Promise of Opportunity in America.* Cambridge, Mass.: Ballinger.

Levitt, Martin Jay. 1993. *Confessions of a Union-Buster.* New York: Crown.

• Lichter, Daniel T., Gail M. Johnston, and Diane K. McLaughlin. 1994. "Changing Linkages between Work and Poverty in Rural America." *Rural Sociology* 59(3): 395–415.

Lurie, Ellen. 1970. *How to Change the Schools: A Parents' Action Handbook on How to Fight the System.* New York: Random House.

McAtee, Arlene. N.d. *Family Development: Empowering Families to Move Out of Poverty.* Washington, D.C.: National Association of Community Action Agencies.

Milkman, Ruth. 1985. "Women Workers, Feminism, and the Labor Movement since the 1960s." In R. Milkman, ed., *Women, Work, and Protest: A Century of Women's Labor History.* Boston: Routledge and Kegan Paul.

———. 1993. "Union Responses to Workforce Feminization in the United States." In J. Jenson and R. Mahon, eds., *The Challenge of Restructuring: North American Labor Movements Respond.* Philadelphia: Temple University Press.

Miller, Dorothy C. 1990. *Women and Social Welfare: A Feminist Analysis.* Westport, Conn.: Praeger.

Mink, Gwendolyn. 1990. "The Lady and the Tramp: Gender, Race, and the Origins of the American Welfare State." In L. Gordon, ed., *Women, the State, and Welfare.* Madison: The University of Wisconsin Press.

Modigliani, Kathy. 1986. "But Who Will Take Care of the Children? Child Care, Women, and Devalued Labor." *Journal of Education* 168(3): 46–69.

Morgen, Sandra, and Ann Bookman. 1988. "Rethinking Women and Politics: An Introductory Essay." In A. Bookman and S. Morgen, eds., *Women and the Politics of Empowerment.* Philadelphia: Temple University Press.

Moynihan, Daniel P. 1970 [1969]. *Maximum Feasible Misunderstanding: Community Action in the War on Poverty.* New York: The Free Press.

Naples, Nancy A. 1991. "'Just What Needed to Be Done': The Political Practice of Women Community Workers in Low-Income Neighborhoods." *Gender and Society* 5(4): 478–94.

———. 1992. "Activist Mothering: Cross-Generational Continuity in the Community Work of Women from Low-Income Urban Neighborhoods." *Gender and Society* 6(3): 441–63.

National Association for Community Action Agencies (NACAA). N.d. "Media Kit." Informational packet distributed by NACAA.

National Head Start Parent Association. 1989. *Twenty-Five Voices Celebrating Twenty-Five Years.* Alexandria, Va.: NHSA.

Neisser, Ulrich, ed. 1986. *The School Achievement of Minority Children: New Perspectives.* Hillsdale, N.J.: Lawrence Erlbaum Associates.

New York State Department of Labor. N.d. "Occupational Outlook: 1993–1997 North Country Region." Saranac Lake: NYS DoL.

———. N.d. "Tomorrow's Jobs, Tomorrow's Workers: 1993–1994 North Country Region." Saranac Lake: NYS DoL.

Nielsen, William L. 1989. "The Longitudinal Effects of Project Head Start on Students' Overall Academic Success: A Review of the Literature." *International Journal of Early Childhood* (June): 35–42.

O'Brien, Leigh M. 1991. "Teacher Values and Classroom Culture: Teaching and Learning in a Rural, White Head Start Program." Paper presented at the Annual Ethnographic Education Forum, Philadelphia.

O'Connor, Alice. 1992. "Modernization and the Rural Poor." In C. Duncan, ed., *Rural Poverty in America*. New York: Auburn House.

Orleck, Annelise. 1995. *Common Sense and a Little Fire: Women and Working-Class Politics in the United States, 1900–1965*. Chapel Hill: University of North Carolina Press.

Oyemade, Ura Jean. 1985. "The Rationale for Head Start as a Vehicle for the Upward Mobility of Minority Families: A Minority Perspective." *American Journal of Orthopsychiatry* 55(4): 591–602.

Parker, Faith Lamb, Chaya S. Piotrkowski, and Lenore Peay. 1987. "Head Start as a Social Support for Mothers: The Psychological Benefits." *American Journal of Orthopsychiatry* 57: 220–33.

Patterson, James T. 1981. *America's Struggle Against Poverty, 1900–1980*. Cambridge, Mass.: Harvard University Press.

Pearce, Diana. 1990. "Welfare Is Not for Women: Why the War on Poverty Cannot Conquer the Feminization of Poverty." In L. Gordon, ed., *Women, the State, and Welfare*. Madison: The University of Wisconsin Press.

Pennsylvania Association for the Education of Young Children. 1992. *Pennsylvania Statewide Staffing Study*. Pittsburgh: PAEYC.

Perrow, Charles. 1986. *Complex Organizations: A Critical Essay*. New York: McGraw-Hill.

Peterson, Paul E., and David J. Greenstone. 1977. "Racial Change and Citizen Participation: The Mobilization of Low-Income Communities through Community Action." In R. Haveman, ed., *A Decade of Federal Antipoverty Programs: Achievements, Failures, and Lessons*. New York: Academic Press.

Piven, Frances Fox, and Richard Cloward. 1971. *Regulating the Poor: The Functions of Public Welfare*. New York: Pantheon Books.

———. 1977. *Poor People's Movements*. New York: Pantheon Books.

Plotkin, Sidney, and William E. Scheuerman. 1990. "Two Roads Left." In J. Kling and P. Posner, eds., *Dilemmas of Activism: Class, Community and the Politics of Local Mobilization*. Philadelphia: Temple University Press.

Polakow, Valerie. 1993. *Lives on the Edge: Single Mothers and Their Children in the Other America*. Chicago: University of Chicago Press.

Posner, Prudence S. 1990. "Introduction." In J. Kling and P. Posner, eds., *Dilemmas of Activism: Class, Community and the Politics of Local Mobilization*. Philadelphia: Temple University Press.

Powell, Douglas R. 1982. "From Child to Parent: Changing Conceptions of Early Childhood Intervention." *Annals AAPSS* 461: 135–44.

Public Broadcasting System. 1995. "America's War on Poverty" (television documentary).

Quadagno, Jill. 1994. *The Color of Welfare*. New York: Oxford University Press.

Quadagno, Jill, and Catherine Fobes. 1995. "The Welfare State and the Cultural Reproduction of Gender: Making Good Girls and Boys in the Job Corps." *Social Problems* 42(2): 171–90.

Rank, Mark Robert. 1994. *Living on the Edge: The Realities of Welfare in America*. New York: Columbia University Press.

Reiner, Michael B., Judith A. List, and Peter LaFrenier. 1983. "An Evaluation of a Parent Education Program." *Studies in Educational Evaluation* 9: 303–18.

Reinharz, Shulamit. 1992. *Feminist Methods in Social Research*. New York: Oxford University Press.

Riessman, Frank. 1962. *The Culturally Deprived Child*. New York: Harper and Row.

Robinson, Ian. 1993. "Economistic Unionism in Crisis: The Origins, Consequences, and Prospects of Divergence in Labor Movement Characteristics." In J. Jenson and R. Mahon, eds., *The Challenge of Restructuring: North American Labor Movements Respond*. Philadelphia: Temple University Press.

Robinson, James L., and Willa Barrie Choper. 1979. "Another Perspective on Program Evaluation: The Parents Speak." In E. Zigler and J. Valentine, eds., *Project Head Start: A Legacy of the War on Poverty*. New York: The Free Press.

Rodgers, Harrell R., Jr. 1988. "Introduction: The Role of Non-Welfare Social Policies in Reducing Welfare." In H. Rodgers, ed., *Beyond Welfare: New Approaches to the Problem of Poverty in America*. Armonk, N.Y.: M. E. Sharpe, Inc.

Rodgers, Harrell R., Jr., and Gregory Weiher, eds. 1989. *Rural Poverty: Special Causes and Policy Reforms*. Westport, Conn.: Greenwood Press.

• Rosier, Katherine Brown and William A. Corsaro. 1993. "Competent Parents, Complex Lives: Managing Parenthood in Poverty." *Journal of Contemporary Ethnography* 22: 171–204.

Ross, Catherine J. 1979. "Early Skirmishes with Poverty: The Historical Roots of Head Start." In E. Zigler and J. Valentine, eds., *Project Head Start: A Legacy of the War on Poverty*. New York: The Free Press.

Rothschild, Joyce, and J. Allen Whitt. 1986. *The Cooperative Workplace*. New York: Cambridge University Press.

Rural Sociological Society Task Force on Persistent Rural Poverty. 1993. *Persistent Poverty in Rural America.* Boulder, Colo.: Westview Press.

Rowbotham, Sheila, and Swasti Mitter. 1994. "Introduction." In S. Rowbotham and S. Mitter, eds., *Dignity and Daily Bread.* London: Routledge.

Ryan, William. 1976. *Blaming the Victim.* New York: Pantheon.

Sapiro, Virginia. 1990. "The Gender Basis of American Social Policy." In L. Gordon, ed., *Women, the State, and Welfare.* Madison: The University of Wisconsin Press.

Schell, Ellen C., Esq. 1995. Personal communication.

Schweinhart, Lawrence J., and David P. Weikart. 1986. "What Do We Know So Far?: A Review of the Head Start Synthesis Project." *Young Children* (January): 49–55.

Sherman, Alec. 1994. *Wasting America's Future: The Children's Defense Fund Report on the Costs of Child Poverty.* Boston: Beacon Press.

Skerry, Peter. 1983. "The Charmed Life of Head Start." *The Public Interest* 73: 18–39.

Smith, Joan. 1984. "The Paradox of Women's Poverty: Wage-Earning Women and Economic Transformation." *Signs* 19: 121–40.

———. 1987. "Transforming Households: Working-Class Women and Economic Crisis." *Social Problems* 34(5): 416–36.

Solomon, Barbara Bryant. 1976. *Black Empowerment: Social Work in Oppressed Communities.* New York: Columbia University Press.

Sorenson, Monica, ed. 1990. "Head Start Success Stories." Washington, D.C.: CSR, Inc.

Sosin, Michael. 1986. "Legal Rights and Welfare Change." In S. Danziger and D. Weinberg, eds., *Fighting Poverty: What Works and What Doesn't.* Cambridge, Mass.: Harvard University Press.

Steinberg, Ronnie J., and Jerry A. Jacobs. 1994. "Pay Equity in Nonprofit Organizations: Making Women's Work Visible." In T. Odendahl and M. O'Neill, eds., *Women and Power in the Nonprofit Sector.* San Francisco: Jossey-Bass.

Susser, Ida. 1990. "Working-Class Women, Social Protest, and Changing Ideologies." In J. Kling and P. Posner, eds., *Dilemmas of Activism: Class, Community and the Politics of Local Mobilization.* Philadelphia: Temple University Press.

Swap, Sue McAllister. 1990. "Comparing Three Philosophies of Home-School Collaboration." *Equity and Choice* 6: 9–19.

Takanishi, Ruby, and Patrick H. DeLeon. 1994. "A Head Start for the 21st Century." *American Psychologist* 49: 120–22.

Tiano, Susan. 1994. *Patriarchy on the Line: Labor, Gender, and Ideology in the Mexican Maquila Industry.* Philadelphia: Temple University Press.

Trolander, Judith Ann. 1987. *Professionalism and Social Change: From the Settlement House Movement to the Neighborhood Centers, 1886 to the Present.* New York: Columbia University Press.

Valentine, C. A. 1968. *Culture and Poverty: Critique and Counter-Proposals.* Chicago: University of Chicago Press.

Valentine, Jeanette, and Evan Stark. 1979. "The Social Context of Parent Involvement in Head Start." In E. Zigler and J. Valentine, eds., *Project Head Start: A Legacy of the War on Poverty.* New York: The Free Press.

Vanneman, Reeve, and Lynn Weber Cannon. 1987. *The American Perception of Class.* Philadelphia: Temple University Press.

Washington, Valora. 1985. "Head Start: How Appropriate for Minority Families in the 1980s?" *American Journal of Orthopsychiatry* 35(4): 577–90.

Washington, Valora, and Ura Jean Oyemade. 1987. *Project Head Start: Past, Present, and Future Trends in the Context of Family Needs.* New York: Garland Publishers, Inc.

Washington, Valora, and Ura Jean Oyemade Bailey. 1995. *Project Head Start: Models and Strategies for the Twenty-First Century.* New York: Garland Publishers, Inc.

Weir, Margaret. 1992. *Politics and Jobs: The Boundaries of Employment Policy in the United States.* Princeton, N.J.: Princeton University Press.

West, Guida. 1981. *The National Welfare Rights Movement: The Social Protest of the Poor.* New York: Praeger.

West, Guida, and Rhoda Lois Blumberg, eds. 1990. *Women and Social Protest.* New York: Oxford University Press.

Whithorn, Ann. 1984. *Serving the People: Social Services and Social Change.* New York: Columbia University Press.

Wickham-Searl, Parnel. 1992. "Mothers with a Mission." In P. M. Ferguson, D. Ferguson, and S. J. Taylor, eds., *Interpreting Disability.* New York: Teacher's College Press.

Winters, Wendy. 1993. *African-American Mothers and Urban Schools: The Power of Participation.* New York: Lexington Books.

Wohlford, Paul. 1974. "Head Start Parents in Participant Groups." *Journal of Applied Behavioral Science* 10: 222–249.

Zigler, Edward, and Karen Anderson. 1979. "An Idea Whose Time Had Come: The Intellectual and Political Climate." In E. Zigler and J. Valentine, eds., *Project Head Start: A Legacy of the War on Poverty.* New York: The Free Press.

Zigler, Edward, and Susan Muenchow. 1992. *Head Start: The Inside Story of America's Most Successful Educational Experiment.* New York: Basic Books.

Zigler, Edward, and Sally J. Styfco. 1994. "Head Start: Criticisms in a Constructive Context." *American Psychologist* 49: 127–32.

Zigler, Edward, and Jeannette Valentine, eds. 1979. *Project Head Start: A Legacy of the War on Poverty*. New York: The Free Press.

Zinsser, Caroline. 1986. *Day Care's Unfair Burden: How Low Wages Subsidize a Public Service*. New York: Center for Public Advocacy Research.

INDEX

247